GOOD [illegible] E

MUNICH AND BAVARIA

GRAHAM LEES

CAMRA
BOOKS

ACKNOWLEDGEMENTS

No book is ever written without the support and encouragement of others, always too many to mention. But I'd like publicly to thank pioneer beer hunter and writer Frank Baillie, whose undimmed enthusiasm — spanning five decades — has been a mighty inspiration; Dave Cunningham, Neil Kellett and Richard Sanders for pointing me in the direction of good pubs;the members of the Munich Cricket Club; Jill Adam, Roger Protz and Jo Bates for their patience and professionalism in sorting out the manuscript and handling production; and last, but definitely not least, my wife Fran, for her graceful tolerance of my selfish indulgence.

DEDICATED
to all who appreciate good beer,
regardless of borders.

Author: Graham Lees
Designer: Rob Howells
Maps by: Perrott Cartographics
Typeset by T&O Graphics, Broome, Bungay, Suffolk
Printed by WSOY, Finland
Published by CAMRA, the Campaign for Real Ale, 34 Alma Road, St Albans, Herts AL1 3BW

ISBN 1-85249-114-0

Contents

Munich's Hofbraüs *Photo: Robert Hetz*

Introduction

The joy in searching for the perfect beer is not so much the possibility of finding it as the great pleasure involved along the way. But although beer is now drunk virtually everywhere humans gather, the chances of finding the Holy Grail of brewing in Siberia or the Australian outback are slim. The search must concentrate in countries and regions where the odds are higher.

One such country is reunited Germany. One such region is Bavaria. Germany has about 1,300 breweries — more than one third of the world total. Over 750 of these German breweries are concentrated in Bavaria, a region no bigger than Scotland (which has just 12 breweries).

It is perhaps no coincidence, then, that the Germans are the world's biggest beer drinkers, downing 253 pints per head of population a year — 20 pints ahead of their nearest rivals in the Czech Republic. But the Bavarians take the crown. They average over 400 pints per head!

Their outstanding capacity to brew and to drink has given Bavarians the folksy image of being a thigh-slapping, barrel-shaped, ruddy-faced people dressed in leather shorts and feathered hats and all living in log cabins in the snow-capped Alps. It is an image reinforced by the staggering statistics which flow from the Oktoberfest, the world's biggest beer festival held annually in Munich.

This picture belies the fact that Bavaria was at the centre of technical advances which changed the face of brewing throughout most of the world, apart from Britain and Belgium. Nineteenth-century Munich, capital of Bavaria, elevated brewing from a hit-and-miss medieval craft to a science. On today's world beer map, Bavaria remains a region of excellence and variety. Two of the world's most famous brewing schools are there, and many of today's brewers are former students.

The world's oldest brewery, with records dating from 1040, is in Bavaria (Weihenstephan in Freising); evidence of the oldest known brewery in Europe north of the Alps has been found amongst second-century Roman remains at Regensburg in Bavaria.

It is a back-handed compliment to Bavarian brewing that when British brewers began embracing the idea of "lager" beer 20 years ago after pasteurised keg beer flopped, they created imitation Germanic beers with phoney Bavarian names and images. The classic "con" was from Greenall's of Warrington, Cheshire, who baptised their lager with a Germanised version of their own name — Grünhalle — and advertised it with, yes, yodelling men in lederhosen. But the name was as close as Greenall's ever came to producing real Bavarian beer. They made such a job of it, they have since ceased brewing altogether.

Although "lager" is a German word, it is rarely used in Germany to define a category of beer the way it has been in Britain. With a few notable exceptions, many home-grown British lager beers are poor imitations of the real thing, which is matured for six-eight weeks and often longer.

Lager in German simply means store or storage. In brewing terms, it stems from the ancient practice of storing beer somewhere cool, such as in caves in cliffs. Originally it was done to prevent it going bad in the warm south German summers, but since the mid-19th century it became a deliberate method of maturing beer — known as cold conditioning.

One of Munich's 12 breweries, Spaten, is still largely owned by the descendants of Gabriel Sedlmayr who was at the forefront of research which isolated the type of yeasts needed for bottom fermenting beer — what we call lager. He played a leading role, along with brewers in Vienna and Pilsen, in recognising that beer brewed with these bottom fermenting yeasts worked better in cold conditions — and that lagering young beer for longer periods improved its taste. The new technologies of the 19th century enabled mechanised refrigeration to be developed and used for this purpose.

Before these discoveries, all beer — whether brewed in Munich, Manchester, Melbourne or Milwaukee — was a similarly unpredictable, murky monster.

In Bavaria, you order beer, not lager. If you simply ask for "Ein Bier, bitte" (A beer, please), you will be given the basic house product, usually a pale brew called a Helles — the nearest thing to what we in Britain call lager. Even so, it will have a good strength of 4.5 to 5 per cent alcohol by volume (abv).

One of the beer styles to emerge from Sedlmayr's researches was a bottom fermented Münchner Dunkel, or Munich Dark. It is a great compliment to Bavarian brewing that breweries as far away as South America still label their products with the epithet "Munich style".

Ironically, while many parts of the world concentrate on reproducing modern Munich or Bavarian style beers, the region itself has quietly maintained a large portfolio of beers whose family trees reach back way beyond the 19th century.

There are fruity-sour wheat beers; the rare smoke-flavoured Rauchbier; dark strong bock beers to celebrate the end of winter; pale strong bock beers to celebrate spring; pale malty lagers; dry, extremely hoppy, unfiltered Kellerbier; rich, spicy Märzen beers (see Beer Styles guide).

Despite the pioneering work of Sedlmayr, some of these beers are still produced in tiny backyard rural brewhouses where the pace and methods of production seem to pre-date the Industrial Revolution.

The British have their unique bitters, the Irish their stouts, and the Belgians their extraordinary Lambics, but I venture to suggest that Bavaria offers the last great beery adventure. Any quest for the Holy Grail of brewing must certainly include a visit there.

Competition is fierce. Some villages and small towns have two, three even four breweries. In many rural areas, beer is still as cheap as a pound a pint in the pub — even since sterling's 1992 devaluation. The real price war is in the take home market. A crate of bottled Bavarian beer — ten litres, or 17.5 pints — can be delivered to the customer's front door for less than a fiver.

There is no time like the present to explore the Bavarian beer world. Some unusual beers face the same uncertain future as African wild life. Most people would be sad to see the rhinoceros become extinct but few bother to lift a finger to prevent its relentless hunting. While no-one is exactly hunting Bavarian beers to death, they nevertheless face late 20th-century predations and pressures which threaten their survival.

Since I first went to live in Munich in 1981, more

than 125 Bavarian breweries have closed — victims, one way or another, of change.

Your perfect pint or mine might have been brewed by one of those vanished breweries. I do know that one of them produced a beautifully rich, fruity-dry, copper-coloured beer which came close to being the title taker for me and over which first I drooled, then lamented. It was produced in one of four brew pubs in a village of only 6,800 people. Perhaps the inhabitants of that north Bavarian parish were swamped with choice, but I detect in many Germans the same kind of apathetic attitude to their beer heritage which almost destroyed Britain's before the arrival of the Campaign for Real Ale in 1971.

With a few exceptions, many German breweries have a 1960s British attitude to the consumer — drink up, but mind your own business. Bavarians puff up their chests at the mere mention of Bavarian beer, yet few of them appreciate just what they have got. The idea of anyone protesting about the threatened loss of a favourite beer or brewery or pub is alien. A Munich resident knows nor cares little about the beers of neighbouring Augsburg. A beer drinker in Bamberg is fiercely loyal to his town's nine breweries (15 years ago there were 12), but has probably never even thought of drinking the delicious beers of Bayreuth 31 miles away. In a perverse way, this parochial attitude has perhaps helped stave off the creation of big regional and national breweries and brands, and all the negative influences which ensue for the consumer.

Today, still, Bavarians can enjoy the delights of 750 breweries. But probably not until the region is reduced to 100 breweries will they wake up to the loss.

Munich
A Beery City of Culture

Munich's lust for drinking beer, rather than the number of barrels brewed, justifies the city's claim to be Beer Capital of the World. Other German cities have more breweries, or produce more beer; but Munich has the world's biggest "pub" (see Mathäser), the biggest beer gardens, and the biggest festival — the huge annual Oktoberfest. Few other places can claim to have had such a worldwide influence on brewing. The words "Munich Style" are inscribed on bottles of beer brewed in countries as far away as South America. Trainee brewers still flock from all corners of the globe to study at two of the world's most influential brewing schools, in the self-indulgent city of the "oompah" band and Lederhosen.

The industrial revolution of the 19th century brought in its wake a greater thirst for beer. All the major industrial countries experienced a big upsurge in brewing to meet demand. By the 1880s, every fourth mug of beer in the world was poured down a German throat. This provided the trigger for the search for more scientific and efficient methods of brewing. Along with Vienna and Pilsen, in what is now the Czech Republic, Munich was in the forefront of technical advances which perfected the brewing of what we British today call lager — bottom-fermented beer. The main pioneering work in Munich was done by Gabriel Sedlmayr whose family still owns one of Munich's major breweries, Spaten. With the advantage of geographical conditions which bless southern Bavaria with an ability to grow barley with a particularly rich maltiness, Munich created its own distinct and distinguished portfolio of beers which have been copied (with varying degrees of success) ever since.

The belated development in Britain in recent decades of "lager" (German word for storing) is often a thin, poorly flavoured version of the styles which Munich breweries offer: from Augustiner's straw-coloured Helles, to Spaten's rich dark Dunkel Export.

Against the trend elsewhere in Europe, the number of breweries in Munich is higher today than for many years. In the mid 1980s, there were six giants and one

David. Today, the city can boast 12 breweries, even if half of them are only brew pubs. Munich's Big Six are: Löwenbräu, probably the most internationally famous, although with a lesser pedigree than some of the others; Hacker-Pschorr; Paulaner; Augustiner (the oldest, claiming a history reaching back to 1328); Spaten; and the state-owned former royal brewery, Hofbräu.

The mini breweries are: Forschung (established in the 1930s); Isarbräu, Unionsbräu (a revived local brewery name), Fliegerbräu, Paulaner Bräuhaus (owned by Paulaner); and Bambergerhaus.

In Munich, the seasons are marked by special, and usually strong, beers. The first of these beer seasons — the Starkbierzeit — coincides with Lent in March. Monks in the 17th century are credited with creating a particularly strong beer to fortify them while they fasted. How on earth they got up in the morning to say their prayers is anybody's guess. It resulted in Paulaner's Salvator, daddy of all doppelbocks, with a strength of 1070 OG (7.5 per cent alcohol by volume). Some other major Munich brewers make their own versions, but acknowledge the original by adding the suffix "ator" to their beer names.

The principal Munich Starkbierfest is organised by Paulaner in its huge Salvator Keller (see Munich Pubs), where thousands of devotees gather for a knees up which makes the Oktoberfest seem like a church fete. Incredibly, they down this potent 7.5 per cent brew by the litre mug (almost 2 pints). Löwenbräu has a rival fest with its Triumphator doppelbock at its huge beer hall on Stiglmaierplatz. The Löwenbräukeller party features strongmen competing to lift ridiculous weights.

In April-May, brewers Hofbräu, Spaten, Hacker-Pschorr, Augustiner and the tiny brew pub Unionsbräu serve up the paler Maibock, which is not quite so strong as the doppelbock but still makes the maypole dancing a little giddy. Hofbräu is the noted exponent of this style. Then, the beer gardens settle down to a summer of normal beer drinking, when the paler, malty Helles and the sour wheat beers are the favourites. In September-October, the cool autumn winds blowing up from the Alps herald Märzenbier, a dark brown malty brew which owes its name to the month of March when it is traditionally brewed and laid down — like a wine — to mature with age. This beer used to be the staple diet at the Oktoberfest, but a weaker, paler

Festbier is now sold there. Müncheners have barely recovered from this before Christmas beer (Weihnachtsbock) is in the shops.

The Prussians to the north have traditionally looked down disdainfully on Müncheners, caricatured as short, fat, red-faced people who dress in leather shorts, long socks and stubby Tiroler hats with what look like large shaving brushes sticking out of the top (the proper name is Gamsbart, made from the bristle-like hair of the Chamois, a mountain goat). However, national surveys consistently show that Munich is the city most Germans would prefer to live in if they could choose. They cite its reputation for "Gemütlichkeit", which roughly translates as cosiness or cheerfulness, and its proximity to the Alps and skiing — just 50 km (30 miles) to the south. This might explain why half of Munich's 1.3 million population is not indigenous.

Some cities manage to brew a lot of beer without really conveying the feeling of being a major brewing centre; Manchester is a little like that. That is not the case with Munich, where beery images — and often aromas in the air — constantly remind the visitor that brewing beer is an important industry and drinking it is a great custom bathed in ritual. In case there might be any doubt, the postcard home will be obligingly franked by the German Post Office: "Bierstadt München" (Munich The Beer City).

Surprisingly, tens of thousands of tourists are attracted to Munich each year for non-beery reasons. Here are a few.

WHAT TO SEE

Munich is an Olympic city, having hosted the Games in 1972, as well as being home to fine examples of Gothic, Renaissance and Baroque architecture, leading museums and art galleries. World War Two bombing severely damaged almost half of Munich, but all the wrecked historic buildings were painstakingly rebuilt in style. The following is a selection of the best sight-seeing in between thirst-quenching.

Frauenkirche Cathedral

The twin towers, resembling a salt and pepper pot set, provide the city with its most famous landmark. Parts of the Gothic structure date from 1494. Look out for the Devil's "footprint" just inside the main entrance.

Royal Winter Palace (Residenz)

This was the winter home of the Wittelsbach family (present-day descendants include Kaltenberg brewer, Prince Luitpold) who ruled Bavaria for almost 1,000 years. The sprawling complex includes a museum, the former royal treasury, a tiny ornate theatre and an exhibition of rare porcelain. Entrance in Max Joseph Platz. Closed Monday.

Deutsches Museum

Biggest science museum in Europe with (19 km) 12 miles of corridors connecting 17,000 exhibits, including the history of flight from birdman contraptions to Russian space modules. There's also an impressive display of steam power. Tram 18 to Ludwigsbrücke. Open daily 0900-1700.

Olympic Park

Built for the 1972 summer games, the site is now a landscaped park housing still-functioning sports stadia of tent-shaped architecture which even now looks innovative. Bayern Munich soccer club's ground is here. A trip up the Olympic tower on a clear day provides a magnificent view of the Alps. U2/3 underground lines to Olympiazentrum.

BMW Car Museum

Exhibitions tracing the development of the car and the motorcycle, particularly those from the famous Bavarian Motor Works, and the shape of things to come. Open daily: 0900-1700. U2/3 to Petuelring.

Nymphenburg Palace

A grand diversion en route to Europe's biggest beer garden (see Munich Beer Gardens section). Dating from the 16th century, this former summer retreat of the ruling Wittelsbachs includes some extravagant rococo architecture, and a gallery of paintings of beautiful women courted by one king, including Irish-born showgirl Lola Montez. Closed Monday. Tram 12.

Alte Pinakothek Art Gallery

One of the world's greatest galleries; it contains paintings by most of Europe's old masters, including Rembrandt, Rubens, Dürer, van Eyck and Giotto. Closed Monday. Barer-str. 27. Tram 27.

Dachau Concentration Camp

This was the first of the Nazi horror camps, built in the year Hitler came to power, 1933, originally to lock up his political enemies. Today it is a memorial museum. Open 0900-1700. Closed Monday. English language tours 1130 and 1530. S-2 train to Dachau, then Bus 722. By car, take the B12.

WHERE TO STAY

Hotel rates in Munich are among the highest in the world, although some of the big chains, such as Hilton and Arabella, offer reduced rates for long weekends. The cheapest rooms are in the numerous bed and breakfast guesthouses, or Pensions, where rooms are basic but always clean; some have family or triple-bedded rooms which further reduce the per person rate. Book as far in advance as possible to guarantee lodgings, especially in high summer or during the Oktoberfest. You can book rooms via the tourist office, by writing (they do not accept telephone bookings) to: Fremdenverkersamt, Postfach, 8000 Munich 1, Germany. Fax (from UK): 010-49-89-239-1313. Or contact the following recommended places (prices are approximate for 1994 and include breakfast):

Pension Am Markt, Heiliggeist-str. 6, 8000 Muhich 2. Tel: 089 225-014, no fax. Located beside the colourful outdoor Viktualien Market and beer garden, five minutes walk from the Weisses Bräuhaus and Hofbräuhaus. Single rooms from 55 Marks, doubles from 95 Marks.

Pension Armin, Augustenstr. 5, 8000 Munich 2. Tel: 089 593-197, fax 595-252. This family-run guesthouse proclaims itself to be "family friendly". Close to the main train station, the Hauptbahnhof. Singles from 60 Marks, doubles from 90 Marks. Three-bedded rooms available.

Pension Beck, Thiersch-str. 36, 8000 Munich 22. Tel: 089 220-708, fax: 220-925. Large guesthouse with 100 beds, some three- and four-bed rooms. Tram 20 stops outside; ten minutes walk to city centre. Singles from 38 Marks; doubles from 68 Marks.

Pension Diana, Altheimer Eck 15, 8000 Munich 2. Tel: 089 260-3107. Centrally situated behind the city's pedestrianised centre, and a stone's throw from Augustiner Gaststätte pub. Singles from 40 Marks, doubles from 70 Marks.

Hotel Uhland, Uhlandstr. 1, 8000 Munich 2. Tel: 089 539-277, fax 531-114. A large, smart Victorian house close to the Oktoberfest ground. Singles from 100 Marks; doubles from 130 Marks.

GETTING AROUND

Every Munich venue, beery or not, listed in this book is accessible by one of the best urban public transport services in Europe. Buses, trams, the underground (U-Bahn) and suburban S-Bahn trains are integrated to allow passengers to switch from one service to another on the same ticket. The best value for visitors is a Day Ticket (Tageskarte) which permits unlimited travel for up to two adults and three children from 9am until 3am next morning. It costs 20 Marks and includes travel to and from all the brewery market towns on the S-Bahn (e.g. Freising, Erding, Aying). A Day Ticket for the inner zone only costs 10 Marks. You can break your journey as often as you like. Alternatively, if you do not want to travel about so much in one day, buy a blue strip ticket (Blaue Streifenkarte) for 14 Marks, and "cancel" strips for each trip. All tickets have to be validated by date stamping them in machines on buses and trams and at station entrances. The number of strips to be stamped depends on the length of journey; system map guides are located at all stations. Plain-clothed ticket inspectors (sometimes little old ladies with bags of shopping) haunt the system and charge a 60 Mark fine for travelling without a valid ticket. Warnings are written in English, so they do not accept excuses from foreign visitors claiming not to understand the system.

ANECDOTES

Beer Hall Politics and Hitler's Unpaid Pub Bill

Munich's beer halls have an unwanted but undeniable connection with Adolf Hitler and his early days as a political rabble rouser. In one, he made his first political speech; in another he began his failed 1923 military Putsch. In the chaotic aftermath of Germany's World War One defeat, the beer halls were centres of political debate and plots, fuelled by disillusioned ex-soldiers. Armed communists briefly seized power in the city in April 1919, only to be ousted by nationalists a few weeks later.

Into this melting pot of ideology and anarchy, Hitler was deposited as an army spy. It was a fateful move.

Hitler's military masters, trying to keep abreast of the plotters, sent him to listen in on a meeting of the newly-formed German Workers' Party at the Sterneckerbräu hall in Tal (the original building, at Number 54, is still there but now a bed linen shop) in September 1919. Hitler became interested in the tiny Party's objectives and was invited to speak at the next meeting, in the nearby Hofbräuhaus. On October 16, Hitler made his first public speech — to an audience of 70. Five months later he left the army to concentrate on his budding political career. Just over a year later he became leader of the re-named National Socialist German Workers' Party (abbreviated to Nazi in German). More Hitler beer hall speeches followed at the Hofbräuhaus and in the Löwenbräu Keller (still serving beer on Stiglmaierplatz on Dachauer-str., near the main train station).

Hitler was never much of a beer drinker, but clearly many of his followers were. On the eve of his failed Putsch — a bid to seize control of Munich by force in November 1923, and then lead an armed rebellion against Berlin — about 500 fellow rebels had quite a knees-up in the Bürgerbräu Keller where the uprising was declared. A recently re-discovered bill for the night revealed that they drank 2,360 pints of beer and broke 143 beer mugs, 98 chairs and two music stands. The landlord also charged them for 148 missing sets of knives and forks. Worse, the bill was never fully paid, which seems to have been a Hitler trait (see Schelling Salon in Munich Pubs).

Beer mug throwing was part of the ritual of a beer hall political rally. In November 1921, a Hitler speech to his fledgling Nazi Party in the Hobräuhaus was disrupted by opponents hurling mugs and smashing tables and chairs. The Bürgerbräu Keller survived the war and became an American forces club. It was demolished only in the mid 1980s (the Bürgerbräu brewery was taken over by Löwenbräu in 1921) and today a Hilton hotel stands on the site at Rosenheimerplatz. Local politicians remain undecided whether to erect a memorial there to Munich cabinet maker George Elser, who almost succeeded in assassinating Hitler in the Keller in November, 1939. Elser, thought to have been a communist but who always claimed to have acted alone, planted a bomb timed to go off while Hitler was giving a Putsch memorial speech. Because of bad weather,

Hitler left 13 minutes early to catch a train for Berlin. Elser was later executed in Dachau.

Beer Consumption and Munich Mothers

Müncheners today are world leaders in beer consumption. They outstrip not only the big beer-quaffing nations such as Belgium and the Czech Republic, but also fellow countrymen in other regions of Germany. But their downing of an average 200 litres (350 pints) per person per year is nothing compared with the records achieved in the mid-late 19th century. In 1860, the per capita consumption was a staggering 535 litres (936 pints).

This record was no doubt helped by nursing mothers and surrogate "wet" nurses who in those days believed it was necessary to drink up to SEVEN pints of beer a day in order to provide sufficient sustenance for breast-feeding children. In 1876, Munich city health department tried to moderate the mothers' thirst by recommending that two pints a day was sufficient to help beef up their offspring.

Old habits die hard; in Bavaria, beer is still nicknamed liquid bread. A German federal government petition to the European Court in 1987 in defence of the Beer Purity Law stated that up to 25 per cent of the average German man's daily nutrients come from beer.

Drunken Sausage

Munich's most famous sausage, the curious white Weisswurst, is said to have been invented by a "tired and emotional" butcher, and is the only known case of someone being given a pay rise for turning up for work with a hangover.

According to legend, the first Weisswurst was the handiwork of a butcher who had drunk too much beer the night before in the Donisl pub in Munich's main square, Marienplatz.

The sausage — made from veal and herbs and wrapped in a thick, inedible elastic skin — is reputed to have been born early one morning in 1857. The butcher should have been making beef sausages but picked up the wrong ingredients. After the strange sausages went on sale later that morning there was a clamour for more.

A blue plaque hangs on the wall of the Peterhof pub opposite the town hall (Rathaus) on Marienplatz commemorating the butcher's mistake.

ALPINE PRESSURE

Although Munich is 50 km (30 miles) north of the Alps, the city's weather is heavily influenced by the mountains.

The most peculiar influence is the Föhn (pron: fern), a hot wind which blows over southern Bavaria. It is caused by a sudden and dramatic change in air pressure due to warm and cold air currents meeting over the mountains. The Föhn sends the thermometer soaring. In winter it can melt a snowy Christmas card scene in hours; in summer the temperature can rise over 30C (90F).

But the Föhn's most curious influence is to give people headaches and fray tempers. Road accidents rise during a Föhn, work absenteeism increases, schools make allowances for its effects when marking exam papers — and beer consumption goes up too.

MOONLIGHTING IN MUNICH

For pubgoers who set their drinking clocks by the moon, Munich's Vollmond bar is the place to be.

The Vollmond (Full Moon) stays open until 3am (0300) every time there is a full moon or a new moon. Customers must leave their broomsticks and black cloaks at the door. Vollmond: Schleissheimer-str. 82 (city end). Normal opening hours: 1900-0100. Spaten beers.

24-HOUR BEER

It is possible to drink beer in ordinary pubs in Munich round the clock. Here's how:

0600: start in the Wirtshaus Ligsalz, Ligsalz-str. 23, U-4/5 to Messegelände station (Augustiner and Kaltenberg beers).

0700: breakfast at the Schelling Salon, Schelling-str 54, tram 27 (Spaten beers).

0800: down to the Donisl, Marienplatz, U-3/6 (Hacker-Pschorr beers).

0900: stroll round the corner to the Altes Hackerhaus, Sendlinger-str. 75 (Hacker-Pschorr).

1000-2400: most pubs are open, but if it is a warm morning why not sit in the cool courtyard of the Hofbräuhaus, Platzl 9, before the crowds arrive and enjoy "Elevenses" of Weisswurst and Weissbier.

2400-0300: Alter Simpl, Türken-str. 57 (Löwenbräu Pilsener on draught); Zum Brez'n, Leopold-str. at Münchener Freiheit, U 3/6 (Hacker-Pschorr Dunkles discounted by the litre mug; hot meals until 0200); or Vollmond, Schleissheimer-str. 82, if there is a full or new moon. U-2 to Theresien-str. (Spaten).

0300-0600: Weissbierkeller, Bayer-str. 1, near the main railway station, (Löwenbräu wheat beers). Closes at 0700.

Key to symbols

Beers available. May be subject to change

Ⓕ Food available – meals or snacks as specified

Opening hours, given as a 24-hour clock

Overnight accommodation available on the premises

Munich
Beer halls and pubs

CITY CENTRE OLD TOWN

Altes Hackerhaus
Sendlinger-str. 75
Tel: 089 260-5026
City centre, near Marienplatz

Hacker-Pschorr Dunkel, Hell and Pilsener on draught; bottled pale unfiltered wheat beer.
Ⓕ *Hot food all day*
Daily 0900-2300
✣ *Beer Garden*

According to local records, a communal brewery first operated on this site in 1570. It became associated with the Hacker and Pschorr families from 1738. Today, the Hackerhaus is a kind of shrine to the origins of Munich's giant Hacker-Pschorr brewery. At weekends, customers are permitted to visit the 2nd floor "Silver Salon", which is a replica of the Pschorr family's living room in the 1880s. The pub is festooned with bric-a-brac from the Hacker-Pschorr Brewery, and can probably lay claim to having the smallest beer garden in Munich - one of the coolest and quietest spots in the city centre to enjoy a beer on a hot day. Ask to see what the landlord claims is the biggest beer mug in the world.

Augustiner Gaststätte
Neuhauserstr. 16
Tel: 089 551-99257
City Centre, between Karlsplatz and Marienplatz

Augustiner Hell, Dunkel and pale, unfiltered wheat beer on draught. Bottled Maximator Doppelbock in March-April. Märzen in September.
Ⓕ *Hot food mid morning-midnight*
Daily 1000-2400
✣ *Beer garden*

Perhaps the most architecturally attractive drinking and eating venue in Munich. The art nouveau-styled Augustiner with an oval-shaped Italian patio at the rear is the flagship hostelry of Augustinerbräu, smallest of the city's six big breweries. It is located in the middle of Munich's busy pedestrian shopping district, between Karlsplatz and Marienplatz S-bahn stations. Dark wood-panelled nooks and crannies conjure up images of turn-of-the century central European political plotters huddled together. The Augustiner has two entrances: the right-hand door leads to the cavernous and ornate restaurant and the Italian garden; the left-hand door opens into a more basic beer hall, where the emphasis is on drinking rather than dumplings. Traditional Bavarian food is served; suckling pork chops cooked in dark beer sauce (Spanferkel) are a tasty house speciality. Quiet times are mid afternoon and after 9pm midweek.

Donisl

Tel: 089 220-184
Corner of Marienplatz and Weinstr.

Hacker-Pschorr Hell, pale, unfiltered wheat beer and Pilsener on draught. Bottled Dunkel.
Daily 0800-0030

The Donisl is a colourful beer drinkers' haunt with a chequered history. The building began life in the 14th century as the local jail, then became a wine keller before switching to beer about 300 years ago. The pub was knocked out by a direct hit from the RAF in the final days of World War Two. When the Donisl re-opened after repairs, the landlord made up for lost time by operating a 23-hour licence – closing between 5am and 6am to sweep out the animal and vegetable debris. That era came to end in 1983 with the "knockout drops affair" which scandalised Munich's pub-going fraternity when it was revealed that lonesome middle-of-the-night customers were having their beer stiffened with a substance which definitely did not comply with the German Beer Purity Law. Victims woke up to discover that wallets or other valuables had disappeared. Police who raided staff homes found an Aladdin's Cave of stolen property. The pub now opens all night only on weekends during the Fasching carnival (immediately preceding Lent). An oompah band sometimes serenades evening customers from the medieval-style first-floor gallery. A stand-up bar just inside the main entrance is a haunt of homosexuals.

Hofbräuhaus

Platzl 9
Tel: 089 220-859

Hofbräu Hell, Dunkel on draught. In season, Delicator (March), Maibock (April-May) and Märzen (Sept-Oct) also on draught. Bottled pale unfiltered wheat beer.
Ⓕ *Hot food all day*
Daily 1000-2300
✤ *Tree shaded courtyard*

Despite being plagued by coachloads of gawping tourists who prefer being photographed holding a beer to actually drinking the stuff, the Hofbräuhaus still manages to create the social levelling of a Bavarian beer hall. Old men in Lederhosen and Tiroler hats adorned with large shaving brushes are still to be found supping in corners of this cavernous drinking cave; buxom dirndl-dressed waitresses still bulldoze through the place carrying ten litre mugs of beer at a time; an oompah band still deafens the swaying crowd. This most famous of beer halls was a favourite of Lenin's, used by Hitler and visited by a bemused Gorbachev. Lenin's live-in girlfriend Krupskaya perhaps summed up the place best when she wrote to a friend while the couple lived in exile in Munich before the 1917 revolution: "We particularly like going to the Hofbräuhaus where good beer is enjoyed by all classes". Ironically, at that time the Hofbräu brewery was owned by the class "enemy" –

the Bavarian royal family. Today it is run by the state government, and although the beer is now produced on a greenfield site on the edge of town, the Hofbräuhaus remains the brewery tap, proudly serving its classic seasonal specialities, like the pale Maibock. Bavarian food is served throughout the day, but is best enjoyed in the quieter first floor beer restaurant. Sometimes at weekends there are Bavarian dances in a second floor beer hall.

Mathäser Bierstadt

Bayerstr. 5
Tel: 089 592-896
Between Karlsplatz and the Hauptbahnhof

Löwenbräu Hell, Dunkel, unfiltered wheat beer, Pilsener on draught. Seasonal beers such as Triumphator Doppelbock and Oktoberfest Festbier also on draught.
Ⓕ *Hot food all day*
Daily 1000-2400
✤ *Summer courtyard*

If the Hofbräuhaus can claim to be the world's most famous beer hall, the Mathäser is without doubt the biggest. On a busy thirsty day, a full house of 5,000 drinkers can down about 16,000 pints - figures guaranteed to make the average pub landlord green with envy. The Mathäser is at times bawdier and certainly earthier than the Hofbräuhaus. The central feature is the giant beer hall, where a band plays for much of the time and - if you are drunk enough - you can take a turn with the baton for a small fee. But it is a warren-like place of smaller drinking rooms, most notably the pretty, vaulted Gewölbekeller where jazz quartets sometimes play. Another barn-like hall is used for jazz concerts. Other less quaint fixtures and fittings include the uniquely Bavarian chunder sinks, complete with handgrip rails, in the washroom, where those who have over-indulged can channel their excesses.

Nürnberger Bratwurst Glöckl

Frauenplatz 9
Tel: 089 220-385
Next to the Frauenkirche Cathedral

Hacker-Pschorr Export on draught. Bottled Hacker-Pschorr unfiltered wheat beer.
Ⓕ *Hot food*
Mon-Sat 1000-2400; closed Sun and Public Holidays

A beer hall in miniature perhaps best sums up the atmosphere of this small, beer drinking gem which stands in the shadow of the cathedral chancel. The place is heaving night and day with solid, ruddy-faced Bavarian types; even some of the womenfolk wear the Tiroler hat. Sadly, this sort of hostelry is becoming a rarity in central Munich, where more emphasis is being placed on up market eating rather than old-fashioned drinking. Regulars come here primarily for the liquid refreshment - it is the only place left in central Munich where beer is regularly served straight from a wooden barrel, a factor which local purists say gives a different flavour to the beer (it lacks the artificial CO_2 bite accompanying beer served in many other pubs). If you get hungry, the house speciality is the spicy Nuremberg finger sausages, after which the pub is named, served on battered pewter plates. They are as much a part of the "Glöckl" as the surly, burly waitresses who challenge every male to melt their fixed scowls. Another rarity here is the little backroom stone-flagged tap where, if it suits the chap manning the barrels, you can stand and drink. Beware of outrageously short measures.

Weisses Bräuhaus

Tal 10
Tel: 089 299-875
City centre, close to Marienplatz

Schneider bottled wheat beers; Karmeliten Hell, Dunkel and Pilsener on draught (from Straubing, Bavarian Forest).
Ⓕ *Hot food all day*
Daily 1000-24000
✤ *Pavement tables*

An historic and cavernous pub for those with serious drinking intentions. Blue-rinse tourists take one look in here and turn tail, thankfully. The pub's name is a little misleading: a brewery stood on this site from 1540 until bombing raids in late 1944 put the brewer out of work. The Schneider family took the opportunity to move post-war production out of the cramped city centre to a site (Kelheim, 120 km or 75 miles north) where they could also expand. The name of the original brewery, Maderbräu, is preserved in the name of the street adjoining the pub. George Schneider took over the failing brewery at a time in the mid 19th century when wheat beers had gone out of fashion in favour of the new, clear bottom-fermented brews developed in Munich. But the Schneiders persevered with a style which, although now extremely popular again, could easily have disappeared altogether. Most customers here prefer the bottled wheat beers to the draught beers on offer, and if you stroll past the serving counter during a busy time, you will see several frantic Fräuleins juggling with dozens of bottles and glasses at various stages of being filled. The Dunkel and Pilsener is served direct from wooden casks - but only after 4pm each day. It can be difficult to leave this pub if you're not sharp: the keen waitresses will deposit a fresh full glass in front of you as you drain the last one.

Weissbierkeller

Bayer-str. 1
Tel: 089 595-431
Five minutes from the main railway station (Hauptbahnhof)

Löwenbräu pale and dark unfiltered wheat beers (draught and bottled).
Ⓕ *Breakfast*
Mon-Sat 0300-0700; closed Sun night/Mon morning

Only insomniacs, shift workers, or travellers who missed their train need to know about this oddest of Bavarian beer haunts, which offers all the fun of the beer keller, complete with oompah band, in the middle of the night. The large Weissbierkeller, bedecked in the blue and white Bavarian flag, only opens its doors at 3am, then there is a kind of slow motion knees up, with brass band music to accompany the chomping of the "breakfast" sausage (Weisswurst) before the place closes...at 7am.

NORTH MUNICH (SCHWABING)

Alter Simpl

Türken-str. 57
Tel: 089 272-3083
University district of Schwabing

Löwenbräu Pilsener and unfiltered wheat beer on draught
Ⓕ *Simple fare*
Mon-Thu 1700-1300; Fri-Sat 1700-0400; closed Sun

Traditionally, the Alter Simpl has been the haunt of showbiz and media folk, whose working hours are said to deny them the pleasures of normal pub opening hours. Nowadays, the pub is popular with a much broader clientele in search of an early morning nightcap. The Alter Simpl is at its liveliest around midnight, when a colourful mixture of sugar daddies and their companions, bar flies and singles who want to double up gather in the cramped surroundings. The back bar is more interesting than the front. Modest meals are served until around 2am.

Annahof

Lerchenfeldstr. 12
Tel: 089 224-498
Tram 20 to Paradies-str. stop

Postbräu Thannhausen Hell, Dunkel and Pilsener on draught; two pale, unfiltered bottled wheat beers: Postbräu and Erdinger.
Ⓕ *Hot food all day*
Mon-Fri 1130-0100; Sat-Sun 1800-0100; closed Sat Whitsun-mid Sept

Some people go to this cosy little pub for the best schnitzels in town. But those in the know turn up to hear the latest local cricket gossip and perhaps get themselves picked for the next Saturday match in the Englischer Garten across the street. The Annahof is the home pub of Munich Cricket Club, the other MCC. Club trophies (including an Essex policeman's helmet) adorn the walls around the Stammtisch, or Club regulars' table, in the room adjoining the bar. But the chief curio and pride of landlord Peter Schubert is the framed correspondence between the MCC and 10 Downing Street when the Club appealed to Prime Minister John Major in 1992 for help in saving their cricket pitch. The Club's ground was commandeered as a heliport for world leaders during the World Economic Summit held in Munich that year. Cricket-loving Mr Major was persuaded not to use the improvised heliport, which would have damaged the pitch, and the Bavarian government was forced to use another site. MCC cricketers meet at the Annahof every Friday from 8pm, and they are sometimes in need of an eleventh man...

Ayinger Extra

Herzog-str. 14
Tel: 089 344-741
Two minutes from Münchener Freiheit station (U3/6)

Ayingerbräu Hell, Dunkles, Pilsener on draught; bottled wheat beer.

Mon-Fri 1200-0100; Sat 1700-0100; closed Sun

A small stand-up "kneipe", or bar, where the emphasis is on drinking the most popular of Ayinger's big portfolio of beers. Big Bavarian Hans will delight in practising his English, and inviting you to share his grand collection of snuff; take a big hanky along.

Bambergerhaus

Brunner-str. 2, Luitpold Park
Tel: 089 308-8966
U2/3 to Scheidplatz

Home brew pub producing dark wheat beer and an unfiltered pale beer classified as a Pilsener.
Ⓕ *Hot food*
Daily 1000-0100 (bierkeller 1730-0100)
✤ *Sun terrace*

Bambergerhaus was the first of the new generation of home brew pubs in Munich (there are now five). It was opened in 1987 by Prince Luitpold, of Kaltenberg beer fame in the cellar of an elegant Baroque house in the city's Luitpold Park. By day, a curious mix of young people and elderly ladies in feathered hats sit in the slightly intimidating and hushed ground floor pub-restaurant with its marvellous stuccoed ceiling. At night, the cellar opens up for business, attracting a more beer-oriented crowd. Drinkers sit at long wooden tables adjacent to the tiny brewery. On summer days, a sun terrace is the most popular spot to drink. In mid-1993, there were reports that the Prince planned to sell the brewery.

Clemensburg

Clemens-str. 61
Tel: 089 348-346
Tram 12 from Scheidplatz, U3/U2

Spaten Hell and Pilsener on draught; bottled Franziskaner wheat beer, and Dunkel.
Daily 1900-0100

Two large dartboards are the focal point of this busy night bar, and they are in constant use by Germans with a steady throw. If you fancy your chances with the "arrers", remember the locals here are no push-over. Many of them are card-carrying members of the Munich Darts League, which has strict rules about competition matches - every player must produce a stamped card with a photograph to verify their team eligibility. In true German style, it is all very serious. It is also a popular haunt with students; customers in sharp suits and ties are as rare as teetotal Bavarians.

Fürstenberg Schwabing

Franz Josef-str. 48
Tel: 089 271-0283
Tram 27 to Elizabethplatz and walk 10 metres

Fürstenberg Export, Pilsener and pale unfiltered wheat beer on draught.
Mon-Sat 1100-0100; Sun and Public Holidays 1800-0100

An impressive line of tall, golden fonts dominates this sparkly little stand-up bar, which offers a pleasant alternative to Bavarian beer. Fürstenberg comes from Donaueschingen, the town on the edge of the Black Foest which lays claim to being the source of the River Danube (Donau, in German). One wall of the pub houses an unusual collection of beer trays, including some from Britain - see if you can spot the name of the defunct English brewery.

Haus der 111 Biere

Franz-str. 3
Tel: 089 331-248
Two minutes from Münchener Freiheit station, U3/6

One hundred and eleven beers from 25 countries, mostly in bottles and cans, but eight beers are served on draught: Warsteiner, Bitburger and König Pilseners from northwest Germany; Budweiser Budvar and the original Pilsener Urquell from the Czech Republic; Munich's Augustiner pale Export; Diebels Altbier, top fermented beer from Düsseldorf; and Guinness.
Mon-Fri 1600-0100; Sat-Sun and Public Holidays 1500-0100

Very much a modern bar with glitzy decor and loud music, but the owners faithfully maintain their beer menu detailing country of origin and style. The bottled range has several distinctive bocks, including Einbeck's Urbock from northern Germany, plus southern wheat beers. Pricey.

Osterwaldgarten

Kiefer-str. 12
Tel: 089 346-370
Five minutes walk from Münchener Freiheit station, U 3/6

Spaten Hell, Dunkel, Pilsener on draught; bottled Franziskaner wheat beer.
Ⓕ *Hot food*
Mon-Sat 1100-0100; Sun 1000-0100
✤ *Beer garden*

Beer and brass greet Sunday morning customers to the Osterwaldgarten, which is more like a cosy, friendly country inn than a town pub. The old Bavarian tradition of Frühschoppen - a morning pint or three accompanied by the strains of an oompah band - is still practised here; hence the early Sunday opening. This is as good a time as any to try a Bavarian breakfast of wheat beer and Weisswurst with sweet mustard. In winter, the Osterwaldgarten is a favourite haunt of ice skaters and curling players returning from a session on the frozen lake in the adjacent Englischer Garten park.

Schelling Salon

Schelling-str. 54
Tel: 089 272-0788
Tram 27 stops outside

Spaten Hell and Dunkel on draught; Spaten Pilsener and Schneider wheat beers, including Aventinus, in bottle.
Ⓕ *Hot food*
Thu-Mon 0630-0100; closed Tue-Wed

Breakfast here on boiled eggs and beer from 6.30am, if you wish, before the first serious chess players of the day arrive. The Schelling, a 19th- century pub with an impressive turreted front, has been in the same family for generations and is noteworthy for its two specialities: 15 varieties of fruit schnapps and not quite as many different pub games. Cards, chess, billiards, snooker - even table tennis in a back room - are the most popular pastimes. A section of the pub is reserved for those who just want to drink, eat and read the newspaper. Adolf Hitler used to lunch here in the late 1920s when he was still a largely unknown and struggling politician. His liking for the place is said to have ended abruptly when the landlord stopped his tap by cutting off his credit because of unpaid bills. Another former Hitler haunt, the Osteria restaurant, is a block away at Schelling-str. 62. It was there that Hitler befriended Unity Mitford, sister-in-law of 1930s British fascist leader Oswald Mosley. Unity, a student at Munich University, was infatuated with the Führer and shot herself in the nearby Englischer Garten after hearing that Britain had declared war on Germany in 1939.

WEST/SOUTHWEST

Deutsche Eiche

Ranert-str. 1, Lochhausen
Tel: 089 864-9000
S3 suburban train from Hauptbahnhof

Maisach Hell and Dunkel, Bitburger Pilsener and Kaltenberg unfiltered dark wheat beers on draught. Plus guest draught beers, including seasonal selections, and usually three bottled wheat beers.
Ⓕ *Hot food*
Wed-Mon 0930-2300; closed Tue
✤ *Beer garden*
Accommodation

This big, independent 19th-century country-style hostelry with its own butcher's shop and slaughterhouse (typical for rural northern Bavaria but unusual in Munich) expresses a rare innovative attitude to beer choice and variety, especially the idea of guest beers. Such enthusiasm for beer is oddly coupled with up-market catering, starched tablecloths and pink napkins. More modest eaters can buy tasty, warm snacks like Leberkäs (see General Information) at the butcher's and sit in the beer garden.

Gollierhof

Park-str. 22
Tel: 089 508-798
U4/5 to Messegelände station

Weihenstephan Hell, Pilsener on draught. Bottled wheat beer (filtered and unfiltered varieties) and Dunkel.
Daily 1100-0100

A street-corner local in one of the older parts of Munich close to the Oktoberfest ground, the trade fair centre, and the main railway station. Traditional wood panelling abounds in the main room, but there is also a bar to sit at. Drawings of Weihenstephan brewery hang on the walls of the carpeted snug. This offers the best chance to sample the beers of the self-proclaimed oldest brewery in the world if you do not have time to visit Freising.

Paulaner Bräuhaus

Kapuzinerplatz 5
Tel 089 530-331
U3/6, Goetheplatz

Paulaner-owned brew pub producing a house pale, unfiltered wheat beer and an unfiltered Hell on draught. Paulaner Pilsener and Dunkel also on draught.
Ⓕ *Hot food*
Daily 1100-2400
✤ *Large beer garden*

The ornate, marble-covered entrance resembles some big bank's ritzy head office - until you see the glistening brewing coppers behind the bar. The Bräuhaus is housed in a picturesque and cavernous 19th-century building which first brewed beer more than 100 years ago under the name Thomasbräu. The brothers Eugene and Ludwig Thomas studied brewing in Pilsen, Bohemia, and returned to Munich to introduce the pale beer style. Thomasbräu was eventually taken over by Paulaner, which opened the brew pub in 1989. Insultingly, the Thomasbräu name survives today only as an alcohol-free beer. There's a rare stand-up drinking section at the Bräuhaus, as well as a restaurant section and an unusual library room at the back.

Zum Mariandl

Schwantaler-str. 150
Tel: 089 504-218
U4/5, Messegelände station

Hacklberg Hell, Pilsener on draught. Bottled pale unfiltered wheat beer.
Mon-Tue and Thu-Sat 1000-0100; Sun 1000-1330, 1730-0100; closed Wed

If you prefer somewhere a little more intimate and snug than the Hofbräuhaus, or the 5,000-seat Mathäser, head for Zum Mariandl. This tiny pub consists of three tables and the same number of stools around the bar. It offers a good opportunity to sample beers from one of Passau's breweries. See if you can spot the Scottish pound among the banknote collection pinned to the wall.

SOUTH/SOUTHEAST

Forschungsbräustuberl

Unterhachingstr. 76, Perlach
Tel: 089 670-1169
S-bahn train line 1, southbound

Brew pub: Pilsissimus Export, St. Jakobus pale bock on draught.
Ⓕ *Simple fare*
March-mid Oct Tue-Sat 1100-2300; Sun 1000-2200; closed Mon except Public Holidays
✤ *Beer garden*

The two distinguished beers, served in litre-sized earthenware mugs, are available only seven months of the year. During the other five months the pub is shut while brewer Heinrich Jakob and son concentrate their skills on brewing research for other breweries. It is a service the Jakob family have provided since the brewery was established in 1936. Neither the prefab-like pub nor the glass-fronted brewery are architecturally exciting - it is the beer alone which attracts enthusiasts from miles around, especially on warm summer evenings when the small beer garden fills to capacity. If you express an interest in the beer to one of the matronly waitresses (who make no attempt to hide their liking for the boss's beer), Jakob senior will be summoned to peer over his half rim spectacles and wax lyrical. The food is Urbayerische, which means fairly basic fodder like sausages and cold pressed meats. The best accompaniment to these beers - and something is necessary with a litre of St. Jakobus - is the cheesy O'batzn (see food section). The pub's annual re-opening, about the first weekend of March, and the winter shutdown are marked by boozy celebrations complete with an oompah band.

Brauereigasthof Gmeineder

Hubertusplatz 5, Deisenhofen
Tel: 089 613-1617
S2 train southbound to Deisenhofen, 20 minutes from Marienplatz. Five minutes walk down Bahnhof-str. to T-junction, turn left and look for the tall blue and white maypole

Gmeineder Weissbräu unfiltered wheat on draught. Plus Augustiner Hell.
Ⓕ *Hot food*
Fri-Wed 1100-2300; closed Thu
✤ *Beer garden*
Accommodation

A "secret" brewery on the southern fringes of Munich which few Müncheners know about. The small, family-run brewery is part of a big, rambling modernised hotel-pub in the old part of this village which has been gobbled up by suburbia. There's only one house beer: an unusual wheat beer, which despite its chocolate-brown colour, defies being labelled a typical dark wheat beer. Well worth the trek, especially on a fine hot summer's day when it is a delight to sit outside beneath big, cool chestnut trees beside the brewery.

Brauereigaststätte Krailling

Margarethenstr. 59
Tel: 089 857-1718

Herrnbräu Hell, Dunkel on draught. Bottled pale unfiltered wheat.
Ⓕ *Hot food*
Daily 1000-2400
✤ *Beer garden*

If you are visiting Zum Alten Wirt in Krailling, another five minutes along Margarethen-str. brings you to this pub offering beers from Herrnbräu at Ingolstadt, north of Munich. The pub has a big beer garden, a surprisingly expensive menu and a naughtily misleading name; it is more than 25 years since there was a brewery attached to it. The No. 67 bus will save you the walk back to Planegg train station.

Isarbräu Gaststätte

Kreuzeckstr. 23
Tel: 089 798-961
On S-7 Grosshesselohe railway station

Home brew pub producing amber unfiltered wheat beer on draught. Occasional special wheat brews, such as the dark Dinkel (late Sept.) Plus a range of draught beers from the parent Hofbräuhaus brewery at Traunstein, near Salzburg on

the Austrian border (no connection with Munich's Hofbräuhaus).
◔ *Mon-Fri 1100-2400; Sat-Sun 1000-2400*
✤ *Small beer garden*

For railway enthusiasts, this is the next best thing to a brewery on a train. The pub and brew house are in the converted booking office of a station. The S-bahn suburban trains (15 mins to central Munich) stop outside. The booking hall has been given the traditional Bavarian treatment - the dark wood panelling and chunky burnished wood furnishings look as though they have been there for generations. The conversion took place in 1988. A quiet time to visit, and admire the gleaming mini brewery housed behind glass partitions, is mid-afternoon. It gets busy early evening when the commuter trains arrive and the kitchen re-opens. Adjoining the main pub is an unusual drinking annexe, which resembles a greenhouse.

Leiberheim

Nixenweg 9, Neubiberg
Tel: 089 603-295
S-1 train to Neubiberg. Right on Haupt-str. to Rathaus (town hall). Behind here, pick up woodland walk to the pub, ten minutes.

Erhartinger Hell and Pilsener on draught. Bottled pale wheat beer. Spring dark doppelbock Doppel Ritter on draught.
Ⓕ *Hot food*
◔ *Tue-Sun 1100-2300; closed Mon*
✤ *Beer garden*

The S1 suburban train line links a rich seam of beer, from Weihenstehan at Freising in the north to Ayinger in the south, with gems in between. One of these is the Leiberheim, a lively local which nestles alongside the Waldperlach, an area of tree-labelled woodland walks. No doubt because of its pleasant location, the pub has one of Munich's biggest beer gardens outside the centre, accommodating 3,000 customers. There's a low-priced menu, or you can eat your own picnic in the beer garden.

Salvator Keller

Hoch-str. 77
Tel: 089 459-9130
Tram No. 27, to Ostfriedhof

Paulanerbräu: five beers regularly on draught are 1639 Urtyp Hell, Dunkel, Pilsener, pale wheat beer and Salvator doppelbock. Dunkel wheat beer bottled.
Ⓕ *Hot food all day*
◔ *Daily 0900-2400*
✤ *Beer garden*

The brewery "tap", also known as Nockherberg after the hill it stands on overlooking the brewery, is a pub, beer hall and large beer garden combined. The small vaulted Keller is open year-round, while the enormous hall is reserved for special occasions, and really comes into its own during the Starkbierfest in March when tens of thousands of Muncheners flock to drink litre mugs of the daddy of all doppelbocks, Salvator. In the Keller, you can get away with a half litre sampling of the 7.5 per cent Salvator. Cooked meals are served in the Keller, where groups of locals gather in the evening for a game of cards.

An adjoining beer garden seats 3,000.

Zum Alten Wirt

Margarethen-str. 31, Krailling
Tel: 089 859-6236
S6 to Planegg. Straight along Bahnhof-str. and bear right past the onion-domed castle, five minutes

Graf Arco Hell and Dunkel on draught. Bottled pale and dark unfiltered wheat beers.
Ⓕ *Food*
Daily 1000-2300
✣ *Beer garden*

The pub is no oil painting and the beer garden has gaudy plastic furniture, but it is well worth the trek here on a sunny summer's day to sit under the horse chestnut trees beside the tiny River Würm and enjoy interesting beers and food for 30 per cent less than average Munich prices. The beer garden food kiosk serves amazingly generous portions.

EAST

Fliegerbräu

Sonnen-str. 2
Tel: 089 903-9600
S-6 train to Feldkirchen. Five minutes walk down Sonnen-str.

Fliegerbräu unfiltered pale wheat beer on draught. A second draught beer is brewed, according to season: Hell, Dunkel or Bock. Sister brewery of Isarbräu, both of which are owned by Hofbräuhaus of Traunstein, whose Dunkel and Pilsener are also on tap.
Ⓕ *Hot food*
Daily 1100-2400
✣ *Beer garden*

This "aerobilia"-festooned pub is the newest of Munich's new wave home brew pubs specialising in wheat beer. The pub, in a tastefully renovated old red-brick building, gets its theme from the now disused Riem airport down the road. The pub envelops the tiny brewery, which produces a wheat beer remarkably similar to Isarbräu. See if you can spot the difference. A light plane is usually parked in the beer garden at the rear. Interesting menu.

Unionsbräu Keller

Einstein-str. 42
Tel: 089 476-662
Tram 18, U4 5 Max Weber Platz

Home brew pub producing copper-coloured unfiltered Hell on draught from wooden cask, and seasonal specials, such as Maibock in May. Löwenbräu Pilsener on draught, plus Löwenbrau pale and dark wheat beers in bottle.
Ⓕ *Restaurant open 1100-2400*
Mon-Sat 1600-0100; Sun 1000-2400

Brewing returned to a corner of this renovated 19th-century former brewery in 1991, although on a much reduced scale. Unionsbräu was taken over by Löwenbräu way back in 1922 and the name faded into history until it was revived by Löwenbräu with the growing Munich fashion for "hand-made" beer. Today's tiny brewhouse and lagering tanks are in the vaulted cellars where customers sit at long wooden benches.

Despite this setting, it must be the quietest beer keller in the world. Ingredients for the house beer are organically produced - an increasingly important requirement for the hand-made image which appeals to the German preoccupation with health and environment. The ground floor restaurant/pub features displays of memorabilia of Munich breweries past.

A Munich beer garden *Photo: Robert Hetz*

Munich
Beer gardens

The smallest can accommodate only a few dozen people; the biggest will cater for a small town of 8,500. Whatever their size, beer "gardens" are a traditional part of summer life in Munich. The city's continental climate can push the thermometer as high as 35°C (102°F) for several days at a time, driving many people who live in small flats to find a cool spot outdoors. During the evening and at weekends, whole families join in the ritual of heading for the beer garden for a picnic.

Traditionally, a beer garden consists of long benches underneath horse chestnut trees. Sometimes there is a brass band playing; occasionally a children's playground. But there is always beer - often served in litre mugs - and food. Some beer gardens are attached to pubs, but the biggest and most popular are oases in parks where people take their own picnics.

The Bavarian beer garden idea developed in the days before the industrial revolution when brewers strove to store their beer in cool places, both to help it mature and stop it going sour. They cut caves into hillsides or dug storage cellars in the ground. Later, some brewers would open a few barrels on site in spring or early summer, and word spread rapidly that this beer tasted much fresher than the warm, flat and sometimes sour stuff which had been kept elsewhere.

Eventually, the brewers decided to tap into this growing outdoor market by providing comfortable facilities. When they began selling food as well, it became enshrined in law that customers were entitled to take their own food. There are 100 beer gardens in and around Munich. Here is a selection chosen for their variety of beer and location. Others, like the half hidden, tree-covered courtyard at the back of the Hofbräuhaus - reputedly the city's oldest beer garden - are referred to in the Munich Pubs section. The beer garden season depends on the weather. Some big gardens, like the Chinesischer Turm, will open in March if the winter thaw has already begun. A warm autumn can keep the beer gardens bustling until early November. The weather dictates opening times. Some, in residential areas, close at 10pm; others may keep serving until midnight if the weather is warm.

Am Nockherberg

Hoch-str. 77
Tel: 089 459-9130
Tram No. 27 from Sendlingertor Platz; stop Ostfriedhof.

Most Paulaner beers on

draught, including Salvator.
Ⓕ *Own food allowed*
◔ *Daily 0900-2400*

One of the original beer gardens which sprang up alongside pre-refrigeration lagering caves dug into the hillside on which this summer haunt stands. Such is the popularity of Paulaner's Salvator that during the adjoining beer hall Starkbierfest in March - hardly a time for outdoor drinking - the Nockherberg garden's 3,000 seats are fully occupied at weekends by an overflow crowd. On hot summer evenings, the horse chestnut tree-shaded beer garden is an outdoor oasis for families living in cramped flats in the neighbourhood.

Chinesischer Turm

Englischer Garten park
Tel: 089 395-028
Buses 54 154 (from Münchener Freiheit) stop outside.

Löwenbräu Export and pale unfiltered wheat beer on draught.
Ⓕ *Own food allowed*
◔ *April-Oct daily 1030-2300*

The "Chinese Tower" is so-called because the 6,500 seats are arranged around a 50-foot tall wooden pagoda, in which an oompah band of stout Lederhosen-clad Bavarians sit and serenade the drinkers (Wednesday evening and weekends). All Munich life gathers here: from punks to business people. Also features a 19th-century wooden carousel and organ.

Heide Volm

Bahnhof-str. 51
Tel: 089 857-2029
Opposite the train station at Planegg, S-6 line.

Hacker-Pschorr's range of beers on draught, including seasonal specialities. A Maibock festival takes place in April.
Ⓕ *Own food allowed*
◔ *Fri-Wed 1000-2300; closed Thu*

One of the biggest, if not the prettiest, beer gardens in southern Munich. A brass band plays on Sunday from 3pm. A large and ugly factory-block pub stands alongside. But inside, if the weather turns wet, there are two skittle alleys, drinking rooms and a beer hall where Hacker-Pschorr stars its lip-smackingly good St. Hubertus Maibock beer at a Bavarian concert festival, usually in April. Call landlord Willy Heide, one of the Oktoberfest ringmasters, to find out if the hilarious Bauern Ballet (a dance featuring hairy-legged farmers) is to be performed.

Hirschgarten (park)

Königsbauer-str., Nymphenburg
Tel: 089 192-591
Tram 12 to Romanplatz, then by foot via Gunther-str.

Augustiner Hell and Dunkles direct from huge wooden barrels; Kaltenberg's bottled pale unfiltered wheat beer.
Ⓕ *Own food allowed*
◔ *Daily 1030-2300*

With seating for 8,500, the Hirschgarten claims to be the biggest beer garden in Europe.

"Hirsch" is German for deer and a small herd nibbles grass on the fringes of this most traditional of Munich's outdoor drinking haunts. It is handy for a refreshing stop after visiting Nymphenburg Palace (see What To See).

Hofbräu Keller

Innere Wiener-str. 19
Tel: 089 489-489

Full range of Hofbräu beers, including seasonal specialities such as Maibock.
Ⓕ *Own food allowed*
Daily 0900-2400

One of Munich's oldest pub beer gardens; the old Victorian Hofbräu brewery stood next door until 1990, when it was demolished to make way for an hotel: Inside, the Keller is more a beer hall than a pub, with a series of large inter-connecting drinking rooms adorned with dark wood panelling. The Unionsbräu Keller is five minutes' walk away.

Königin

Königin-str. 34
Tel: 089 333-403
Buses 54 154

Thurn & Taxis beers.
Daily 1100-2300

The smell of horses sometimes drifts over this walled garden from a neighbouring riding school. The beautiful people gather here, and on hot, steamy evenings young men might be troubled by the state of undress of some of the pretty young fräuleins sipping beer. Own food not allowed.

Neue Schiess-stätte

Zielstatt-str. 6
Tel: 089 786-940
S-7 to Mittersendling station, then five minutes southwards along trackside path.

Kaltenberg Helles, Dunkles (from wooden barrels) and pale wheat beer on draught.
Ⓕ *Own food allowed*
Daily 1100-2200

One of the most pleasant beer gardens, with a friendly family atmosphere and children's playground. Imbibing from a litre mug of the cool, dark, dry König Ludwig beer and tucking into a plate of barbecued pork ribs while sitting beneath a spreading chestnut tree has to be one of life's great simple pleasures. The ornate Victorian pub in the grounds has long associations with local shooting clubs, hence the name. In winter, there is a Bavarian theatre and bock beer fests.

Viktualienmarkt (Open air food market near Marienplatz)

Tel 089 297-545

Munich's big six breweries take it in turns to supply beer. Hell on draught; Dunkles and wheat beers in bottle.
Ⓕ *Own food allowed*
Mon-Fri 0900-2000; Sat 0900-1500

The local custom here is to buy a wedge of cheese from one market stall and a bunch of radishes (a popular Bavarian accompaniment to beer) from another. You wash the radishes in one of the surrounding fountains, and queue at the kiosk for beer.

Waldwirtschaft

Georg-Kalb-str. 3
Tel: 089 795-088
S-7 to Isartalbahnhof station; follow signs for ten minutes.

Spatenbräu, including Dunkles on draught and seasonal specialities such as Maibock.
Ⓕ *Own food allowed*
Daily 1100-2200

Not the most accessible of watering holes, but a must for jazz fans and combines well with a visit to the Isarbräu brewery pub on the train station. Instead of the traditional oompah band, this beer garden offers jazz nightly (from 5pm) and during the day at weekends (Saturday from 2pm, Sunday from 11 am). Call ahead to find out if jazz is on offer in the adjoining pub in wet weather. After complaints from local residents about car noise, the landlord was considering running a customer bus service to and from the station.

Zum Alten Wirt

Margarethen-str. 31
Tel: 089 859-6236
S6 train to Planegg. Walk along Bahnhof-str. and bear right past the onion-domed castle; five minutes. Or Bus 67 from Planegg station.

Graf Arco Hell and Dunkel on draught (sometimes served direct from wooden barrels), plus pale and dark unfiltered wheat beers.
Ⓕ *Snacks served and own food allowed*
Daily 1000-2300

It is well worth the trek here on a warm sunny day (perhaps stopping en route at the Heide Volm, also listed) to sit under the horse chestnut trees beside the tiny River Würm and drink one of the most malty pale lagers imaginable - like chewing a handful of malted barley. Beer prices at Zum Alten Wirt are up to 30 per cent cheaper than in the city, and a kiosk in the pub garden serves whacking great snack portions at unbeatable prices.

Oktoberfest

EVERY year, one Saturday lunchtime in September, at precisely midday, the Lord Mayor of Munich takes off his jacket, puts on an apron and rolls up his shirt sleeves before swinging a big wooden mallet to drive a brass tap into a large wooden beer barrel.

"O'zapft is", he shouts in Bavarian dialect (meaning: the beer is tapped) and hands the first litre mug of foaming Oktoberfest beer to the guest of honour, usually the Prime Minister of Bavaria.

This ritual, on a tent-covered field a mile south of Munich city centre, is solemnly observed by German and foreign dignitaries and recorded by television crews - and is the signal for the world's biggest orgy of drinking and eating to begin. During the next 16 days, more than ten million pints will be drunk in ten cavernous canvas beer halls, each holding more than 6,000 people and a very noisy brass band. And the several million visitors to the annual Oktoberfest beer festival can be relied on to munch through 600,000 sausages, 750,000 roasted chickens, and 65,000 pork knuckles.

The origin of the Oktoberfest was a royal wedding in 1810 when the future Bavarian king, Ludwig I, married Princess Theresa. Local people joined in the celebrations with a party of their own on the site where today's festivities are held. Ironically, that first fest, on what has become known as the Theresienwiese, or Theresa's Meadow, took place without beer - it was a horse race and fair. But beer was soon an important component of what became an annual horse race and agricultural show.

Except for wars and pestilence (outbreaks of cholera in 1854 and 1873 stopped the festivities), Munich has been Oktoberfesting ever since. The advent of railways brought revellers from farther afield and the state government seized the opportunity to turn the Oktoberfest into a kind of Bavarian National Festival to underline Bavaria's proud independence from Prussian efforts to create a pan-German super state. Much as the Windsors never miss Ascot, the Bavarian royal family, the Wittelsbachs, maintained their own tent at the Oktoberfest every year until the monarchy abdicated in 1918.

Today, the Oktoberfest is an international event, attracting visitors from as far away as Australia and Japan. The horse racing has disappeared, replaced by a huge fun fair, and beer drinking is the chief activity. Only the big six Munich breweries are allowed to sell beer at the fest - a city council edict which increasingly upsets the many smaller breweries surrounding Munich.

A campaign to break this cosy cartel has been led for a number of years by Kaltenberg brewer Prince Luitpold, who not only has two breweries just outside the city but is the great-great grandson of the last Wittelsbach king (Luitpold made Diätpils drinking popular among figure-conscious British women in the 1980s).

In a bold bid to get round the monopoly rules, he opened a pub brewery in the city in 1987. But the city council then moved the goal posts, saying that only breweries established in Munich before 1970 qualified to supply the Oktoberfest. The sly change in the rules lost the Prince a bet with a Munich brewer which required him to walk 30 miles from his Kaltenberg Castle brewery to the Theresienwiese - carrying a litre mug full of beer. It is claimed that not a drop passed his lips en route. The reason behind the Munich cartel which excludes smaller brewers appears to be plain, old fashioned monopoly - the Public Enemy Number One of consumer choice, as British beer drinkers have repeatedly learned to their palate's cost.

Nowadays, it is virtually impossible to obtain the traditional strong, dark Märzenbier at the Oktoberfest. Each of the big six Munich brewers produce their own copper-coloured Festbier, which is a little richer and maltier than the everyday pale beer (Helles) supplied to the city's pubs. Märzenbier, which is brewed in March and allowed to mature longer, stopped being served at the fest at the end of the 1980s when the brewers thought it would be a good wheeze to introduce an alcohol-free "beer" as an alternative to the regular Festbier. Who ever heard of anyone going to a beer festival to drink what cynical Germans have dubbed lead-free beer? Stunningly, half a million pints of the stuff were drunk at the 1992 Oktoberfest. Märzenbier is still produced by the big brewers and it can generally be found in the city's bigger pubs during September and October, most notably in the Hofbräuhaus where that brewery's version is served on draught.

Despite its name, the Oktoberfest is always held in the second half of September. The starting date varies slightly from year to year, but the two-week drinking binge always ends on the Sunday evening of the first weekend in October. A parade of gaily-decorated brewers' drays, accompanied by brass bands and the Bavarian equivalent of Morris dancers - Schäfflertanzer - winds it way through the city centre to the festival ground on the first Saturday morning, watched by thousands of spectators. Before the parade convoy even reaches the festival grounds, Munich's thirstiest 60,000 drinkers are already sat in the beer tents impatiently waiting for the Lord Mayor's symbolic tapping of the first barrel before they begin lubricating their throats.

A second parade takes place on the first Sunday, featuring groups from many parts of Europe dressed in traditional costumes, plus folk and brass bands. It has been known for a Scottish bagpipe band to lead the parade; but then Edinburgh is twinned with Munich.

Munich goes a little mad during the Oktoberfest, which is one of the rare great levellers in German society, attracting people from all walks of life. Traditionally, many local firms give employees a half day off to visit the fest, and for a few hours office workers are on first name terms with bosses who, next day, revert to being Herr Schmitt, or whatever.

Beer tents are open all day from about 11am, but they are at their busiest from about 4pm until last orders at around 11pm (the fair and one or two smaller beer tents stay open until midnight, while some pubs and bars in the vicinity of the festival ground keep serving until 3am - just in case anyone is still thirsty).

Streets, trams and underground trains become littered with tipsy and, usually, cheerfully garrulous folk. The stiff formality of the German language breaks down - as well as a number of marriages. Each year the newspapers report a surge in the divorce rate which it is claimed stems from shenanigans which started round an Oktoberfest beer bench.

Despite all the drinking and eating records, nothing can compare with the record price paid for a single beer at an Oktoberfest: 21 million Marks. This occurred during the hyper-inflationary years of the early 1920s when Germany's post-World War One economy careered out of control and people needed wheelbarrows to collect their wages. 1994 may well see the second time in the Oktoberfest's history that beer prices have been in double figures: the cost of a litre (almost two pints) of beer is hovering around just below the 10 Mark level.

If you plan to visit Munich during the Oktoberfest, the most important advice is to book accommodation early. There are plenty of moderately priced guesthouses, but these get booked up many weeks in advance. It is not uncommon for some tour groups to be billeted in accommodation up to 80 km (50 miles) away! If you do not mind sleeping under canvas, the city council operates an overspill campsite in a southern suburb - and even lays on a commuter bus to ferry campers home when the beer tents close!

Key to symbols

Beers available. May be subject to change

Ⓕ Food available – meals or snacks as specified

Opening hours, given as a 24-hour clock

Overnight accommodation available on the premises

Munich Regions

This section details 21 breweries which flourish within a 40 km (25 mile) radius of Munich. Virtually all of them can be reached by public transport - 13 of them by Munich's fast, frequent S-Bahn train system.

The breweries and pubs have been selected for their choice of beer and accessibility. Other breweries within the 25-mile radius are at Dachau (S2) in the castle in the old town, Grafing (S4, east), Schloss Kaltenberg, a few miles beyond Geltendorf (S4, southwest) and at Altomünster, near Odelzhausen (see below) northwest of the city. A train service goes to Altomünster from Dachau.

S-Bahn trains run at 20 and 40-minute intervals, depending on the time of day. Maximum journey time to any terminus from Munich city centre is about 45 minutes.

The predominant flavour of beers in the Munich region is malty-sweet, particularly the everyday pale lagers, or Helles. There are, however plenty of exceptions to this rule: the sharp, coarse wheat beers to the east; the hoppy-dry Maisacher beers; Kaltenberg's malty-dry black lager; the fruity Märzen in Maxlrain; the rich bocks of Reutberg, Odelzhausen and Markt Schwaben. There is the deliciously broad portfolio of beers produced at Weihenstephan in Freising.

Aying organises several beer-oriented festivals through the year; the moated fairytale-like Schloss Kaltenberg stages jousting tournaments every June, when thousands of litres of dark bock are consumed; the monastery brewery at Andechs is a year-round centre of thirst-quenching pilgrimage.

ANDECHS

Klosterbräustuberl

Kloster-str. 1
Tel: 08152 1012
S-5 train from Munich to southern terminus at Herrsching (40 mins), then bus No. 956, or a one-hour walk through woodland.

Andechs Doppelbock, pale Spezial and dark Export on draught. Bottled pale Bergbock.
Ⓕ *Self-service canteen*
Daily 1000-2200
✤ *Beer garden*

Andechs is one of the few genuine monastic breweries where the brewing is still done by monks. Although many people pilgrimage to this small Benedictine monastery to admire the little 15th-century hilltop church and its religious relics, the adjoining brewery and beer cellar has become a cult attraction, drawing large numbers of beer drinkers from miles around. Weekends get very busy, so a daytime midweek visit is recommended, and a stroll through the woods from Herrsching Station does wonders for the thirst. There is canteen-style catering; try the monks' own blue cheese. The church houses 1,000-year-old religious relics from the Holy Land Crusades.

AYING

Brauereigasthof

Zornedinger-str. 2
Tel: 08095 7057
S-1 train southbound from Munich.

The brewery produces 13 different beers. Hell, Dunkel, Pilsener always on draught; others only in season, such as Fortunator doppelbock. Most are available in bottle most of the time. There are three bocks and three wheat beers. In addition, separate beers – including an unfiltered brown beer – are produced for two annual brewery-sponsored festivals which take place in the village: a jazz week in the second week after Whitsun, and an event in mid-October.
Ⓕ *Hot food*
Daily 1130-1430, 1730-2300; tap room closed Thu
Beer garden
Accommodation

This family-run country brewery has created a very high profile for itself to match its highly drinkable beer range. "Munich's Country Brewery" is more than a slick slogan; people do travel out from the city to drink from the font. The up-market ivy-covered pub-hotel has rooms with four-poster beds, but there is a more basic tap room, popular with locals, and a skittle alley. The pub menu recommends specific beers to match dishes, a welcome idea which should be copied everywhere.

DORFEN

East of Erding, on and around the B-15 road, there is a rich but sadly thinning seam of village pub-breweries: Isen, Dorfen, St. Wolfgang, Stierberg, Au am Inn, Haag, Gars. Traditionaly, this is wheat beer country. Dorfen, although with a very small population, had three breweries until very recently; now only one remains: Bachmayer. During the research for this book, one large brewery tap on Dorfen's pretty cobbled square was gathering cobwebs and the other (Bachmayer's own) had been converted into an office equipment shop. Perhaps the Dorfen beer price rioters of 1910 have finally reaped revenge. The village can be reached by train from Munich, but to explore the surrounding breweries you need a car, or else hire a bike.

Bachmayer Bräustuberl

Erdinger-str. 10
Tel: 08981 2110

Bachmayer Hell on draught. Bottled Dunkel, Pilsener and a seasonal bock.
Wed-Sun 0900-2400; Tue 1600-2400; closed Mon

A basic, cash-strapped local of formica-topped tables. Round the corner from the Marienplatz town square brewery, but a long way spiritually from the grand building flanking the square which used to be Bachmayer's brewery tap and premier outlet.

ERDING

A two-brewery market town at the end of Munich's S-6 suburban train line; renowned for many years as a home of good wheat beers. The breweries are Erdinger and Stiftungsbräu. Rooms are available at the Festlbräu Hotel in the market square (Lange Zeile), tel: 08122 2718), which despite its name serves Kaltenberg's König Ludwig Dunkel on draught, as well as Stiftung beers.

Erdinger Weissbräu

Lange Zeile 1
Tel: 08122 12208

Erdinger's pale unfiltered wheat beer, Stiftungsbräu Hell, Krombacher Pilsener and Maisach's Dunkel on draught; four other Erdingerbräu wheat beers, including Pikantus bock, in bottle.
Daily 0900-2400

Ignore Erdinger's ugly modern factory block brewery on the edge of town, and seek out this solid seat of tradition in the market square. A feast of wheat beer drinking awaits you in Erdinger's brewery tap, a delightfully unspoilt multi-roomed pub which also offers hot meals all day. Do not be too surprised if you overhear English accents at neighbouring tables; the travel ticketing conglomerate Amadeus, owned by several major European airlines, is based nearby and employs many British technical staff.

Gasthof zur Post

Friedrich Fischer-str. 6
Tel: 08122 2316

Stiftungsbräu Hell, Pilsener on draught. Bottled Dunkel and St. Prosper doppelbock (on draught in March) and Erdinger wheat beers.
Sat-Thu 1000-2300; closed Fri

Barn-like pub attached to the Stiftung brewery but surprisingly subdued and a little twee, seemingly more interested in candlelit dinners than beer. The atmosphere is more boisterous during March when there is a doppelbock fest.

FREISING

Northern terminus of Munich's S-1 train line; 40 minutes. Freising is an ancient ecclesiastical centre with its own cathedral and a claim to the oldest functioning brewery in the world. The Bavarian government-owned Weihenstephan Brewery, on a hill overlooking the town, has its roots in a monastery with records reaching back to the eighth century. The link with brewing is "only" since 1040, although today's brewery is far from medieval. It has working links with the world-famous neighbouring brewing school of the same name, which is part of Munich's Technical University. The "oldest brewery in the world" claim may be a little dubious, but there are no challengers for the title. Freising is also home to another brewery with a catchy if less distinguished slogan. Moy Brewery (which has a sister brewery in Haag, see South section) advertises that "Mein Bier ist Moy Bier" - My beer is Moy beer.

Bräustuberl Weihenstephan

Tel: 08161 13004
Ten-minute walk from the station. Follow Banhof-str left into Oberehaupt-str. At the junction with Johannes-str., pick up the Weihenstephaner Füssweg footpath.

A beer menu offers up to 10 brews, depending on the season. Hell, Dunkel Export, Pilsener are usually on draught; two bottled bock beers (pale Stephansquell, dark Korbinian – the latter on draught in Spring). Several wheat beers, including a bock version, are usually on sale, and sometimes a bottled top fermented Dusseldorf-style Alt is available.
Ⓕ *Food*
Daily 1000-2300
✤ *Beer garden*

The world's oldest brewery envelops this cosy brewery tap of dark polished wood and beery smells, which attracts fans from miles around. Before you order, ask for the Bierkarte (beer menu) to see what is on offer. There is also a food menu. In summer, you can sit outside under chestnut trees. The experience here is well worth the stiff climb up the hill from the town.

NB Moy beers are widely available in Freising. Try the Hofbrauhaus, Mainburger-str. 26. Tel: 08161 6010, or the station bar.

FÜRSTENFELDBRUCK

A market-cum-dormitory town 27 km (17 miles) with a pretty centre, west of Munich on the S-4 train line; home to one of two breweries owned by Prince Luitpold von Bayern, who might be familiar in Britain for promoting his Kaltenberg Diätpils. The Prince's other brewery is in a fairy tale-like moated castle just beyond the end of the S-4 line at Geltendorf.

Marthabräu Keller

Augsburg-str. 41
Tel: 08141 25490
10-minute walk through the town from the station

Kaltenberg König Dunkel, Helles and (in March) the Ritterbock on draught; the brewery pale and dark unfiltered wheat beers in bottle.
Ⓕ *Daily 1000-2400*
Beer garden

A plain, but friendly Bavarian pub attached to the biggest, but least photogenic, of Prince Luitpold's two breweries. In summer, the dark is served straight from the cask in the adjoining beer garden, although it is not a particularly pretty spot.

Hotel Post

Haupt-str. 7
Tel: 08141 24074

Herrnbräu, from Ingolstadt: Hell and Pilsener on draught; Kaltenberg's pale and dark unfiltered wheat beers in bottle.
Ⓕ *Hot food*

Daily 11000-2330
Accommodation

An old coaching inn on the town's main street, the Post is a typical Bavarian pub-restaurant and also has moderately priced rooms. The lunchtime menu is very good value.

HOLZKIRCHEN

Two-brewery town on the S-2 line southbound from Munich, 40 minutes, or take the mainline Bayrischzell train, which calls at Miesbach and Hausham breweries too. The picturesque tiny brewery at Reutberg is also reached via Holzkirchen. The two recommended Holzkirchen brewery pubs are in the centre; turn left out of the station and walk along Münchner-str.

Brauerei Gasthof Oberbräu

Marktplatz 18
Tel: 08024 64711

Oberbräu Hell, Dunkel, Pilsener on draught. Bottled wheat beer.
Ⓕ *Hot food*
Tue-Sun 1000-2400; closed Mon

Along with the church, this pub dominates the town square. Stretching out behind it is the picturesque 19th-century brewery, painted bright yellow. The pub's snug pine furnished Gaststube, on the left as you go inside, is the place to drink. There is a dining room to the right. The brewery has an interesting series of 12 bottle labels which detail the ingredients of beer and the brewing process.

Alte Post

Marktplatz 10a
Tel: 08024 6035

Genossenschaft Hell, Dunkel, Märzen
Ⓕ *Hot food*
Wed-Sun 1030-2400; Mon 1030-1400; closed Tue

A hotel and the flagship pub of the Genossenschaft brewery, which has an unusual kind of German-style cooperative ownership. This cooperative has played a part in helping to keep the financially troubled Reutberg brewery nearby in operation. As the name implies, the Post is an old coaching inn. The big, airy lived-in interior has the inevitable dark wood panelling. Sometimes there is great bustle, sometimes you could fall asleep in a corner and no-one would bother.

ISEN

12 km (7 miles) east of Markt Schwaben. Or by train from Munich via Markt Schwaben.

Gasthof Schnellinger Brückenwirt

Bahnhof-str. 10
Tel: 08135 247

Schnellinger pale wheat beer.
Thu-Tue 1000-2300; closed Wed

For wheat beer enthusiasts, it is well worth making the effort to reach this unexceptional pub by the railway station to sample the village brewery's pale wheat beer, which is a very good example of the style but little known beyond a few miles outside Isen.

MAISACH

S-3 westbound from Munich

Maisacher Bräustuberl

Haupt-str. 24
Tel: 08141 90111

Maisacherbräu Hell-Export, Dunkel Export, and Pilsener on draught. Erdinger pale and dark wheat beers in bottle.
Daily 1100-2300

This big, jolly pub can be spotted by the adjoining traditional tower brewery rising above surrounding buildings. Maisacher beers are much drier than the typical south Bavarian malty style. The pale export in particular, has an unusual bitterness. The dark lager is named after a 19th-century robber of local infamy. The cellar houses a skittle alley.

MARIABRUNN

This delightful brewery and pub, literally in the middle of a hilltop wood, takes its name from a well which is dedicated to the Virgin Mary and whose waters are said to have miraculous healing qualities. The small brewery is part of an old manor farm which grew up around the spring where legend has it that a woodcutter was healed when he bathed a severe wound after injuring himself in 1662. The spring became a place of pilgrimage for people with all kinds of injuries. The Well of the Virgin Mary (Mariabrunn) - which still functions today - was built, and a tiny pilgrimage church followed.

Schlossbrauerei Mariabrunn

Schlossgaststätte
Tel: 08139 261
S-2 northbound to Röhrmoos, then 3 km (2 mile) walk or bike ride, or B-304 to Dachau and follow signs to Schönbrunn. A good map is needed.

Mariabrunn Hell and Dunkel and Erdinger pale unfiltered wheat beer on draught.
Ⓕ *Food*
Tue-Sat 1100-2300; Sun 1000-2300; closed Mon
Beer garden

The main feature and attraction of this place, once you find it, is the peaceful beer garden set among tall stands of horse chestnut, beech and sycamore. There is a small, traditional pub and typical Bavarian food.

MARKT SCHWABEN

S-6 train northbound from Munich towards Erding.

A two-brewery market town-turned commuter dormitory, 30 minutes from the centre of Munich. To reach the old town centre where the Widmann and Schweiger breweries are located, turn left outside the main entrance of the station and head towards the onion-domed church tower.

Widmann Bräustuberl

Pfarrer Hueber Weg 2
Tel: 08121 23586

Widmann Hell on draught. Bottled Dunkel, pale unfiltered wheat beer and a Doppelbock called Lorenzi.

Wed-Sun 1000-2300; closed Mon and Tue

A rambling pub attached to the tower brewery. Some evenings the strains of Turkish music from an ethnic community knees-up in a back room - the Nebenzimmer - confuses the Bavarian setting. A notice on the front door giving opening times says the pub will open for funeral parties!

Bräustuberl Schweiger

Erdinger-str. 26
Tel: 08121 2210

Schweiger Hell, Dunkel, pale unfiltered wheat on draught. Bottled doppelbock.
Sun-Fri 1000-2400; closed Sat
Beer garden

The attraction of this cluttered, fussy brewery tap is the little beer garden in front of the brew house's gleaming coppers, which stand proudly on public display behind huge plate glass windows.

MAXLRAIN

On the Grafing-Bad Aibling-Rosenheim road, southeast of Munich.

Schlosswirtschaft

Aiblinger-str. 2
Tel: 08061 8342

Schlossbräu Maxlrain Hell, Pils on draught; bottled bock, Märzen and unfiltered wheat beer.
Ⓕ *Hot food*
Wed-Sun 1000-2300; Mon 1000-1400; closed Tue
Beer garden

A venue to recall the ancient link between brewing and the Bavarian aristocracy, which was as strong as monastery brewing. This pub stands next to a delightful lived-in Renaissance castle and its adjoining, much-expanded brewery. If the weather is right, the best place to sit is outside in the beer garden taking in the rural view. The kitchen does excellent schnitzels; cold snacks are good.

ODELZHAUSEN

24 km (15 miles) northwest of Munich just off the A-8 (exit Odelzhausen).

Schlossbräustüberl

Am Schlossberg 1
Tel: 08134 6606

Odelzhausen unfiltered pale Export on draught. Operator doppelbock in bottle (on draught in spring).
Ⓕ *Food in hotel*
Sun-Fri 1000-2400; closed Sun and most of January
Beer garden
Accommodation

According to local records, there has been a brewery and a castle on this site since 1450. Today, an up-market manor house hotel with a swimming pool and riding stables adjoins the brewery tap, where the brewer's pride is doppelbock Operator which was originally brewed to celebrate the re-opening of Munich's post-war re-built Opera House in 1963. The heady brew is still sold at the Opera House, but regular opera-goers travel to the charming, pine-panelled Bräustüberl in March for an Operator festival.

PFAFFENHOFEN

45 km (28miles) north of Munich on the B-13, or via A-9.

Hotel Bräustuberl Müller

Hauptplatz 2
Tel: 08441 8738

Müllerbräu pale Export, Pilsener on draught; bottled Dunkel Beissen Export and pale unfiltered wheat beer.
Ⓕ *Hot food*
Daily 1000-2400
Accommodation

The flagship pub of this expanding brewery on the fringes of Bavaria's Hallertau hop-growing district. It stands in a corner of the oblong town square, next to the white town hall. Take the left entrance if you want to drink with the town's beautiful people; take a right if you prefer the company of "Oldies". Extensive restaurant menu.

Zum Wohlherrn

Hauptplatz 13
Tel: 08441 75313

Urbanusbräu pale Export and Pilsener on draught; bottled Dunkel.
Sun-Fri 1000-2300; Sat 1000-1400

Quiet brewery tap of Müllerbräu's rival across the street, where card-playing is a favourite pastime.

SCHEYERN

Off B-13 near Pfaffenhofen, 42 kms (26 miles) north of Munich.

Scheyernhof

Tel: 08441 9791 (Hotel: 08441 4037)

Scheyern Hell and Dunkel on draught. Doppelbock Dunstler available March-April, also on draught.
Ⓕ *Food*
Sun-Fri 1000-2300; Sat 1000-1400
Beer garden
Accommodation

A large ancient religious complex dominates this tiny village. At its heart stands the Scheyernhof and a cobwebbed brewery. Scheyern beers are now brewed by Hasenbräu, of Augsburg. However, Scheyern's distinctive beer portfolio is still maintained, allowing Hasenbräu to trade on the quaint Klosterbier, or "monastery beer" image which is, of course, a fraud. However, the cavernous beer hall-like pub still retains a monastic air and is worth a visit to drink these beers "in situ". A small, simple hotel forms part of the Scheyernhof. There is a quiet beer garden with a charcoal grill on summer weekends.

ST. WOLFGANG

On the B-15, 6 km (4 miles) south of Dorfen.

Brauereigasthof Bauer

Haupt-str. 7
Tel: 08085 210

Bauerbräu Hell and Pilsener on draught. Bottled pale unfiltered wheat beer.
Ⓕ *Hot food 1130-1400 and after 1800*

Wed-Mon 1000-2300; closed Tue

A quiet village local which has had the pale pinewood refurbishment. A pleasant pub for all that. Good solid menu.

REUTBERG

Outside Sachsenkam village, B-13 road between Holzkirchen and Bad Tölz. Bus from Holzkirchen railway station stops outside.

Bräustüberl Kloster Reutberg

Tel: 08021 271

Reutberg Hell and Dunkel on draught; bottled Reutberger bock. Bottled Ayinger Pilsener and wheat beers.
Thu-Tue 1000-2230; closed Wed
✤ *Beer garden*

This small brewery, now commercially separate from the adjoining 17th-century monastery, must have the best beer garden view in Bavaria. Perched on a south-facing ridge, it offers a panoramic sweep along the northern edge of the Alps. The small, dark panelled one-roomed pub has a timeless feel, and on weekdays you could have the place and the view virtually to yourself. But the chestnut tree shaded garden can get crowded on summer weekends. The monks no longer brew themselves, but the brewery's future - and that of the classy dark lager and pale bock - now seems assured following a period of uncertainty.

VALLEY

Village close to A-8, Holzkirchen turn off, south of Munich.

Bräustuberl Arco

Tel: 08024 6316

Graf Arco Hell, Dunkel, Pilsener and unfiltered pale wheat beer on draught.
Ⓕ *Hot food lunchtime and evening*
Thu-Mon 1000-2300; Tue 1000-1400; closed Wed
✤ *Beer garden*

A charming old wood-beamed country inn, surrounded by lime and chestnut trees, a castle and a brewery. The locals are curious and friendly towards strangers, particularly if they have come specially to drink the beer.

Reinheitsgebot
the German Beer Purity Law

An epitaph on an ancient Bavarian tombstone bears the eternal damnation: "Here lies a wicked brewer". It is a reminder of how gravely, pardon the pun, Bavarian drinkers have regarded the quality of their beer down the ages.

In medieval times, German brewers were as mischievous or misguided as all others about beer ingredients. Across Europe, all manner of unsavoury substances were tossed into the brewing cauldron to cut costs or "improve" the flavour. Some of the end results often left drinkers rebellious, if not ill. Many a brewer suffered public wrath.

A survey in the early 15th century ordered by the Munich royal house, which controlled the profits if not the procedures of brewing, revealed the extent of the problem in Bavarian brewhouses. The survey found that among ingredients regularly being used to make beer were pitch, chalk, soot, potions of snake juice and ox's liver fluid. And these were just the seasonings. The fermentables included beans, peas and the occasional dead sheep.

Thus, in 1447, Munich council acting under royal instruction issued a decree restricting town brewers' ingredients to barley, or wheat, hops and water (they didn't know about the workings of yeast in those unscientific days). Slowly over the next few decades, this edict spread to other Bavarian towns.

In 1516, still beset by disputes over the quality of beer, which was becoming a growing source of royal revenue, the monarchy stepped in once again to regulate brewing. This action would guarantee the then ruler, Duke William IV, a lasting place in brewing as well as German history.

On April 23, 1516, William issued a proclamation laying down "forever" rules governing the ingredients of beer, as well as controls on prices and marketing. It was the world's first consumer protection law, and became known as the Reinheitsgebot, or Purity Law. The price of beer has changed somewhat since that distant spring day, and marketing is a little more hyped, but William's Purity Law is today adhered to by brewers throughout Germany.

Some of the early methods of checking whether a brewer was working to the new law were a little unscientific, even if universally popular. Three "weights and measures" men appointed by the council visited a brewer's premises wearing Lederhosen, which for some unknown reason had to be yellow. The brewer would pour some of his beer on to a wooden bench and the testers would sit on it for two hours. If when they stood up the bench stuck to their backsides, the beer had passed the purity test. If the bench stayed firmly on the ground the brewer was fined.

The survival of the Reinheitsgebot was a condition of Bavaria joining the new German republic after World War One. It was the early 1950s before its principles were finally adopted throughout the rest of western Germany. Breweries in eastern Germany are only now beginning to brew according to the Reinheitsgebot, following the collapse of the Berlin Wall.

In 1987, the West German government presented a petition with two and a half million signatures in defence of the Purity Law to the European Court. A French brewer had complained that the German authorities contravened European Community free market rules by banning his beers from Germany because they were not brewed according to the Reinheitsgebot. The German government said German

The Purity Law in full

beer was a health food — the source of up to 25 per cent of the average German's daily nutritious needs — and alleged that many foreign beers contained harmful additives. But whatever the merits of the Pure Beer Law, the court's view was that it was being used as a form of trade protectionism. The Frenchman won his right to sell his beer in Germany. Perhaps he is now doing good business, but even today there are not many foreign beers on sale in Germany. The German beer-drinking public not only has strong local brand loyalty, it firmly believes that Reinheitsgebot is right.

Some German brewers may well ignore their own domestic Purity Law when brewing for export (Bavarian brewers do not), but in my view European Community legislators missed a golden opportunity to raise the quality of brewing across Europe by failing to adopt the Reinheitsgebot as an EC standard. The Reinheitsgebot could, however, still be used as a kind of *appellation controllée* for beer.

Southern Bavaria

The guide's Southern Region covers all of Bavaria south of an imaginary line drawn across the state from Augsburg in the west to just below Passau (excluded) in the east. It embraces most of Germany's favourite summer and winter playground, the scenic Alpine region, but excludes Munich and a 25-mile radius of the city which is dealt with under Munich Region, an area mostly accessible by the rapid suburban rail system.

The Alpine region glistens with lakes for sailing, wind-surfing and swimming; mountains for hiking through in summer and skiing in winter. Smaller lakes freeze over in winter for ice skating and some resorts have long, hair-raising toboggan runs. For the less energetic, the area is peppered with castles, monasteries, churches - even breweries - in Renaissance, Baroque and Rococo styles; some of the world's best Baroque architecture can be found here. Then there is Neuschwanstein; the preposterous neo-Gothic castle of teetering turrets, built by an eccentric 19th-century king and copied by Walt Disney for Sleeping Beauty, is probably the single most photographed building in Germany. It is near the brewery town of Fussen in the southeast.

Accommodation in the Alpine area is plentiful and suits all pockets, from simple wayside bed and breakfast places to resort hotels. An efficient rail network penetrates into many mountainous places on a north-south system based on Munich. Buses link many stations on an east-west basis. The regional tourist authority is: FVV München Oberbayern, Sonnenstr. 10, 8000 Munich. Tel: (89)-597-347.

ALTENMÜNSTER

This sleepy village 25 km (16 miles) northwest of Augsburg, is now the adopted home of a rare beer - top-fermented Rauchenfels Steinbier, or stone beer - which has nevertheless acquired a high profile because of the unusual process involved. The beer gets its interesting burnt or smoky flavour because the wort is poured over red-hot rocks heated to 1,200 degrees centigrade, a process which caramelises the malt. This modern version of an old central European brewing method, pre-dating the use of metal kettles for heating the wort, was revived by brewery-chain owner Gerd Borges in the 1980s. The stone beer process was moved in spring 1993 to Altenmünster from its first modern home at Neustadt, near Coburg in northern Bavaria when Borges closed three of his five breweries for economic reasons. The switch has led to a variation in the technique. In Neustadt, the glowing stones were lowered into the wort in a metal basket. In Altenmünster, the pre-heated stones are placed in an open stainless steel bath and the wort is then washed over the stones. The effect is the same: the malt sugars in the wort stick to the stones, which are then removed while primary fermentation takes place. The stones are later put into the maturation tanks, where the green beer remains for two-three months, triggering a secondary fermentation. Only greywacke stone can be heated to such a high temperature without splintering.

Borges imports his stone from Austria, where the technique was quite common until the late 19th century. The stones are always heated over a beechwood fire. Originally, hot stones were used simply as a means of boiling the wort in wooden containers which could not be heated directly. Today, the practice is employed to recreate the flavour of the beer style which resulted. The Altenmünster brewery also produces a dark wheat beer involving the heated stones method, but after two weeks in maturation tanks with the stones the wheat beer is roughly filtered into bottles where a secondary fermentation continues. The Altenmünster brewery produces two other exceptional beers, including a very hoppy Pilsener, untypical of the region.

Bräustüberl Kronen

Haupt-str.
Tel: 08295 425

Altenmünster Pilsener and Jubelbier Dunkel on draught. Bottled Rauchenfels Steinbier and Weizenstein.
Ⓕ *Hot food lunchtime and evening*
Tue-Sun 0900-2300; closed Mon
✤ *Beer garden*

In mid-1993, "stone beer" was available only in bottles, but there were plans to serve it on draught at this brewery tap. The beer is also sold in some large Munich department stores (try Karstadt), and the supermarket chain HL, and is exported to eight countries including Britain. The quiet, unassuming Bräustüberl is a typical country Bavarian pub, an unlikely place in which to find and sample such an interesting range of beers. For those without a car, a bus service runs from Augsburg railway station, via a change at Zumarschen. The complete journey takes about 40 minutes. Traditional Bavarian food is served.

ALTÖTTING

For a little town (11,000), Altötting has an enormous and magnificently facaded traffic-free square. It is not quite as big as St. Peter's Square, Rome, but it is important enough in the Catholic church's scheme of things for 500,000 pilgrims a year to flock here. They participate in the Veneration of the Virgin and gather around two medieval churches laden with religious and art treasures from the 14th century. Pilgrims also get thirsty and many of them gather at three nearby brewery taps. One of them, Hellbräu, is just off the square.

Hellbräu Gasthof

Herrenmühl-str. 15
Tel: 08052 5832

Hellbräu pale Export and Lagerbier, an unfiltered Dunkel, and a Märzen on draught.
Ⓕ *Daily 0900-2300 (but closed Sat and Sun afternoons)*
✤ *Beer garden*

In summer, the nicest part of this somewhat pilgrim-infested hostelry is the horse chestnut tree shaded garden in front of the early 19th century building. It is furnished with adapted old brewing equipment such as sawn off coppers. The pub is a three minute walk from the pilgrims' square.

NB Hellbräu's beers are also served in the keller of the Hotel Post directly on the square.

Weisses Bräuhaus

Graming 79
Tel: 08671 6930

Three bottled house wheat beers: a medium dark unfiltered, a paler filtered variety, and a bock wheat, Kirtaweissbier.
Ⓕ *Snacks*
◔ *Fri-Wed 0900-2300; closed Thu*
✤ *Beer garden*

The old locals have been supping wheat beers in this old fashioned, spartan pub since long before the mid-Eighties dash to re-embrace the style as a popular drink throughout southern Germany. Simple snacks, such as sausages and sauerkraut, accompany the tasting sessions.

Brauereigasthof Müllerbräu

Burghausener-str. 2, Neutötting
Tel: 08671 2433

Müller Hell and Dunkel on draught. Bottled pale unfiltered wheat, Pilsener and Märzen.
Ⓕ *Hot food*
◔ *Tue-Sun 0930-2400; closed Mon*

More solid offerings of food match the sturdy variety of beers on offer in this busy, traditional pub. But you must go into the dining room to eat – leaving the serious imbibers to get on with their noisy card-playing at long tables, reminiscent of a Munich beer hall.

AU AM INN

Between Wasserburg and Mühldorf on a back road hugging the River Inn, off the B-12.

Bräustüberl Klosterbräu

Tel: 08073 1209

Klosterbräu Hell and Dunkel on draught. Own bottled Märzen, plus Unertl wheat beer.
◔ *Daily (opens midday or later)*
✤ *Beer garden*

This tiny village is little more than a large monastery church, a small brewery and a charming, ancient and unspoilt one-roomed inn. Dark wood panelling, creaky nooks, bare floorboards, a green heating stove, and a little rickety serving hatch combine to offer a snapshot of a bygone era. One end of the room overlooks a beer garden of gnarled chestnut trees, the other has a timeless view across fields of waving barley towards the River Inn. The monastery church, Kloster St. Maria, has a 1,200-year history. The brewery, once run by monks, is now privately owned.

AUGSBURG

One of the three oldest cities of the German-speaking world, Augsburg was founded by advancing Roman legions in 15BC and for centuries afterwards was a key business centre on the north-south trading route across the Alps. The world's first social housing programme was established here, in 1519. The Fuggerei, named after a wealthy business family, still provides shelter for the poor within its renovated almshouses. Another Augsburg first was engineer Rudolf Diesel's engine, produced here in 1893, and now on display in Munich's huge science museum, the Deutsche Museum. Noteworthy sights include the 14th century Gothic cathedral, the city walls, and the impressive Renaissance town hall. A yellow flag flies from its tower when you can view the Alps from the top. Until a few years ago, Augsburg had nine breweries. Today, the number has dwindled to five, including a quite new brew pub. Augsburg is reached from Munich in half an hour by fast Intercity train. Tourist office: Verkehrsverein, Bahnhof-str. 7. Tel: 0821 502-070.

Charlybräu

Ulmer-str. 43
Tel: 0821 426-346

Charlybräu pale and a darker bock unfiltered wheat beers on draught.
Mon-Fri 1700-0100; Sat-Sun 1000-0100

This curiously named brew pub (no-one seems to know who Charly is, or was) stands adjacent to the Oberhausen suburban railway station and is one of a growing chain of brew pubs run by the Hofbräuhaus Brewery of Traunstein. Munich's Isarbräu and Fliegerbräu are in the same group. Wheat beers are the speciality. Charly's is more of a night bar, popular with younger people - who have spearheaded the big swing to wheat beers in southern Bavaria.

Wirtshaus zum Hasenjagd

Kapuzinergasse 15
Tel: 0821 32990

Hasenbräu Hell and Pilsener on draught. Bottled Hasenbräu pale bock Fortissimo, and Weisser Hase pale wheat, plus Scheyern Dunkel, Doppelbock and dark wheat beers.
Ⓕ *Hot food*
Mon-Fri 1100-1400 and 1800-0100; Sat-Sun 1800-0300
✤ *Beer garden*

One of the oddest of brewery taps, where the beer is not the sole attraction. It stands at Hasenbräu's brewery gates, offering an excellent beer menu, yet this hostelry is a bit of a Jack the Lad looking for Jill sort of place. Customers regularly run the gauntlet of live music from the Fifties and Sixties. Sunday brunches are also interestingly unusual, at least for this part of the world: vegetarian and Indian dishes.

Goldener Gans Bräustüble

Weitgasse 11
Tel: 0821 512-266

Goldener Gans Urhell and Pilsener on draught. Bottled Dunkel and pale unfiltered wheat beer.
Ⓕ *Hot lunches*
Mon-Sat 1100-1400 and 1800-2300; closed Sun

Hasen means hare and it is barely more than a hare's breadth from the brewery of that name to the neighbouring Golden Goose Brewery (Goldener Gans), which claims to be the oldest brewery in Augsburg, founded in 1346. Why are teetotal creatures so closely associated with drinking beer (the British can count mucky ducks, black sheep, horny rams, and daft dobbins among their pub names)? However, the malty smells of the Goldener Gans brewery waft into the tap of the same name, although there is not the slightest sign of the 14th century. Popular with brewery workers. Good lunchtime menu.

NB The "Sieben Schwaben Stuben" is the most traditional pub in which to try Herren Pils, the most popular beer produced by Augsburg's large Riegele Brewery. The pub is five minutes from the railway station on Burgermeister-Fischer-str. 12. Closed Sundays.

Thorbräu beers can be sampled at the Thorbräukeller, Heiligkreuz 20, or the brewery tap at Wertachbrücker Tor 9 (closed Monday).

BAD TÖLZ

Spa town one hour by direct train from Munich, or by car on the B-13. There's a giant lido, the Alpamare, and a colourful Wednesday street market along Markt-str., which boasts a wonderful line of medieval buildings, including six pubs each bearing the name of a defunct brewery - a legacy of the 19th century when there were 21 local breweries exporting their beers by raft down the River Isar to Munich. The discovery of iodine-rich hot springs and the new status of health spa appears to have undermined the town's thriving brewing industry. Tourist office: Kurverwaltung, Ludwig-str. 11, tel: 08041 70071.

Gasthof Grünerbräu

Markt-str. 8

Tel: 08041 6091

Grünerbräu pale Export and unfiltered Pilsener, plus Bitburger Pilsener on draught; bottled Grünerbräu Dunkel, two wheat beers, dark bock, and a pale bock.
Daily 1000-2400

The brewery is adjacent to the railway station, but its main pub is in the main street of the old town. A quiet pub which livens up in the evening, the Grünerbräu is noteworthy for its range of beers, in particular the unfiltered Pilsener.

NB Gasthaus zum Höcknen, Markt-str. 41, also sells

Grünerbräu beers, plus a selection from Weihenstephan. Closed Friday.

BAD WÖRISHOFEN

South of Augsburg (40 km or 25 miles), just off the B18 between Mindelheim and Landsberg.

Hotel Löwenbräu

Hermann-Aust-str. 2
Tel: 08247 5056

Löwenbräu unfiltered Urtrunk, Pilsener, Dunkel on draught. Bottled unfiltered wheat beer. In spring, the Doppelbock Leusator is also on draught.
Ⓕ *Wed-Sun 0700-2400; Tue 1600-2400; closed Mon*
✤ *Sun terrace*
Accommodation

A brewery hotel-pub catering for middle-aged Germans taking the so-called Kur, or "cure", bathing in, or drinking the mineral waters of the little town's spa (the Bad prefix signifies it is a spa town). Certainly more refreshing are Löwenbräu's broad range of beers, most notably the Urtrunk and Pilsener. Too much Leusator and the spa comes in very handy. The rustic Löwen-Grube keller features a strumming yodeller nightly. A hotel double room costs about 65 Marks per person.

BERCHTESGADEN

Set among craggy peaks in an area of great scenic beauty, Berchtesgaden is the beginning of the German Alpine Road (Deutsche Alpenstrasse), the tourist route which winds its way westwards for 480 km (300 miles) through the Bavarian Alps to Lake Constance (Bodensee). This pretty, dinky town which gets crowded out with visitors in July and August is noted for two other things, one savoury the other unsavoury. Salt has been mined from the surrounding hills for more than 450 years. A visit to the mines, including a boat ride on a subterranean lake, is now part of the tourist agenda.

Many visitors, especially Americans, whose armed forces have relaxed in these parts since 1945, also visit the one remaining symbol of the Third Reich and Adolf Hitler's love affair with the area. The dizzy heights of the Kehlstein, sometimes known as the Eagle's Nest, was Hitler's 6,000-ft high mountain chalet retreat. It is reached by a perilously narrow, winding road which climbs more than 2,000 feet. The last few hundred feet of the journey to the peak – which offers terrific views – is via a lift built into the rock. Hitler's main holiday home, at nearby Obersalzberg, where the hapless British Prime Minister Neville Chamberlain negotiated "peace in our time" in 1938, has been destroyed. Berchtesgaden can be reached by train from Munich, via Bad Reichenhall. Local tourist office: Kurdirektion, Königsseer-str. 2. Tel: 08652 5011.

Bräustüberl im Hofbräuhaus

Brauhaus-str. 13
Tel: 08652 61903

Hofbräu Hell-Export, Dunkel

and Pilsener on draught. Plus Thurn und Taxis beers.

Tue-Sun 1000-2400; closed Mon and November-mid December

The name of the brewery - which has no links with Munich's Hofbräu but is owned by Thurn und Taxis - is the clue to its origins. In German, Hof historically referred to a royal court, household or property; in this case it was the prince-bishop Catholic hierarchy who ruled this region for centuries. Brewery records date back to the 16th century. Until the mid 19th century, the local brewer-monks maintained a beer monopoly through a deal between the church and the Bavarian Wittelsbach monarchy, which itself did well out of the beer tax. Nothing much changes. The pub's elegant Fürstenzimmer (Prince's Room) sums up the past, like a picture, saying more than 1,000 words.

ETTAL

Monastery-dominated village close to the Passion Play centre of Oberammergau, The Linderhof Palace of "Mad" King Ludwig, and Garmisch-Partenkirchen.

Hotel Ludwig der Bayer

Kaiser Ludwig Platz 10
Tel: 08822 6601

Klosterbräu Ettal Dunkel and Pilsener on draught. Bottled Curator Doppelbock.

Daily 1000-2300

Accommodation

A large church dome - painted inside in Rococo-style heavenly blue and soft pink - is the architectural focal point of this 14th-century monastery complex which includes a school, a brewery and a distillery. The pub grew up in the shadow of the dome to cater for pilgrims, and now tourists. The more basic Bräustüberl is the most atmospheric room in a pub of stone pillars, vaulted ceilings and dark wood panels. Most visitors take away a bottle of the monks' liqueur, made from mountain herbs and said, inevitably, to have health-giving properties.

FUSSEN

Quaint Alpine holiday town of Elizbethan-style half-timbered buildings on the border with Austria. Close to the utterly eccentric Neuschwanstein Castle, which Walt Disney used as his model for cartoon fairytale classics such as Sleeping Beauty.

Bräustüberl Bräuhaus

Rupprecht-str. 5
Tel: 08362 7843

Bräuhaus Hell-Export and Pilsener in draught. Bottled Märzen and a spring season Doppelbock, Alpinator.

Ⓕ *Hot food*

Tue-Sun 1030-2400; closed Mon

A small locals' pub which is nevertheless friendly to outsiders who come to Fussen to stand in endless summer queues to gawp at Mad King Ludwig's 19th-century turreted castle. The food is excellent local fare.

HAAG

Two-brewery village on B-15 between Dorfen and Wasserburg.

Gasthaus Weissbräu Unertl

Lerchenberg-str. 4
Tel: 08072 8297

Unertl's unfiltered pale wheat beer and Kloster Au Hell on draught. Bottled Unertl bock wheat.
Thu-Tue 1100-2400; closed Wed

Down a sleepy lane, separated from the tiny brewery by a field, this pastel blue and white painted building seems more like a Georgian gentleman's country house than a pub. But inside there is no mistaking its purpose: scrub-topped tables, wooden floor, tiles and an upturned sawn off copper forming a funnel roof over the bar.

Gasthof Freundl

Haupt-str. 17
Tel: 08072 1011

Moy Hell on draught. Bottled pale and dark wheat beers.
Ⓕ *Hot food*
Tue-Sun 0900-2400; closed Mon
Accommodation

A typical, all-purpose Bavarian country town pub, combining locals' drinking corners and an everyday restaurant. Big portion pork dishes are served via the pub's own butcher's shop – a common tradition in rural Bavaria. The Hofbrauhaus Graf von Moy brewery (which also has a brewery in Freising) is the impressive turreted building up the hill.

HAUSHAM

A-8, Irschenberg junction, B-307 to Schliersee Lake; or Munich-Bayrischzell train.

Brauhaus Bräustüberl,

Schlierseer-str. 8,
Tel: 08026 8203

Hausham Brauhaus Hell and Märzen on draught; bottled pale unfiltered wheat beer.
Ⓕ *Food*
Wed-Mon 1000-2300; closed Tue

The brewery and tap are directly opposite the railway station. Most of the pub was recently rebuilt, although the locals tend to sit in a retained older taproom. The Hell beer is the village's favourite, but wheat beer connoisseurs highly rate Hausham's Weissbier. There is a limited food menu. A few miles down the road, the large, picturesque Schliersee lake is well worth a visit. In summer there are boat rides, in winter it freezes over.

IRSEE

A tiny village dominated by a large former monastery near Kaufbeuren, off the B-12 Munich-Kempten road.

Brauereigasthof Klosterbräu

Klosterring 1
Tel: 08341 432-200;
Fax: 08341 432-269

Irseebräu unfiltered Kloster Urtrunk (an interesting cross between a Kellerbier and a Märzen), Pilsener, and an unfiltered doppelbock on draught. Bottled pale and dark unfiltered wheat beers. Finally, the Abtstrunk, a stiff, thick brew with the character of barley wine or a liqueur, and served sparingly in brandy glasses.
Ⓕ *Food in hotel*
Daily 1100-2300
Beer garden
Accommodation

An up-market complex of brewery, pub, hotel and museum. The sort of place for a full day's outing, perhaps even an overnight stop if you venture to trying the Abtstrunk and house schnapps. There are several unusual beers here. Drink them in the magnificent stone-vaulted keller, after taking the one-hour tour of the little brewery which, despite the name, is no longer associated with monks. A monastery was founded here in the late 12th century and for hundreds of years until secularisation in 1803 the monks brewed beer. During the 19th century, the mentally ill were locked up in its myriad cell-like rooms. Today, the renovated monastery building has a far worse function: training people to be government bureaucrats. Attached to the privately-run brewery is a museum of brewing history, open daily 0900-1900.

MIESBACH

A-8 to Irschenberg junction; the Munich-Bayrischzell train stops here.

Gasthof Bräuwirt

Marktplatz 3, Unterer Markt.
Tel: 08025 1435

Hopf Weizenbierbrauerei: Unfiltered pale, dark and dark bock wheat beers, draught and bottled; plus Hell and Dunkel beers from Holzkirchen's Genossenschaft brewery.
Tue-Sun 0930-2330; closed Mon

A large friendly town square pub. The Bräuwirt boasts its own butcher's shop, and fresh meat dishes from the kitchen. The brewery, which the train passes on the right just before Miesbach station, is a specialist wheat beer producer and was in the forefront of technical developments in the early 1980s which resulted in unfiltered wheat beer on draught. Until then, most Bavarian brewers had insisted that such a lively, unstable style of beer could only be sold bottled (see Wheat Beer Wave). Hopf's beer can be tried in draught and bottled form. Some Bavarian purists say draught wheat beer generally is not as well matured as bottle conditioned varieties. If you have time before jumping on the train to visit the next brewery stop down the line (Hausham), the waxworks on the Oberer Markt is an interesting diversion.

MURNAU

On the B-2, 20 kms (12 miles) north of Garmisch-Partenkirchen. A large water sports lake, Staffelsee, is nearby.

Bräustüberl Karg

Untermarkt 27
Tel: 08841 8272

Karg pale wheat beer, and a dark Karg wheat beer mysteriously called Schwarzer Woiperlinger.
Ⓕ *Hot food*
Tue-Sun 0900-2300; closed Mon

Karg brewery produces other beers, but it is the wheat beer which draws people from near and far to drink at the font – although bottled versions can now be bought in Munich and farther afield. This old-fashioned, dimly lit pub gets busy early evenings and especially Sunday lunchtimes when the locals flock in for their fix of Schweinebraten and Knödl.

NESSELWANG

A pretty mountain holiday village on the B-309 "Deutsche Alpenstrasse" tourist road between Kempten and Füssen with two small breweries. Train connections from Kempten. In summer, city Germans come here for a fresh air "cure"; in winter it is a ski centre.

Brauereigasthof Hotel Post

Haupt-str. 25
Tel: 08361 30910

Postbrauerei Dunkel, Gold (pale), Pilsener on draught. In summer, an unfiltered Zwickel also on draught; in winter this is replaced by a Bock. Bottled dark unfiltered wheat beer (Postillion); other seasonal brews for spring, autumn and Christmas.
Ⓕ *Hot food*
Daily 0730-2300
Accommodation

The Meyer family, who have owned and managed the Post for over 100 years, think more about their beer than just something to wash down the roast. They actively encourage customer interest in the whole business of brewing, and beers are matched to food. The pleasantly renovated coaching inn has its own brewery museum, and there are weekend "beer seminars" with lectures from the brewer, tasting sessions, a beer quiz, and a seven course dinner with beers to match. The house nightcap is Nesselwanger Hopfen-Geist – a beer schnapps which is matured for a year.

Brauereigasthof Zum Bären

Haupt-str. 3
Tel: 08361 3255

Bärenbräu Hell and Pilsener on draught. Bottled Dunkel, Bock and pale unfiltered wheat.
Thu-Tue 0900-2400; closed Wed

Slightly poorer neighbour to the more up-market Hotel Post up the street, but a pleasant old pub nonetheless. Similar tasting beers to the Post here, but the wheat beer is distinctive.

OBERAUDORF

Village close to the Austrian border, south of Rosenheim and next to the A-93.

Bräustüberl

Rosenheimer-str. 19
Tel: 08033 2918

Bottled Bals unfiltered wheat beer. Rosenheim's Auerbräu Hell and Pilsener on draught. Bottled Auer and Erdinger pale wheat beers.

Thu-Tue 0900-2300; closed Wed

The village's tiny wheat beer brewery stands adjacent to this separately-owned modern pub; hence the sign advertising Auer beers. Ask by name for a Bals wheat beer (the brewery's only product), or you are likely to be served something else.

OTTOBEUREN

A few kilometres southeast of Memmingen and close to Bavaria's state border with Baden Württemburg. The town boasts a Benedictine monastery noted, not for beer, but its basilica which boasts a whopping great organ.

Ottobeurer Braugasthof

Marktplatz 12
Tel: 08332 7990

Ottobeurer Kellerbier and Pilsener on draught. Bottled Ottobeurer pale unfiltered wheat beer.

Daily 1000-2400

Accommodation

The family-run brewery also operates the Hotel Hirsch next door, which seems designed for keep fit fanatics. There is a big indoor swimming pool, saunas, solarium, a steam bath, medical baths, gymnasium, a table tennis room and, to relax in the evening, a bowling alley in the cellar. There is also a keller bar to enjoy the Kellerbier and the brewery's other delights.

PEISSENBERG

Train south from Munich, or B-2 road from Starnberg

Bräustüberl Plötzbräu

Haupt-str. 81
Tel: 08803 3068

Plötzbräu Hell-Gold and Dunkel on draught; bottled unfiltered pale wheat called Rigi, and a dark wheat called Schützenkönig (shooting champion). Plus Warsteiner Pilsener on draught.

Tue-Sun 1000-2400; closed Mon

It would be worth coming here even if the pub served only Whitbread Tankard keg. It is a rare gem: arched stone drinking alcoves heavy with time and mystery; a vaulted panelled ceiling; boisterous customers in traditional dress whose drinking enthusiasm would make any brewer content. This is central Europe anywhere between 1800 and now. Hollywood's "Dracula" set makers must surely have been through here. Treat with respect.

RAITENHASLACH

Off the B-20 which hugs the Austrian border and River Salzach between Salzburg and Burghausen. Many people come here to listen to Bach concerts in the Baroque setting of the former Cistercian monastery church; others are attracted by the six beers on the menu at the brewery tap across the way. The monks have gone, and the brewery is today privately run.

Bräustüberl Raitenhaslach

Raitenhaslach 2
Tel: 08677 5507

Klosterbrauerei Hell, Pilsener, pale unfiltered wheat beer on draught. Bottled Kellerbier, a dark lager and a dark unfiltered wheat.
Ⓕ *Hot food*
Mon-Thu 1030-2300; Fri-Sat 1030-2400; Sun 1000-2200
✤ *Beer garden*
Accommodation

Records show that monks first brewed here 700 years ago – and were running an inn in the 16th century. Today's pub, dating from 1585, is a collection of carefully renovated, high-ceilinged stone vaulted rooms, with bare wooden floors and high-back settles. The food is good quality, sturdy Bavarian. A good place to tackle the entire beer menu and stay the night.

ROSENHEIM

Forty minutes by train from Munich. By road, south of Wasserburg on B-15 road. Three breweries.

Fischküche Bierbichler

Gillitzer-str. 10
Tel: 08031 32761

Bierbichler pale unfiltered wheat beer.
Ⓕ *Hot food*
Mon-Sat 1100-2400; closed Sun

Fish and wheat beer were once a popular combination. Here is one place where that tradition survives, and there are plenty of takers. As the name implies, the Fischküche (literally Fish Kitchen) specialises in fish dishes – and the only beer on sale to accompany the food is Bierbichler's Weissbier. The result is that virtually everyone in Rosenheim can direct a stranger to this spacious, bustling turn-of-the-century pub.

Gasthof Stockhammer

Max-Joseph-Platz 13
Tel: 08031 12969

Flötzinger Hell, Pilsener and pale unfiltered wheat beer.
Ⓕ *Hot food*
Mon-Sat 1000-2400; closed Sun

A centuries-old pub which has been renovated in that way the Germans often have of making a place look as though it was built yesterday. The schnitzels and Hell beer go together well.

NB Beers from Rosenheim's third brewery, Auerbräu, are widely available in the town and elsewhere. See also the entry for nearby Oberaudorf.

TEGERNSEE

A big lake and backcloth of mountains makes Tegernsee a popular day trip destination from Munich, and for many there is a compulsory stop at the lakeside brewery keller. A direct train runs from Munich; turn right out of the station to reach both the brewery tap and the lake. Ferries criss-cross the lake, except when it occasionally freezes over. Steam trains occasionally operate on the private section of rail line alongside the lake, from the junction station Schaftlach, near Bad Tölz. Check the timetable at the Regional Tourist Office in Munich: Fremdenverkehrsverband, Sonnen-str. 10, tel: (089) 597-347.

Herzogliches Bräustüberl

Schlossplatz 1
Tel: 08022 4141

Brauhaus, or Herzoglich Bayerisches Brauhaus (HB): pale Spezial and dark bock on draught; bottled Dunkel export and pale bock.
Ⓕ *Snacks*
Daily 1000-2330
✤ *Lakeside beer garden*

The vaulted cellars of the 17th-century Bräustüberl, where monks once sat in silent contemplation, is a classic south Bavarian beer drinking haunt: noisy, jolly, constantly crowded. There is little time for eating here, as witnessed by the very basic snacks menu. If you are really hungry, visit the more spacious, cellar beer restaurant next door. The adjoining former Benedictine monastery has its origins in the 8th century. The brewery was "acquired" by the Bavarian monarchy after 19th-century secularisation and is still in aristocratic hands: Duke Maximilian, of the Wittelsbach family which ruled Bavaria until the monarchy was abolished in 1918. The family coat of arms is used to maximum PR effect, hence the brewery name: Herzoglich Bayerisches Brauhaus, or Brewhouse of the Bavarian Duke.

TRAUNSTEIN

Gasthof Schnitzlbaumer

Stadtplatz 13
Tel: 0861 4534

Schnitzlbaumer Hell and Pilsener on draught. Bottled Georgitrunk, a Märzen.
Ⓕ *Hot food*
Wed-Mon 1000-24000; closed Tue

Lively town square locals' pub, with the brewery at the bottom of the hill behind. Card-playing and the consumption of roast pork and dumpling go on in equal proportions here. One of the few watering holes open in Traunstein on Saturday afternoons. Lengthy, generous menu.

NB There are three other breweries in Traunstein. The biggest is Hofbräuhaus (no relation to Munich's Hofbräu), whose beers can be drunk in two Munich wheat beer brew pubs, Isarbräu and Fliegerbräu, which it owns. Another Traunstein brewery, Weissbräu, is owned by the expansionist Ayingerbräu, of Aying near Munich, and produces Ayinger's wheat beers. Kieselbräu is widely available in Traunstein and produces a yeasty, turbulent rusty-coloured wheat beer.

WASSERBURG

S-4 to Ebersberg terminus, and change to local main line train; by road, the B-304 from Munich. A visit to this picturesque time-warp town is worthwhile if only to marvel at its largely unspoiled survival in the late 20th century.

Wasserburg is a jumble of Gothic, Renaissance and Baroque architecture wrapped up in a lazy loop of the River Inn. The setting is best seen by climbing the hill to the castle, from where you can look down over a once important medieval town which fell into a centuries-long slumber after its river trade slumped.

Hotel Brauerei Fletzinger

Fletzingergasse 1
Tel:08071 8010

Fletzingerbräu Pilsener draught; bottled Hell and Dunkel.
Ⓕ *Hot food*
Daily 1030-2330
Beer garden
Accommodation

A cosy, old fashioned town centre hotel/pub, dotted with antiques, and with moderately-priced rooms. The kitchen serves excellent food.

WEILHEIM

Train from Munich, or B-2 road from Starnberg.

Gasthof Bräuwastl

Schmied-str. 15
Tel: 0881 4591.

Bräuwastl unfiltered brown wheat beer; Munich Spaten Hell and Dunkel on draught.
Ⓕ *Hot food*
Sat-Thu 1000-2400; closed Fri

A lovely old two-roomed pub, boasting gnarled wood furnishings and ornate Baroque plasterwork. The small brewery produces only wheat beer, bottled conditioned. The food menu includes dishes from Schwaben, the far southwest region of modern Bavaria.

Dachbräu Stüberl

Murnaur-str. 5
Tel: 0881 2693

Dachbräu Hell and Dunkel on draught; an unfiltered wheat beer and a darker bock wheat beer, both in bottle.
Sun-Fri 1000-2300; closed Sat, and sometimes winter Sun
Beer garden

This is the sort of undistinguished hostelry you visit strictly for the beer.

Photo: Stefan Moses

Central Bavaria

The Central Region extends southwards from just below Nuremberg to Landshut, which is 65 km (40 miles) north of Munich. It excludes Nuremberg (which is in the Franconia Region) but includes the historic, picturesque and beery, medieval towns of Regensburg and Passau in the east. Regensburg claims to be the home of the first known brewery in Europe, north of the Alps. Passau has arguably the most architecturally attractive brewery in Germany (Hacklberg). The region embraces the Bavarian Forest-Czech border area, and guides scenery-loving travellers through the chalk-cliffed Altmühltal river valley (see below). The not-so-blue River Danube meanders through the region, linking a string of brewing pearls in Kloster Weltenburg, Kelheim, Regensberg and Passau.

One of the world's biggest hop-growing districts, the Hallertau, is to be found here. Fields of hop poles line both sides of the roads in an area extending north of Freising up to the Danube around Abensberg. Some breweries here grow their own hops (Schlossbräu at Au, for example), and the abundance of the great aromatic climbing herb clearly influences local beer tastes. Overall, there is a broad range of styles: from the comparatively dry Pilseners in the Hallertau (Au, Abensberg) and again along the Czech borders (Furth im Wald, Passau), to some outstanding Märzens (Plank in Laaber, Goss in Deuerling), fine wheat beers (Schneider in Kelheim, Andorfer, Passau) and interesting unusual brews (Dampfbier, Kupfer Spezial in Zwiesel). Fürth im Wald is a good base from which to explore western Bohemia, and tours to Czech brewery towns, including Pilsen, are organised from there.

ALTMÜHLTAL

Wooded cliffs line this scenic valley through which the River Altmühl meanders, and along whose banks is a string of excellent small breweries – from the Schneider wheat beer brewery at Kelheim in the east, to the Schattenhofer brewery at Beilngries, and beyond to Eichstatt. The valley is popular with walkers and cyclists (there are cycle paths). In 1992, water poured into the final section of the Rhein-Main-Donau Canal, part of which runs through the valley, to complete an engineering dream first envisaged 200 years ago. The canal is 3,500 kilometres long and links Rotterdam on the North Sea with the Black Sea. For advice about walking and cycling in the area, write to the Tourist Office, Rathaus, 93309 Kelheim.

ABENSBERG

Off the B-16 between Regensburg and Ingolstadt

Another Bavarian market town of just 10,000 people which boasts three breweries. The biggest, Kuchlbauer, has recently decided to promote itself as a wheat beer brewery, as though it always had been. A pity, because this is hop-growing country and Kuchlbauer, more than its two rivals, uses the hop to wonderful effect in its more traditional brews. Sadly, it seems to have given up brewing dark lager. But all three breweries still produce Märzen, which is the main liquid refreshment at an annual town festival on the first weekend in September.

Gasthof zum Kuchlbauer

Stadtplatz 2
Tel: 09443 1484

Kuchlbauer Hell and Pilsener on draught. Bottled unfiltered pale wheat and a bock wheat called Aloysius. Märzen in autumn.
Wed-Mon 0900-2400; closed Tue
Accommodation

A terrific community pub which formerly housed the brewery and today remains the architectural focal point of the small, traffic-free town square. Its crenellated roof resembles a castle. In mid-afternoon the new arrival is greeted by the sound of fists pounding a table or two: a game of cards is in progress, Bavarian style.

Hofbrauhaus Stuben

Stadplatz 13
Tel: 09443 6824

Hofbräu (no connection with Munich's Hofbräu) Hell and Pilsener on draught. Bottled Dunkel, plus pale and a dark unfiltered wheat beers.
Thu-Tue 1000-2300; closed Wed
Pavement terrace

On the opposite side of the town square, the Hofbräu is everything the Kuchlbauer is not: twee, with pretty tablecloths and neatly folded napkins.

Brauereigasthof Ottenbräu

Ulrich-str. 15
Tel: 09443 6242

Hell on draught. Bottled Dunkel, Märzen and Pilsener.
Tue-Sun 0900-2300; closed Mon

The brewery tap of the most run-down of Abensberg's three breweries; the sort of basic but inoffensive boozer most upwardly mobile Germans would shun nowadays.

ADLERSBERG

A tiny village, 8 km (5 miles) northwest of Regensberg just off the A-3 autobahn.

Brauereigasthof Prösslbräu

Dominikanerinnen-str. 1
Tel: 09404 1822

Prössl Hell, Dunkel, Pilsener on draught. A dark doppelbock,

Palmator, is also available on draught (from Palm Sunday).
Ⓕ *Hot food*
◐ *Tue-Sun 0700-2400; closed Mon, and 20 December-15 January*
✤ *Beer garden*
🛏 *Accommodation*

Once part of a Dominican convent, this small unpretentious country inn is nowadays popular with Regenbergers attracted by the peaceful beer garden, budget-priced meals and the home-brewed beer. The Palmator is well worth the trip, but if you drink too much you might need to book a room. The brewery has been in the same family since 1838.

AU IN DER HALLERTAU

Small town on the B-301 between Abensberg and Freising

Schlossbräu Keller

Schlossbräugasse 4
Tel: 08752 9822

Schlossbräu unfiltered Hell and Dunkel Kellerbier on draught. Bottled Pilsener, pale Export Hopfengold and a pale unfiltered wheat beer.
◐ *Wed-Thu 1700-0100; Fri-Sun 1100-0100; closed Mon-Tue*
✤ *Beer garden*

A delightful, if up-market, beer keller in the cellars of this picturesque brewery beside a Renaissance manor house (hence the Schloss prefix) in the heart of Germany's Hallertau hop-growing district. The brewery produces some of the cloudiest non-wheat beer this writer has encountered and many a Briton who drinks with his eyes might be put off. But persevere, the two draught beers are outstandingly tasty. And like all unfiltered varieties they have no detrimental effect. Schlossbräu uses hops from its own neighbouring fields and uses water drawn from its own well. There is an excellent cheese selection in the keller.

BEILNGRIES

B-299 in the Altmühltal valley, between Regensburg and Eichstätt

Brauereigasthof Goldener Hahn

Hauptstr. 44
Tel: 08461 419

Schattenhofer Pilsener on draught. Bottled Dunkel. Seasonal specialities.
◐ *Daily 0700-2400*
✤ *Beer garden*
🛏 *Accommodation*

If you are travelling along the scenic River Altmühl valley (Altmühltal) this is a good spot to spend the night. Apart from Schattenhofer beers, the town's main street is peppered with pubs serving a variety of beers from the region. The moderately priced accommodation is in a converted former brewery building. The Schattenhofer family has been brewing here for nearly 400 years.

BERCHING

B-299, south of Nuremburg, north of Beilngries

Brauerei Gasthof Winkler

Reichenauplatz 22
Tel: 08462 27331

Bären Pilsener, pale unfiltered wheat and Alt-Berchinger Dunkel on draught. Bottled Hell, Märzen. Seasonal Josefi Bock beer on draught in March.
Ⓕ *Hot food*
Mon and Wed-Sat 0900-2400; Sun o900-1500; closed Tue and first two weeks of September
Accommodation

A traditional Bavarian country-style tavern in the centre of a 1,100-year-old walled town of half-timbered houses. Budget priced rooms and meals, and friendly staff, plus the interesting range of in-house beers makes it a pleasant overnight stop.

BÖBRACH

Village in the Black Forest, 12 km (7 miles) north of Regen

Brauereigasthof Eck

Eck 1
Tel: 09923 685

Eckbräu Hell, Dunkel, Pilsener on draught; bottled pale and dark unfiltered wheat beers, and Magistrator doppelbock.
Ⓕ *Food*
Tue-Sat 1000-2330; Sun 1000-1500; closed Mon and week following Easter
Accommodation

An old fashioned country brew pub in the heart of the Bavarian Forest close to the Czech border. Bed and breakfast here is excellent value (about 38 Marks per person). In late March, the pub has its own Starkbierfest featuring the house Magistrator on draught. In late August, there is a shooting competition.

DEUERLING

B-8, 15 km (9 miles) northwest of Regensburg

Brauereigasthof Goss

Haupt-str. 1
Tel: 09498 2315

Goss Hell on draught. Bottled Dunkel and Märzen.
Wed-Mon 0900-2300; closed Tue

A village local which has no identifying signboard, but which is very friendly once you find your way in. It is wedged between the brewery and the river bridge in the centre of Deuerling, which you might also miss if you blink. The Märzen is a must.

DRACHSELSRIED

Black Forest, 20 km (12 miles) north of Regen. Close to Böbrach brewery. Blink and you could miss this hamlet of several hundred souls, yet it boasts two breweries, and one provides excellent stopover facilities. Breweries and pubs are practically glued together, so there is little distance to stagger if you attempt to sample all ten beers produced.

Zum Schlossbräu

Tel: 09945 1038

Bruckmayer Hell on draught. Bottled Pilsener, two unfiltered wheat beers (dark and pale) and Respektator doppelbock.
Ⓕ *Hot food*
Daily 0900-2200
Accommodation

A homely tap room (Bräustuberl) is the focal point of this big rambling pub which claims a history extending back to 1650, when it was home to the local lord of the manor. For today's transient residents, there is a heated indoor swimming pool and a budget priced menu, offering trout from the pub's own pond.

Gasthof Falterbräu

Tel: 09945 406

Falterbräu Hell and Arber Pilsener on draught. Bottled Dunkel and pale and dark unfiltered wheat beers.
Ⓕ *Snacks*
Tue-Sun 0900-2230; closed Mon

This solid 18th-century tavern is the more basic of Drachselsried's two brewery taps. A cheerful watering-hole nonetheless; noteworthy for the Dunkel and good-value cold snacks.

ESSING

Altmühltal valley, west of Regensburg off B-16.

The longest wooden bridge in Europe, at 193 metres (617 feet), is one of the attractions of this ancient village tucked beneath towering white cliffs with stands of 1,000-year-old oak trees on the peaks. A thriving little family brewery is another appealing reason to stop by here. The footbridge, spanning the Rhein-Main-Donau Canal, was built in the 1980s. The brewery dates from 1640. If you want to overnight here and the pub is full, try the Holz Apfel guesthouse a few strides away on Marktplatz 5, tel: 09447 386, where the friendly landlady likes to practise her English.

Brauereigasthof Schneider

Altmühlgasse 10
Tel: 09447 354

Schneiderbräu Dunkel on draught. Bottled dark unfiltered wheat, and Josef Schneider's Privat, a higher gravity pale beer. In May, there is a pale Bock on draught.
Tue-Sun 0900-2400; closed Mon
Accommodation

Here is a rural backwater brewery given a new lease of life by get-away-from-it-all tourists. To cater for them, brewer Josef Schneider has built a new up-market pub of fashionable pale polished pine and pink tablecloths. Thankfully, Herr Schneider's dark lager retains an uncompromisingly old-fashioned style.

FÜRTH IM WALD

Black Forest town bordering the Czech Republic. B-20, northeast of Regensburg.

The collapse of the Iron Curtain which once stood

menacingly at Fürth's backyard door has given new life to this old and attractive border town. Ancient cultural and social ties with Bohemia have been re-established, and cross-border soccer matches are a regular weekend feature. So, too, are visits to one another's breweries and pubs. Cheap day and two-day bus trips run from Fürth into Bohemia, especially to the nearby Czech brewing towns of Domazlice and Pilsen. Fürth itself has three breweries, serving some tasty Pilsener-style beers. The town is also noted for Germany's oldest folk festival, the 500-year-old Drachenstich, when the town square is closed off to become an open-air theatre re-enacting the slaying of a fire-breathing dragon which legend alleges once stalked the forests. Today, 1,400 townsfolk, dressed in medieval costume, and 200 horses are needed for the week-long event held annually between the second and third Sundays in August. Tourist office: Fremdenverkehrsamt, Schlossplatz 1, tel: 09973 3813.

Brauereigasthof Hofer

Waldschmid-str. 20
Tel: 09973 1327

Hofer Hell and Pilsener on draught. Bottled Dunkel.
Ⓕ *Hot food*
Daily May-September 0900-2400; closed Sat October-April
Accommodation

A lively brewery tap with budget priced overnight accommodation, conveniently placed on the road leading out of town to the Czech Republic border. Hearty breakfasts and good, solid Bavarian cooking.

Dimpflbräu Kellerschenke

Bräuhaus-str. 34
Tel: 09973 2775

Dimpfl Hell and Pilsener on draught.
Daily 1200-0100

This charming pub, like a favourite aunt's parlour stuffed with comfy old easy chairs, is hidden in the brewery courtyard. Perhaps the nicest place in town to drink beer.

NB Fürth's third brewery, Späthbräu, is at Lorenz Zierl-str. 20, tel: 09973 1269. Its most noteworthy product is an amber Märzen.

GUNZENHAUSEN

An old walled town close to the large Altmühlsee lake, southwest of Nuremburg on the B-466.

Brauhaus Gaststätte

Marktplatz 10
Tel: 09831 7043

Brauhaus Hell, Pilsener and pale Bock on draught. Bottled Märzen.
Ⓕ *Hot food*
Tue-Sun 0800-2400; closed Mon
Accommodation

A cosy brewery pub where the pale bock is always on draught and popular with the locals, despite its strength. It offers budget priced rooms and good regional cooking; unusually for rural Bavaria, vegetarians are catered for. If you are not one, ask about the wild game menu. The venison in rich, dark sauce is a fine accompaniment to the bock. Or is it the other way round? The Brauhaus beers are heavily consumed during the week-long annual local church festival between the second and third weekends of September.

KELHEIM

This attractive riverside town, with a beautifully renovated 18th-century pedestrianised centre, is home to one of Germany's oldest and most illustrious names in wheat beer brewing - Schneider. The brewery is part of the manicured old town centre, although Schneider moved to Kelheim only in the late 1940s after the RAF had bombed the firm out of its historic headquarters in the heart of Munich (Schneider's brewery "tap" remains in Munich. See Weisses Bräuhaus, Munich Pubs). The Kelheim complex houses a classic Teutonic beer keller. Two other breweries survive in the town, which not so long ago boasted five.

Weisses Bräuhaus

Emil-Ottl-str. 3
Tel: 09441 3480

Schneider's pale unfiltered wheat and the darker Aventinus bock, both in bottle. Karmelitenbräu Hell, Dunkel and Pilsener on draught.
Ⓕ *Hot food*
Daily 1000-2400
✣ *Tree-shaded beer garden*

There is a series of drinking and eating places in this big, rambling establishment off the main town square (Ludwigsplatz) which looks like a monastery. Perhaps the most appropriate place to savour your classic German wheat beer is in the Turm Stuben, a stone vaulted keller, heavily inlaid with Teutonic wall paintings. Better still, seek out the Jägerzimmer - a serious baronial room of solid, dark burnished woodwork. You can almost hear the knights' armour clanking. The menu is as solid as the architecture.

Hotel Aukofer

Allee-str. 27
Tel: 09441 1460

Aukoferbräu Hell and Pilsener on draught. Bottled Dunkel and pale and dark unfiltered wheat beers.
Ⓕ *Hot food*
Daily 1000-24000
Accommodation

A monumental brewery hotel with cavernous drinking and eating rooms, serving meals so large and heavy you might need to book a bed to recover.

Ehrnthaller Hotel

Donau-str. 22
Tel: 09441 3333

Ehrnthallerbräu Hell and Pilsener on draught. Bottled Dunkel.
Daily 0900-2300
Accommodation

Kelheim's smallest brewery certainly makes it difficult to sample its products. This is the only remaining town outlet, apart from a Chinese restaurant. What must have once been the brewery tap next to the classic tower brewery off the main square is now owned by Thurn und Taxis from Regensburg. Will Ehrnthaller survive the Nineties? The Hotel is quite cosy in a slightly quaint 1960s style.

LAABER

Brauerei Gasthof Plank

Martplatz 1
Tel: 09498 8707

Plank Hell and Dunkel on draught. Bottled Märzen and Pilsener. Hot food
Thu-Tue 0900-2300; closed Wed
✤ *Tree-shaded beer garden*
Accommodation

Cheerful locals' pub on the cobbled village square which can get busy at weekends with daytrippers from Regensburg who roar up the nearby Autobahn looking for a traditional rural lunch. Good solid Bavarian dishes, best accompanied by a bottle of the house Märzen.

LANDSHUT

By car from Munich via the A-92 or B-11. Alternatively, this picturesque town with three breweries is quickly reached by train in 30 minutes from Munich. Landshut is notable for architectural records: the longest and most perfectly preserved medieval street (Altstadt) in Europe; and the tallest brick church tower in Europe: St. Martin's 14th-century church (133 metres, 436 feet). See if you can spot Adolf Hitler depicted as the Devil in the church's stained glass windows. The Altstadt is a street of arcaded 15th- and 16th-century gabled houses. Every three years the town stages a huge festival and fancy dress parade (the next one is in 1996) re-enacting a royal wedding of 1475. The town's breweries help celebrate by producing "wedding beer" – Hochzeitsbier. There is a terrific view of Landshut's medieval layout from Trausnitz Castle which overlooks the town.

Kochwirt

Altstadt 388
Tel: 0871 25783

Wittmann Hell, Pilsener and pale unfiltered wheat beer on draught. Bottled Dunkel and dark wheat beers.
Ⓕ *Hot food*
Daily 1000-2400

A bustling pub and meeting place on Landshut's most dramatic and busy street. Good, budget priced menu.

Gasthaus zur Freischutz

Neustadt 446
Tel: 0871 26487

Helm (Landshuter Brauhaus) Hell on draught. Bottled Dunkel, Pilsener, pale unfiltered wheat and Bock.
Wed-Sun 1100-2330; Mon 1100-1500; closed Tue

A small, friendly local on a street in the old town which runs parallel to Altstadt.

Try also the Martinsklause, Kirch-gasse 229 (behind St. Martin's Cathedral), which serves Helm beers and is open daily, 1100-1430 and 1700-2400.

NB Landshut's third brewer is the elusive Reichardtbräu. The brewery is at Watzmann-str. 52.

LENGENFELD/VELBURG

Just off the A-3 Nüremburg-Regensburg autobahn, south of Neumarkt. The turn off is marked Velburg.

Winkler Bräustüberl

St. Martin-str. 6
Tel: 09182 170

Winklerbräu Hell, Hefe-Pilsener (an unfiltered Pilsener-style beer) and Kupfer Spezial on draught. Bottled pale Export and a clear Pilsener variety.
Ⓕ *Hot food*
Mon-Sat 0800-2300; Sun 0800-2100
Beer garden
Accommodation

A strikingly attractive country inn. The former farmhouse, whose pedigree goes back to the Middle Ages, has a dizzyingly steep gabled roof, and inside there are stone vaulted rooms. The accommodation is late 20th century, but then so are the indoor swimming pool, sauna and solarium. The roast lunches and dinners attract regulars from 50 km down the autobahn. The little family brewery has its own maltings. Bicycles for hire.

LOIFLING, NEAR CHAM

Off the B-20 road 7 km (4 miles) south of Cham

The home of Hofmarkbräu, one of those little breweries which has created a high market profile exceeding its out of the way location. Hofmark concentrates on producing two beers, packaged in old style, shapely swing-top bottles: one is branded as bitter, or Würzig Herb, the other mild, Würzig Mild.

Zum Hofmark Bräu

Hofmark-str. 29
Tel: 09971 32696

Hofmark "bitter" and "mild" on draught, Bitburger Pilsener. Bottled Arco pale wheat beer.
Tue-Sat 1000-2400; Sun 1000-1800; closed Mon

The cosy wood-beamed pub with stone pillars and a capacious vaulted cellar was once part of a 16th-century manor house. The brewery was once here, too, before it moved into its more modern buildings a mile away across the village. In quiet moments the landlady is keen to practise her English, but be warned: this otherwise idyllic watering hole is opposite a Bavarian fun park, the Churpfalzpark. Try a wet Tuesday afternoon in June for a quiet time.

MALLERSDORF

Village just off the B15 Regensburg-Landshut road, 15 km (9 miles) north of Landshut

Kloster Mallersdorf Bräustüberl

Nardene-str. 1 Klosterberg
Tel: 08772 69185

Kloster Hell on draught, plus a pale 7% bock in May and

November-December. Bottled Schneider wheat beers, plus a very hoppy, dry Pilsener from the tiny Stüttner brewery in the neigbbouring village of Pfaffenberg.

◔ *Tue-Fri and Sun 0900-2100; Sat and Mon 0900-1300*

The house beer here is brewed by nuns. Much of the small brewhouse's output is consumed by the nuns themselves with their meals, but a small, simple hostelry attached to the convent is open to the public to share the amber liquid served up by head brewer Sister Doris, a shy young nun who came top of her class at the Weihenstephan Brewing School a few years ago. The nuns have been brewing at their hilltop convent farm since they took over the site from monks in the mid 19th century. They grow their own barley.

PASSAU

"Capital" of the Black Forest. B-388 or A-92 and A-3 east of Munich.

A town which has the rare good fortune of being built at the confluence of three rivers. Old Passau is a colourful jumble of medieval cobbled streets squeezed on to a finger of land flanked by the rivers Danube and Inn. The third, less famous, river is the Ilz. The cathedral town on the border with Austria has a 2,000-year history; its Roman past is still being excavated. Some say it has an Italian air, like several old towns on the Inn, because of the strong influence of Italian architects in the 17th and 18th centuries. Passau's promoters like to claim the town is the gateway to the Bavarian Forest; it is certainly the departure point for cruise boat rides up the Danube (to Regensburg) and down (through Austria). Passau has an impressive castle (Veste Oberhaus) and the cathedral boasts the biggest church organ in the world: 17,388 pipes and 231 stops. It is played every weekday at noon - an inspirational interlude, perhaps, before you set out to sample Passau's five breweries: Innstadt, Löwen (no connection with Munich's Löwenbräu), Peschl, Hacklberg, and the small Andorfer wheat beer producer. Passau prides itself on being a "Radlerstadt", a bicycle-friendly town. You can hire bikes by the day for a small sum at the railway station.

There is a big range of accommodation, from simple guesthouse rooms, to plush hotels. Passau tourist office: Fremdenverkehrsverein Passau, Am Rathausplatz. Tel: 0851 33421.

Hacklberger Bräustüberl

Bräuhausplatz 7
Tel: 0851 58382.

Hacklberger Hell, an unfiltered Zwickelbier, and Pilsener on draught. Bottled pale unfiltered wheat beer. During Lent, a doppelbock called Humorator is available on draught.

Ⓕ *Hot food*

◔ *Daily 1000-2330*

✤ *Beer garden*

It is a brisk ten-minute walk

across the Schanzlbrücke bridge over the Danube out of the old town to reach what must rank as one of the most architecturally-attractive breweries in Europe. The yellow-stuccoed Renaissance tower brewery, behind ornate wrought iron gates, was built in 1668 for a prince. The brewery draws on spring water from the steep hillside behind. The 18th-century Baroque brewery tap is a warren of stone vaulted rooms and gnarled wooden furniture. There is an excellent menu, including some unusual and ancient local dishes which seem to be known only to cook Anni Biereder. Ask for her "Saure Watschn", a spicy concoction of offal meats with onions and sour cream. The tangy Zwickelbier is a perfect accompaniment.

Goldener Schiff

Unterer Sand 8
Tel: 0851 2436

Peschl Hell and Dunkel on draught, two bottled wheat beers; Bitburger Pilsener on draught.
Mon-Sat 1100-0100; Sun 1700-0100

A haunt of beards and pipes in an old town back street, offering Sixties music, the ubiquitous polished woodwork, and a late night tap in a town which tends to go to sleep about 11pm.

NB You can also drink Peschl beers on a rather tatty roof terrace adjoining the brewery (which also does tours by appointment: tel: 0851 2489) and overlooking the Danube at Rösstranke 4. Closed Monday.

Brauerei Gasthof Andorfer

Rennweg 2
Tel: 0851 51372

Located on northern tip of Passau. Take the steep, hairpin bending Neue Rieser-str. opposite Schanzlbrücke bridge over the Danube.

Andorfer unfiltered wheat beers: a pale, and a darker bock. Draught and bottled.
Ⓕ *Snacks*
Sun-Fri 0930-2400; Closed Sat
✤ *Beer garden*

In summer, fields of waving wheat surround this wheat beer home brew pub. The Andorfer, in the same brewing family since 1919, is a rambling hostelry of five dark wood panelled rooms, each with their own character and friendly, bustling waitress. It is fashionable with the young, but they come here purely for the beer and the chat. There's no muzak and only a limited snack menu.

Bräustüberl Löwenbrauerei

Kleiner-Exerzier-Platz
Tel: 0851 6497

Löwen Hell, Pilsener on draught. Bottled Dunkel, wheat beer.
Ⓕ *Hot food served 1100-2200*
Daily 1000-2300

The brewery tap is a traditional Bavarian pub adjoining the brewery in the centre of the town, 5 minutes from the railway station. Serious beer drinkers gather in the

Bierschwemme, an old Bavarian word for tap room. Hot food is served in the adjoining restaurant room. A tour of the brewery can be made by appointment. At the other end of the square is a piece of dour Nazi architecture, the Nibelungenhalle, which achieved more recent fame as the reception centre for the first waves of east German refugees who flooded across the border from Hungary in September 1989 heralding the collapse of the Berlin Wall.

Innstadt Brauerei Gasthof

Schmied-gasse 23
Tel 0851 3890

Innstadt Hell, Pilsener on draught; Dunkel in bottle.
Daily 1000-2300

Across the Innbrücke bridge over the River Inn which flanks Passau old town's southern edge, is an equally ancient huddle of narrow streets forming the village of Innstadt. This is the only point where the German border with Austria crosses the river to claim a slice of land. Here you will find the small Innstadt redbrick tower brewery and its unassuming tap, serving an excellent hoppy Pilsener.

REGEN

On the B-85, 48 km (30 miles) north of Passau. Apart from the Bürgerbräu brewery, the pretty cobbled square is the chief attraction of this little Bavarian Forest holiday town.

Bürgerbräu Gasthof Falter

Am Sand 15
Tel: 09921 4313

Bürgerbräu Hell and Pils on draught. Bottled Dunkel, and unfiltered pale and dark wheat beers.
Ⓕ *Hot food*
Tue-Sat 1000-2300; Sun 1000-1500; Mon 1600-2300
Accommodation

This big old rambling brewery pub has been given the tourist facelift with a forest of fashionable pale, polished pine furnishings. The emphasis is on food, but the Alt Regener Dunkel beer is well worth sampling. Cosy rooms offer a good base from which to explore the area.

REGENSBURG

Ninety minutes by road from Munich; take the B-11 from Munich to Landshut, then the B-15 to Regensburg, or the A9 and A93 autobahns. Frequent trains from Munich and Nuremburg. Regensburg should be a place of pilgrimage for all beer lovers. The compact, scenic cathedral town on the River Danube claims to have been home to the first brewery in Europe north of the Alps, supposedly built by the Romans who founded Regensburg as Ratisbon. It is a tall claim, but backed by some archaeological evidence – and a lack of rival bids for the title. Excavations which began in 1978 unearthed a 2nd-century Roman fortress and a combination of artefacts and structures which together, say archaeologists, mean only one thing: a brewery. The remains of a well, a fireplace, a kiln and a mill can be seen in situ in a museum which has been built over the site at Kornweg, off Prüfeninger-str., west of the old town. At the turn of this century Regensbyurg had 28 breweries. Today, there are five, including a home brew pub which opened in 1992.

Out on a geographical limb on the edge of the Bavarian Forest, Regensburg suffered little war damage. Its jumble of medieval cobbled streets, church spires, Renaissance and Baroque architecture is therefore more original than most. The Gothic St. Peter's Cathedral, or Dom, is the focal point of the ancient centre around which are scattered numerous old pubs. A medieval pack horse bridge spans the Danube, connecting with a large island in the river which is home to the St. Katherinen Spital Brewery. The town boasts a royal pile bigger and more ornate than Buckingham Palace. The 500-roomed Schloss St. Emmeram is home to Germany's richest and last feudal aristocratic family, the Thurn und Taxis dynasty, which made a fortune by running a private postal monopoly across central Europe for several centuries until 1867. They also brew beer.

Regensburg is a colourful and interesting base for a short holiday in this largely rural region. Bikes can be hired from the railway station. Excursion boats chug up and down the River Danube, taking beer hunters to Kelheim and on to the Weltenburg monastery upstream. Passau can be reached downstream. Today's Regensburg brewers are Bischofshof, Kneitinger, Thurn und Taxis, the newcomer home brew pub, Brauhaus Albrecht, and St. Katherinen. Regensburg also has a beer museum (undergoing renovation at the time of writing) and a German brewing history archive, which is looked after by the St. Katharinen brewery.

Regensburg's tourist office director claims that his town has the biggest concentration of pubs and bars in Germany, and one of the oldest – the 850-year-old Wurstkuchl beside the Steinerne Brücke bridge on the Danube. The town certainly enjoys any excuse for a beer festival. The most notable are: Maibockfest (beginning of May) in the Hofbräuhaus, Waaggasschen 1, Rathausplatz; Bischofshof Bierbrunnenfest (mid-Sept.), Hotel Bischofshof; Kneitinger Bockanstich, the tapping of the first barrel of Kneitinger Bock (first Thursday in October) at Arnulfsplatz. And every spring and autumn the local brewers dominate a two-week Volksfest, the Dult. For a list of pubs which have accommodation, contact the Fremdenverkehrsverein Regensburg, Altes Rathaus, 93047 Regensburg, tel: 0941 5070; fax: 507-4419. This tourist office is unusually enthusiastic about local beer.

Spitalgarten

St. Katherinenplatz 1
Tel: 0941 84774

Spital Hell on draught. Bottled Dunkel, Pilsener, pale unfiltered wheat and Kloster Weltenburg Bock.
Daily in summer 0900-2300; closed Sat October-May
Beer garden

Set amidst ancient churches and almshouses on the island in the River Danube, this old beer hall has a bustling atmosphere, especially early evening. The beer garden offers views of the cathedral's twin spires.

Bischofshof Gaststätten

Am Dom
Tel: 0941 59080

Bischofshof Hell and Pilsener on draught. Bottled Dunkel, pale unfiltered wheat, and Weltenburg beers.
Ⓕ *Hot food*
Daily 0700-0100
Beer garden

A cosy old pub of large rooms bedecked in dark polished wood. The cathedral is next door. Extensive, solid Bavarian menu.

Zur Bräuschänke

Galgenberg-str. 3
Tel: 0941 7823

Thurn und Taxis Pilsener and pale and dark unfiltered wheat beers on draught. Bottled Hell, Dunkel and the brown-coloured Schierlinger Roggenbier (rye beer, also a Thurn and Taxis beer).
Daily 1000-2400

This three storey yellow-stuccoed building is the flagship pub of the most profitable part of a £1,400 million estate owned by Europe's once most profligate family. Until 1990, Prince and Princess von Thurn und Taxis poured money into lavish lifestyles and wild parties (one four-day binge up at the castle nearby cost £460,000), fuelled by an estate which embraced the biggest private forest in Europe, two banks, two breweries, six castles, South American cattle ranches, numerous small business, and 250,000 Bavarian acres. But then Prince Johannes Baptista de Jesus Maria Louis Miguel Friedrich Bonifazius Lamoral, the 11th Prince von Thurn und Taxis, Prince zu Buchenau und Krotoszyn, Duke zu Wörth und Donaustauf, died after a second failed heart transplant. His widow, Gloria, 30 years his junior, discovered enormous debts, and the white dust sheets were pulled over many a darkened palace room. Only the brewery still makes a decent profit and the Princess who not so long ago spent over £24,000 on a party dress has been selling off precious family antiques. So spare her a thought when you sip a glass of her beer.

Kneitinger Keller

Galgenberg-str. 18
Tel: 0941 76680

Kneitinger Pilsener and Dunkel served direct from wooden casks. A Bock beer is available October-Easter, also on draught.
Ⓕ *Hot food*

Daily 0900-2400
Beer garden

One of the brewery's two main outlets (the other, more historic, pub is in the old town centre at Arnulfsplatz 3) and Regensburg's biggest beer garden with seating for 1,500 people. Inside, there are several traditional Bavarian drinking rooms - benches, acres of polished dark wood, and a cheerful, thigh-slapping atmosphere which gets noisier as the day turns into evening. Cooked meals are served.

Brauhaus Albrecht

Schwarz-Bären-str. 6
Tel: 0941 51055

Kupfer Dunkel and Messing Hell (pale) unfiltered beers on draught.
Ⓕ *Hot snacks*
Daily 1100-0100

Regensburg's home brew pub, opened in 1992 in an old pub in the historic quarter near the cathedral. It is popular with the young who seem keen to embrace the trend towards murky, unfiltered yeast-rich "healthy" beers which their fathers would probably have sent back as unfit to drink.

RIEDENBURG

In the Altmühltal valley between Kelheim and Beilngries. A village popular with holiday cyclists and hikers and boasting two wheat beer breweries.

Raststätte Talblick

Tel. 09442 2540

Riemhoferbräu Hell on draught. Bottled pale (Schwanen Weisse) and dark unfiltered wheat beers, plus Warsteiner Pilsener.
Ⓕ *Hot food lunchtime and early evening*
Thu-Tue 1000-2300; closed Wed
Terrace

Basic Bavarian country pub opposite the brewery. A sun terrace provides panoramic views across the valley.

Gaststätte Hopfenkeller

Riedenburger Brauhaus
Tel: 09442 2873

Riedenburger Pilsener on draught. Bottled pale unfiltered wheat.
Wed-Sun 1400-2300; closed Mon-Tue
Beer garden

A big, shady beer garden is the highlight of this otherwise slightly decrepit, rambling old pub beside a recently rebuilt brewery. On dry summer days, the beer garden opens daily from 1100.

ROTH

On B-2, 20 km (12 miles) south of Nuremburg.

There are two breweries in Roth. One is owned by the local ratepayers and successfully run by the town council, a practice which goes back many years, and maintains a rich portfolio of beers. Stadtbrauerei Roth (Büchenbacher Weg 8, tel: 09171 2379) sells its beers in more than 30 outlets in Roth and the surrounding countryside, but doesn't have its own pub. The beers include: Märzen, Dunkel, Bock (November-March only), pale and dark unfiltered wheat beers, and a Pilsener). The two breweries promote their beers heavily at two town fests: the second weekend in August and the first Sunday in September.

Zum Schwan

Haupt-str. 49
Tel: 09171 2301

Valentinbräu Natürtrüb (unfiltered), Pilsener and Dunkel on draught. Bottled Märzen.
Ⓕ *Hot food*
Daily 0900-2400

A brewery tap which has been tastefully renovated to return it to its turn of the century style. The dark beer not only tastes good as a drink, it is used to excellent effect in the house Biergulasch.

TEISNACH

Black Forest. 10 km (6 miles) north of Regen, off the B-85.

Brauerei Gasthof Georg Ettl

Deggendorfer-str. 1
Tel: 09921 1818

Ettl Hell and Pils on draught. Bottled Ettl Bayerisch Dunkel, Erdinger pale and dark wheat beers.
Ⓕ *Hot food*
Wed-Mon 1000-2300; closed Tue

An unexceptional roadside pub next to the brewery, but for dark lager enthusiasts worth seeking out for the house Dunkel. Good lunchtime menu.

WEISSENBURG

On the B-2, 45 km (28 miles) south of Nuremberg. Three breweries. The best time to visit is during the week following the third Sunday in August, during a beer-oriented church fest, the Kirchweih.

Brauereigaststätte Schneider

Bach-gasse 15
Tel: 09141 2407

Schneider Vollbier and Märzen on draught. A draught Festbier is produced for Christmas, Easter and the Kirchweih church fest.
Ⓕ *Hot food*
Thu-Tue 1000-2400; closed Wed

A lively old pub with a reputation for robust beer and food; several old Franconian dishes survive here, mainly offal-based. If you dare, choose from Saure Zipfel, Schlachtschüssel and - if it happens to be Tuesday - Metzelsuppe. The pub has its own pig slaughterhouse.

Sigwart-Bräustüberl

Luitpold-str. 17
Tel: 09141 4061

Sigwart Hell and Pilsener on draught. Bottled Märzen, pale bock, and pale and dark unfiltered wheat beers
Wed-Mon 1000-2300; closed Tue

It is recorded that there has been a brewery here since

1451, although the steep-gabled black and white half-timbered coaching inn is relatively young, dating only from the 17th century. The pub is at its liveliest early evening. Accommodation is available at Sigwart's Wittelsbacher Hof pub, Friedrich-Ebert-str. 21.

NB The future of Weissenburg's third brewery, Mack & Michel, Luitpold-str. 13, tel: 09141 2058, was uncertain at press time. The brewery produces Märzen and Dunkel beers.

WELTENBURG

4 km (2.5 miles) south of Kelheim on the River Danube.

The ancient monastic fraternity certainly had an eye for locations when they set about building their religious orders. This Benedictine monastery stands beneath white cliffs on a lazy bend of the Danube, and not much has happened to disturb the tranquil landscape since monks first settled here in the 7th century. Records show that brewing was in progress here in 1050, and the inevitable claim is that this is the oldest surviving monastery brewery in the world. There are no challengers to the title, although a former monastery closer to Munich, Weihenstephan, claims by ten years to be the oldest brewery in the world. What has certainly changed since the 11th century is the number of travellers stopping by for succour. Many people stumble on the rich, dark beers by accident since their chief reason for visiting the monastery is to view the Baroque chapel, one of the most noted examples of the extravagant 18th-century style taken to lavish extremes by Bavaria's Asam brothers. Some must find the chapel's interior so dizzying that they need a glass of the strong Bock beer to regain their equilibrium. Weltenburg beer is still produced in a small brewhouse within the active monastery, but these days it is managed by the Bischofshof Brewery of Regensburg.

Klosterschenke Weltenburg

Asam-str. 32
Tel: 09441 3682

Weltenburger Spezial-Dunkel and Asam Dunkel Bock on draught.
Ⓕ *Hot food*
April-October daily 0800-1900; November-March Wed-Sun 0800-1900; closed 20 December-1 March
✤ *Beer garden*

The dark, oak-panelled and stone vaulted beer hall-like setting is the right environment in which to drink these sturdy, almost black beers. The kitchen serves up equally sturdy traditional Bavarian food, such as thick chunks of roast pork (Schweinebraten) in a black sauce. A pungent home made cheese is on offer, too, plus two house schnapps - Klosterbitter - which are matured in oak casks. On warm summer days, visitors prefer to sit under the cool horse chestnut trees in the large courtyard. Note the early closing time.

ZWIESEL

A small, rather nondescript town in the Bavarian Forest which has nevertheless carved a niche for itself as a touring centre. It is the wealth generated by tourism which has doubtless enabled the town's two breweries to survive and prosper. And Zwiesel's family-run breweries, Jankabräu and Pfefferbräu, are certainly enterprising and innovative in a way which proves that small-town competition between two similar-sized breweries can be good news for beer drinkers. Nearby stands the village of Bayerisch Eisenstein, where the border between Germany and the Czech Republic uncompromisingly cuts through the middle of the railway station. The 19th-century station was rejuvenated when the Iron Curtain came down in 1989, but the grand entrance is still barred and bolted in a kind of No-Man's Land.

Gasthof Deutscher Rhein

Stadtplatz 42
Tel: 09922 1651

Jankabräu Pilsener and Kupfer Spezial on draught; four different bottled wheat beers: an unfiltered dark and pale, a pale filtered variety called Finkenweizen and Jankatinus pale wheat doppelbock (seasonal).
Ⓕ *Hot food (not served Sun evening)*
Daily 0900-2330
Accommodation

The Jankabräu tap is the only licensed premises where I have encountered draught beer dispensed by a computer-controlled digital measure gauge. I asked for a half litre mug of the copper-coloured Kupfer Spezial to quench my traveller's thirst and was told "we can only draw a programmed .3 of a litre measure from the tap". Point three still tasted delicious, however. The food, with Bohemian touches, is excellent, and you should round a meal off with a house-made Bärwurz - a clear schnapps made from the root of a plant which grows in the surrounding hills, Ligusticum mutellinum. Bärwurz has a spicy, parsnip-like flavour. "The best schnapps I have ever tasted", said my shotgun rider, Frank Baillie. The pub's 300-year-old vaulted cellar houses a small collection of ancient brewing implements. The pub has comfortable rooms.

Bräustuberl Pfefferbräu

Regenerstr. 9
Tel: 09922 3325

Pfefferbräu Export Hell, top-fermented Dampfbier, and a pale unfiltered wheat beer on draught. Bottled Märzen (all-year-round), Silvator doppelbock (March only) and a pale Weihnachtsbock (Christmas only).
Ⓕ *Hot food*
Wed-Mon 1000-0030; closed Tue

Walk down the hill from the Deutscher Rhein and the town centre to reach this lively locals' pub, where noisy card-playing and loud chatter punctuates the chimes of midnight most nights. A more sedate restaurant, bedecked in twee pale pine, caters for the tourist trade. The Dampfbier, using a rediscovered old family recipe, was originally produced as a one-off celebration brew to mark the brewery's 100th anniversary in the 1980s, but was so popular it is now on tap all the time. Pfeffer's reply to the Janka's Kupfer.

Key to symbols

- Beers available. May be subject to change
- Ⓕ Food available – meals or snacks as specified
- Opening hours, given as a 24-hour clock
- Overnight accommodation available on the premises

Picturesque Bamberg *Photo: Graham Lees*

Franconia
Northern Bavaria

For the beer enthusiast, Franconia is close to Paradise - and fortunately not so inaccessible. Not only does this rural region about the size of Wales house more than 450 breweries - the biggest concentration in the world - there is a wealth of brewing styles, some of which are now only found here.

In the still fiercely proud, independent-minded rural regions of central Europe, tribal tags remain very important. Like Welsh and Scottish attitudes to being British, people in Bavaria are Bavarians first, Europeans second and only then Germans. In Franconia, people are Franconian before they are even Bavarian.

It was only after Napoleon's conquest and occupation in the early 19th century that Franconia became part of Bavaria in his efforts to tidy up the map.

Historically, Franconia occupies the area of northern Bavaria from Coburg in the north to just south of Nuremberg, and from the Wagner music festival town of Bayreuth in the east to Würzburg in the west. Some Franconians still draw imaginary borders around their principality. In some minds, there is even a Lower, Middle and Upper Franconia.

For beer hunting purposes, this book's Franconia encompasses the border area with the Czech Republic and the fringes of the Bavarian Forest.

Beer drinkers can thank Franconia's relative isolation in modern times - prolonged after World War Two by the Iron Curtain on two sides - for the survival of a unique brewing culture.

Until now, Franconian brewing has sauntered on gracefully in a kind of time warp. Here we can find beers which have disappeared elsewhere, and a brewing industry which in many cases remains almost pre-industrial in its scale and practices. Some villages of no more than 2,000 people have two or three breweries. Many of them produce no more than a few hundred barrels a year, usually just for the one family-run pub. This cottage industry has survived because many of these tiny brew pubs are an integral part of a hand-me-down rural family culture little changed for centuries.

Alongside the brewery and the pub, the family enterprise might also include a farm with a herd of pigs, or a schnapps distillery; sometimes a butcher's shop or a slaughterhouse. No single part of these family enterprises is profitable alone, but added together they provide a reasonable income. Many of the brew pubs are the focal point of village life, and many are interlocked with ancient parish festivities: scores of them produce special beers to mark church events or anniversaries.

Inevitably, perhaps, as we approach the 21st century Franconia is sliding into the 20th, placing much of this pleasant way of life under threat from familiar fronts: rising costs, pan-European Community laws, changing habits and tastes - the inexorable march towards a homogenised society.

In the last few years more than 50 small breweries have closed in Franconia, extinguishing some excellent beers. One of them might have been your perfect pint; one now vanished beer came close to being mine. All the more reason, then, for those who relish the search for good beer to visit Franconia before too much more is lost forever. I have selected a range of local styles from a variety of town and country breweries. There are numerous breweries I have not included, chiefly because time or space did not allow it. Some of the breweries omitted are close to others which are recommended and the intrepid searcher will always make a new discovery. That remains the joy of Franconia - the knowledge that, for the time being at least, there is another, different beer just up the road in the next village.

Franconia's chief beer specialities are Rauchbier (smoke beer), Kellerbier, black lager and Märzen (see Beer Styles).

In terms of variety and numbers of breweries, the main brewing towns are Bamberg (nine breweries), Bayreuth (seven), Amberg (five), Forcheim (five), and Kulmbach (four). Small town Kulmbach's beer output almost matches that of Nuremberg.

The greatest concentrations of breweries are to the immediate north and west of Bamberg.

In addition to the recommendations below, there are another 25 small breweries or so in the scenic Steigerwald area west of Bamberg, where overall the taste tends towards dryish beers regardless of whether they are pale or dark. Worth seeking out are: Bräutigam Pilsener in Weisbrunn, near Eltmann (closed Tuesday); Schlossbräu Lagerbier and Märzen in Trabelsdorf (open only after 1600, closed Monday); Beck Hell, also in Trabelsdorf (closed Friday); Sonne Vollbier and Märzen in Bischberg (closed Tuesday); Roppelt Lagerbier in Trossenfurt (closed Tuesday). With the exception of Schlossbräu, which has several outlets, these beers are generally available only in their village of origin.

North of Bamberg, there are 24 breweries along the B-173 road to Lichtenfels - a distance of only 33 km (20 miles). Staffelstein is in the middle and makes a useful and economical base from which to explore this rich seam of beer. Brewery locations along the B-173 not listed in detail are: Ebensfeld, Breitengussbach, Pferdsfeld, Wiesen, Nedensdorf, Herreth, Uetzing, Kemmern and Dorfleins.

There are brewery museums

in Bamberg and Bayreuth, and Bamberg organises beer seminars (only in German). The Bayreuth breweries publish walking and cycling tour guides to rural pubs in their area, and the town's tourist office arranges brewery visits.

The regional tourist is at: Fremdenverkehrsverband Franken, Am Plärrer 14, Nuremberg. Tel: 0911-264-202.

AMBERG

55 km (34 miles) east of Nuremberg via B-14 or A-6. Or by train.

In 1986 there were nine; today, five breweries survive in this town of 50,000 which still has an attractive medieval core surrounded by ancient defensive walls and several gates. Amberg is an interesting town to amble through, making your own discoveries in the myriad narrow cobbled streets and alleys. One architectural attraction is the Ring Bridge across the River Vils which flows through the centre. Its nickname is Stadtbrille – which for any student of German means "town spectacles" – because the fortified bridge's twin arches resemble a pair of specs. The surviving brewers are: Schiessl, Winkler, Brückmüller, Brauhaus, Malteser. The tourist office (which had great difficulty confirming how many breweries Amberg still has) is at: Zeughaus-str. 1.

Brauereigasthof Schiessl

Untere Nabburger-str. 8
Tel: 09621 12512

Schiessl Vollbier on draught. Bottled Bock and a pale unfiltered wheat beer.
Ⓕ *Hot food lunchtime*
Mon-Fri 0800-2400; Sun 0800-1500; closed Saturday and April
✤ *Courtyard*

A well-worn hostelry in the old town. Customers sit outside in an old Hof, or courtyard, on warm days when beer is served straight from the barrel in earthenware pots. Noted for cheap, wholesome midday meals. The brewery runs a modernised hotel nearby – the Altstadt Hotel, Batterie-gasse 2, tel: 09621 13056.

Brauereigasthof Winkler

Untere Nabburger-str. 34
Tel: 09621 23239

Winkler Vollbier, Pilsener, Dunkel on draught.
Wed-Mon 0800-2400; closed Tue
✤ *Beer garden*

Basic boozer category. Unrenovated (a rarity in rich Bavaria), under-priced (a half litre of beer was DM2.50, or less than a quid, in spring 1993), and seemingly unloved (teeming street outside, empty seats inside).

Gasthof Brückmüller

Vils-str. 2
Tel: 09621 12147

Brückmüller Vollbier and Pilsener on draught. Bottled pale wheat beer and a Bock.
Daily 0900-2300
Beer garden

One of the smartest of Amberg's old town's old pubs, this rambling 500-year old inn of wide arched corridors used to be a monastery. The beer garden is part of a former cloister. Lots of dark wood panelling and vaulted stonework.

Brauereigasthof Malteser

Malteser Platz 2
Tel: 09621 25933

Malteser Hell and Pilsener on draught. Bottled wheat beer and Rittertrunk, a bock which is served on draught during the brewery's own Starkbierfest in March.
Ⓕ *Food*
Daily 1000-2400

Both brewery and impressive pub are set amidst a knot of 17th- century buildings which once formed part of a castle. The main drinking room in this warren of stone vaulted chambers and corridors is the knights' drinking hall, dating from 1693. It is no surprise, therefore, that the local "spring cure" or doppelbock is called Rittertrunk - literally Knight's Drink. You will need a suit of armour to handle more than two litre mugs of it and avoid hurting yourself falling over.

Goldener Ritter

Georgen-str. 39
Tel: 09621 3295

Brauhaus Hell and Pilsener on draught. Bottled EKU Pilsener and pale wheat beer.
Tue-Sun 0900-2300; closed Mon

A drinking man's pub. So if you are only here for the beer, step inside. The Brauhaus Pilsener is excellent, but eat at the Malteser round the corner.

BAMBERG

A-9 from Munich, A-73 from Nuremberg. Frequent trains.

Bamberg is the jewel in the Franconian crown which used to be able to boast it had more breweries than churches - no mean feat for a former seat of the Holy Roman Empire and power base of the medieval prince-bishops. Today, the town of 75,000 has "only" nine breweries - a tenth closed in 1991. Bamberg is also one of Bavaria's most picturesque towns. Its historic heart is an architectural jumble of steep-roofed, half-timbered medieval houses on narrow, cobbled streets cluttered around Renaissance and Baroque masterpieces built for a Catholic hierarchy who once ruled southern Germany. Little Bamberg's long, but important past can be measured from one date in history: Heinrich II was crowned Holy Roman Emperor here in 1012, in the cathedral, or Dom, he ordered to be built. The present towering structure, one of the most impressive examples of early

Gothic architecture in Germany, dates from the mid 13th century. North of the Alps, the unspoken link between churches and breweries stretches into murky history. Catholicism has always had an easy relationship with beer drinking. It was the medieval religious orders which first put brewing on a firm footing in Bamberg, as in many other parts of Germany; records show that local Benedictine monks were brewing beer in 1122.

Perhaps it was the devastating fire which put paid to the first, wooden cathedral, that gave some unknown brewer the idea of drying his germinating barley over a beechwood fire, thereby accidentally creating Rauchbier, or smoked beer – Bamberg's most noted beer speciality. Using beechwood fires was common practice throughout Franconia, and neighbouring Bohemia, until about the middle of the 19th century, when brewing began to acquire the trappings of a modern science.

Although Bamberg enjoys a nice little earner from tourism, the good burgers remain conscious and proud of the town's beery heritage. There is a museum dedicated to Franconian brewing, and beer seminars for the layman are organised jointly by the town's breweries and tourist office. Appropriately, the Fränkisches Brauereimuseum (Michaelsberg 10f, tel: 0951 53016) is housed in one of the vaulted cellars used by those early monk brewers. Exhibitions trace the history of brewing, malting and cooperage in the region. It is open daily except Monday, 1pm-4pm (1300-1600). For an English-speaking guide, telephone 0951 25437 as far in advance as possible. The four-day seminars are usually held in the autumn. The unusual package includes visits to breweries and maltings, a lecture from a brewer, beer tastings, and general sightseeing. Accommodation and some meals are included. The seminars are only in German. For full details contact Bamberg tourist office: Geyerswörth-str. 3, 8600 Bamberg. Tel: 0951 871-161 (the office is on the island in the River Pegnitz, which flows through the old town).

Non-beery attractions worth seeing in Bamberg are the Altes Rathaus, or Old Town Hall, a Baroque decorated Gothic building which sits precariously on a footbridge over the River Pegnitz; the treasures of the cathedral which include a larger than life stone carving of a knight on horse back, known as the Bamberg Rider; and the onetime palace of the prince-bishops, the Neue Residenz.

Like many ancient towns with a long religious past, Bamberg is well endowed with scores of old taverns. The best time to visit them is early evening when the locals slake their thirst. But on sunny summer afternoons and evenings, especially at weekends, Bambergers indulge in the very Bavarian habit of sitting outdoors to drink beer. Several of the breweries, short of space in the old town, have built beer gardens atop one of the seven hills - Stephansberg - which Bamberg is built upon. The biggest are: Mahr's Keller, Obere Stephansberg 36, and Spezial-Keller, Obere Stephansberg 47; open daily from 3pm (1500), May-September.

Bamberg's breweries are: Fässla, Greifenklau, Heller (Schlenkerla), Kaiserdom, Keesman, Klosterbräu, Mahrs, Maisel, Spezial. Several take part in an annual town beer festival on the last weekend in August and brew special beers for the occasion. Kaiserdom, Heller and Spezial produce Rauchbier. Three of the pubs listed below - Fässla, Spezial and Bürgerbräu - have reasonably priced rooms.

Schlenkerla (Hellerbräu)

Dominikaner-str. 6
Tel: 0951 56060

Heller Märzen on draught. Dark bock (October-Christmas only, also on draught) and a slightly smoky bottled Hell.
Ⓕ *Food*
Wed-Mon 0930-2400; closed Tue

The Schlenkerla is one of those rare pubs which have paid little heed to the 20th century. Only the electric light and customers' clothes betray a timeless scene where the dominant colour is black - from the waitresses dresses to the beer, which is poured straight from oak casks hoisted on to a simple serving counter and replaced at regular intervals. Owner-brewer German Trum carries on a family tradition which stretches back five generations. Trum says he tries to provide a community pub. "We expect customers to push up and make room at the tables. Our regulars include window cleaners, lawyers, students and pensioners." He has three "Nos" in his pub: no Coca Cola, no chips, no coffee. Schlenkerla Rauchbier is the darkest and richest of all the Franconian smoked beers. Some people never acquire the taste. For a completely integrated eating and drinking experience, order smoked ham and black bread. Part of the pub is a former monastery, complete with an ornately painted vaulted stone ceiling dating from the 14th century. An inner courtyard offers a cool corner in summer. Schlenkerla is the nickname, in local dialect, for a brewer of long ago who had elongated arms and a monkey-like gait.

Brauereigaststätte Fässla

Obere König-str. 19
Tel: 0951 26516

Fässla Lagerbier and Pilsener on draught. Bottled Märzen called Zergla, and Bambergator, a 7.5 per cent doppelbock (November-May only).
Daily 0900-2300
Accommodation

Fässla means small barrel, and from about 9am every day there are always two wooden ones perched on the serving hatch in the main bar of this earthy pub. Bamberg's oldest family-run brewery is in the backyard. As the day wears on, and the customers slide in and out, the barrels are frequently changed. The Fässla had a major refit in the mid 1980s, but the bar was unobtrusively renovated with wood panelling and scrub-top tables. The rooms above the pub are among the best value in town. A big plus for car travellers in a town where traffic chaos reigns is an off-street car park.

Brauereigaststätte Spezial

Obere König-str. 10
Tel: 0951 24304

Spezial Lagerbier on draught. Bottled Märzen and a pre-Xmas dark bock. All three are lightly smoked.
Ⓕ *Hot food*
Sun-Fri 0900-2200; Sat 0900-1400
Accommodation

Although the Spezial is an ordinary sized pub, it has a beer hall atmosphere. Everybody from housewives to neatly-dressed pensioners sits at long wooden tables laid out in rows like a school. As you sit down, one of the jogging waitresses will plonk a Lagerbier in front of you. The Lagerbier is served direct from a firkin-sized wooden cask. Simple Bavarian food of sausages and sauerkraut is available. Book well in advance if you want B&B; the pub has only seven rooms. The Spezial is directly opposite the Fässla, but they cater for completely different customers, the Spezial being a little more, er, refined.

Mahrs Brauerei Ausschank

Wunderburg 10
Tel: 0951 130-538

Mahrs Lagerbier (unfiltered), Vollbier and (from 5pm each day) Pilsener on draught. Bottled Märzen called Liesl. A dark bock is available November-Christmas.
Ⓕ *Hot food*
Daily 0830-2300
✤ *Beer garden*

From the worn stone floor to the low-slung pitched ceiling beams and the polished mahogany bar, this is a tavern with a long drinking past. No-one entering this hostelry can have any doubt that the sole objective is to drink beer; well, perhaps eat a sausage or two with dumplings and sauerkraut too. The 17th-century Mahrs bar (excuse the pun) is part of a complex of courtyard, horse chestnut trees, cobbled beer garden and brewery - a heavenly setting in which to explore the beer menu at your leisure. The draught beers are dispensed from wooden casks in the taproom.

Braunbierstübla

Obere Mühlbrücke 3
Tel: 0951 57722

Klosterbräu dark lager (Ächd Bambärcha Schwärzla) and Pilsener on draught. Bottled Märzen and a pale winter bock (November-January).
Mon-Sat 0900-2300; closed Sun
✤ *Beer garden*

Despite the name, there is no brown beer here. This

Klosterbräu brewery tap's title stems from the early 16th century when it was owned by the bishopric, monks were the brewers and Braunbier (brown beer) was the everyday drink. The tongue-twisting Ächd Bambärchä Schwärzla, which sounds like the name of a Cairo bar, is Bamberg dialect for "real Bamberg black". The adjoining little brewery is the oldest in Bamberg and stands beside the river. There's a small beer garden in the brewery yard. A pub party heralds the tapping of the first bock at the end of October.

Bürgerbräu Stübla

Urban-str. 18
Tel: 0951 22237

Bürgerbräu Export, Pilsener and Rauchbier on draught. Bottled Dunkel, Bock and two pale wheat beers, filtered and unfiltered varieties.
Ⓕ *Hot food*
Daily 1000-2300
Accommodation

A takeover in the mists of time has left Bamberg's biggest brewery, Kaiserdom, with its chief outlet seemingly bearing the name of another brewhouse. But it is certainly Kaiserdom that produces the seven beers, including Bamberg's only wheat beer. The kitchen specialises in grilled and baked carp, traditionally eaten in Bavaria at Easter. The Stübla, off Wilhelms Platz near the Marienbrücke over the Rhein-Main-Donau Canal, has its own carp ponds. Fish and Rauchbier dovetail nicely. The pub has 20 bedrooms.

NB Of the remaining three Bamberg breweries, Maisel (Maisel-Keller, Moos-str. 46, tel: 0951 15027, open daily) has the biggest and most interesting choice: 10 different brews, including a hoppy Kellerbier on draught and bottled Bock, Märzen and Dunkel. The Keesmann brew pub (Wunderburg 5, tel: 0951 26646, practically opposite Mahrs) has a lightly hopped, fruity Herren Pilsener on tap, plus a bottled Märzen. Greifenklau (Laurenziplatz 20, tel: 0951 53219) is the smallest of Bamberg's breweries and produces only one beer regularly – a dark amber Lagerbier with faint smoked-fish aroma, served straight from the cask. A bock also comes on draught from the end of November until New Year. Greifenklau's only outlet is a pleasant old-fashioned pub at Laurenziplatz 20, (tel: 0951 53219), open daily.

BAYREUTH

Town with seven breweries. A-9 from Munich or Nuremberg; B-505 from Bamberg. Frequent trains.

Better known internationally for its annual Wagner music festival than for its beer, Bayreuth (pron: Bye-roit) is one of the high spots of serious German culture. The otherwise quiet market town lost its anonymity forever when 19th-century composer Richard Wagner chose to settle here after flitting around Europe's royal courts for years. Bankrolled by Bavaria's so-called "Dream King", Ludwig

II, he built an aesthetically drab, but acoustically perfect theatre in which to stage his monumental operas. Since 1876, his fans have flooded Bayreuth every July, when prices rocket and tourist beds get booked out. If you are thinking of overnighting here, check with the town's tourist office (see below) in advance for festival dates. For Wagner fans, the exorbitantly-priced festival tickets are like gold dust - even millionaires have to grovel behind the scenes. For beer fans, Wagner has unwittingly helped Bayreuth's brewing industry. It can be no coincidence that the annual beer-oriented local knees up, the Bürgerfest, is held on the first weekend of July. Surprisingly, not one of the 30 local brands is named after the town's most famous son.

Five of Bayreuth's seven surviving breweries date from Wagner's day. The seven are: Bayreuther Bierbrauerei, Becher, Götschel, Glenk, Maisel, Schaller, Schinner, The biggest by far (260,000 barrels a year) is Brauerei Gebrüder Maisel - the Maisel Brothers Brewery. The smallest is Götschel Brau, a one pub operation. Given the contraction of brewing in many other countries, it is amazing to keep encountering Franconian towns the size of, say, Chester, with so many breweries. But it is still a tough business, and Bayreuth's smallest might struggle to survive; even the two biggest - Maisel and Bayreuther - now have close business links. Most of Maisel's production goes out of Bavaria. Two of the smallest brewers - Becher and Götschel - have found a way round spiralling costs by having a third, Schinner, produce their beers on contract.

Whatever the difficulties, Bayreuth's brewers are enthusiastic - whether it is collectively producing beer tour brochures for the district, organising their individual district beer fest or, in Oscar Maisel's case, lovingly preserving his family firm's defunct 19th-century red brick tower brewery in perfect working order as a museum. Between 1981 and midsummer 1993, 300,000 people visited the museum, which includes remarkable collections of brewery insignia and beer drinking vessels. The museum tours begin 10am, Mon-Thu; starting place Kulmbacher-str. 40 (next to the Göldener Löwe pub). For an English-speaking guide call 0921 401-234 one or two days in advance.

The beer tour brochures can be obtained from the tourist office: Fremdenverkehrsverein, Luitpold-str. 9, 8580 Bayreuth. Tel: 0921 88588. In conjunction with the breweries, the tourist office organises what it humorously calls "Bier-kul-tours", poking fun at its highbrow cultural image while offering a serious programme of brewery visits, lectures and beer tastings for tourists. The Maisel brewery organises a wheat beer festival in the grounds of the brewery (Hindenburger-str. 9) on the weekend before Ascension Day (usually in May). Two of the pubs listed below have reasonably priced accommodation. Wagner's home (Richard-Wagner-str. 48) is now a museum.

Bierbrauereischänke am Markt

Maximilian-str. 56
Tel: 0921 64919

Bayreuther Pilsener, Helles and Zwickel, and Maisel Dunkel on draught. Bottled Maisel unfiltered wheat beers
Ⓕ *Hot food*
Daily 0900-2300

A curious haunt of beer lovers. Lavish fitments of pale pine and pastel-coloured walls adorned with Wedgewood crockery, gives the place more of a tea shop air than a pub. But there is no doubting the excellent selection of beers on draught. The house dish of Camembert cheese, onion and paprika, called O'batz'n is a perfect accompaniment to the dark brew. Breakfast (and beer) is served from 9am in this handily located pub on the old town market square.

Goldener Löwe

Kulmbacher-str. 30
Tel: 0921 41046

Maisel Pilsener, Dunkel and pale unfiltered wheat. Bottled Dampfbier and bock wheat.
Ⓕ *Hot food all day*
Mon and Wed-Sat 0630-2400; Tue 0630-1400; closed Sun
Accommodation

Located behind the Maisel brewery museum, this small, jolly pub is the nearest thing to a brewery tap. It offers the full Maisel beer range and a comfortable, reasonably priced room ready for the museum tour next morning. The bar is Bavarian rustic with pine furnishings. An extensive menu offers hot food until 10pm (2200). Shift workers at both Maisel and the neighbouring Bayreuther Bierbrauerei make use of the Golden Lion's 6.30am opening.

Gasthof Herzog

Herzog-str. 2 (off Kulmbacher-str.)
Tel: 0921 41334

Bayreuther Pilsener on draught. Bottled Maisel wheat beers and Dampfbier.
Mon-Fri 100-2400; Sat 1000-1400; closed Sun
Accommodation

A real locals' pub, wedged between the Maisel and Bayreuther breweries and serving a range of beers from both. While regulars play cards, landlord Peter Friedauer will gladly tell visitors about the beers of his town, and how he has watched Maisel's forest of tall wheat beer lager tanks grow closer to his kitchen door as the beer's popularity grows. Double rooms are a budget traveller's dream at around 50 Marks per night; photographers should ask for No. 17 as it offers the best view in town of Maisel's beautifully preserved old red-bricked brewery, illuminated at night.

Braunbierhaus

Kanzlei-str. 15
Tel: 0921 69677

Schinner Braunbier on

draught. Maisel bottled wheat beers.
Ⓕ *Hot food*
◔ *Daily 1100-2200*

The Braunbierhaus is the showhouse pub of the Schinner brewery, and the oldest building in Bayreuth. The sturdy four storey grey stone pile seems to have stepped out of an Edinburgh back street, but the brown beer after which the pub is named is authentic Bavarian. The brewery claims its Braunbier is brewed to an 18th century recipe, presumably excluding the bottom fermenting yeast used today. The beer is on tap in the snug bar on the ground floor. Upstairs is a fancy restaurant best left alone unless your budget is substantial.

Gasthof Becher

St. Nikolaus-str. 25
Tel: 0921 68993

Becher unfiltered Pilsener and bock (November-March only) on draught. Bottled Dunkel.
Hot food lunchtime and early evening
◔ *Mon and Wed-Sun 0900-2400; closed Tue*

An old, traditional Franconian pub which usually serves at least one of its beers direct from the cask, Gasthof Becher is not easy to find. Take the Erlanger-str. road from the centre, signposted to Bamberg. St. Nikolaus-str. is a right-hand turning just beyond a major crossroads called Freiheits Platz. A small, solidly Bavarian menu is served. Becher is one of two tiny Bayreuth "breweries" whose beers are actually produced on contract by a slightly larger town brewery (see Bayreuth notes above). Ironically, the Glenk brewery is round the corner in Eichelweg.

Gasthof Götschel

St. Georgen 25
Tel: 0921 22750

◔ *Tue-Sun 1000-2300; closed Mon*
✤ *Beer garden*

This is the sole outlet for Bayreuth's tiniest "brewery", but Götschel's only beer, an amber Lagerbier style called Beck'nbier, is brewed under contract by the town's Schinner Brewery. The traditional pub is also noteworthy for seasonal game dishes. The Götschel is less than half a mile from the railway station, via Brandenburger-str.

Gasthof Erlanger Hof

Erlanger-str. 65
Tel: 0921 68377

Glenk Pilsener on draught. Bottled wheat beers.
◔ *Daily 1100-2300*

This basic local, on the way to Gasthof Becher, is one of Glenk's rare Bayreuth outlets, although the brewery distributes to some 45 pubs in the surrounding countryside. The Hof is worth visiting to complete a Bayreuth tasting tour.

Zur Sudpfanne

Oberkonnersreuther-str. 3
Tel: 0921 66805

Schaller Pilsener on draught. Hell and Spezial (a darker, stronger Export-style beer) in bottles.
Tue-Sun 1100-1400 and 1700-2400; closed Mon
Beer garden

The Sudpfanne, or mashtun, is the brewery tap of Bayreuth's smallest actual brewery, Brauerei Klaus Schaller (two other tiny town "breweries" have their beers brewed for them on contract. See above). It is a traditional Franconian hostelry, in the suburb of Oberkonnersreuth 3 km (2 miles) southeast of the centre, off Nürnberger-str. The brewery has its own beerfest on the third Sunday in August.

BUTTENHEIM

Small, two-brewery village off the A-73 or parallel B-4, halfway between Bamberg and Forcheim.

There is nothing remarkable, in this part of the world, in a one-horse village having two breweries - but the beers they produce are. Their speciality is the heavily hopped Kellerbier style, but the liberal use of the bitter herb influences all 12 beers produced in Buttenheim, from the basic Vollbier through Pilsener to Märzen. Buttenheim probably produces the most hoppy beers in all Bavaria; a visit here is a must for all lovers of dry, hoppy beer. Both breweries - St. Georgen and Löwen - stem from the same family Modschiedler and stand next to one another. Both brewery taps offer budget priced accommodation; the St. Georgen pub serves mountainous meals.

Brauereigaststätte St. Georgen

Markt-str. 12
Tel: 09545 4460, or 4183

St. Georgen Vollbier, Kellerbier (unfiltered and gravity dispense), Pilsener on draught. Bottled Märzen and Dunkel. Seasonal specialities: dark doppelbock in spring and Weihnachstfestbier (Christmas).
Ⓕ *Hot food*
Fri-Wed 0900-2400; closed Thu
Accommodation

A bustling, hearty pub of crowded long wooden tables. A varied clientele clearly relishes the beer; waitresses are constantly busy refilling the earthenware mugs favoured especially for the unfiltered Kellerbier. It is particularly busy early evening when people flock in from beyond the village to eat lion-sized Bavarian meals. Not one, but two thriving Stammtische (regulars' tables). Brewery visits are possible. Call in advance.

Brauerei Gasthof Löwenbräu

Markt-str. 8
Tel: 09545 332

Löwen Kellerbier on draught. Bottled Vollbier, Pilsener, Märzen and a winter pale Bock

(November-December). Kellerbier accounts for 95 per cent of the brewery's production.
◔ *Tue-Sun 0800-2400; closed Mon*
🛏 *Accommodation*

The smaller pub and brewery of Buttenheim's family duo. Very friendly, plain tap room of scrubbed tables, with brewery workers popping in and out all day. The Kellerbier is served straight from the barrel secreted in a cubbyhole behind the kitchen sink bar. The entire family seems to be involved in running the pub and brewery. Septuagenarian brewer Johann Modschiedler – who still also plays soccer – will happily regale enquiring visitors with a history of Buttenheim brewing (in German).

COBURG

Historic, two-brewery town on B-4, 40 km (25 miles) north of Bamberg.

All monarchists should stop here. It is the birthplace of Queen Victoria's Prince Albert, one of the Saxe-Coburg family whose chief occupation was blue-blood stud to Europe's royal households. The Saxe-Coburg base is the 16th-century Veste Coburg, one of the largest fortress castles in Germany, which stands on a hill dominating the picturesque old town. The family still lives there. Albert was born in a more modest manor house, Schloss Rosenau at Rödental, 9 km (6 miles) north of Coburg, but spent much of his youth in Coburg's Ehrenburg Palace – yet another little Saxe-Coburg pad. The Saxe-Coburgs were a bastion of Protestantism, underlined by Martin Luther's sojourn at the Veste Coburg. "Luther's Room" is part of a castle tour.

Of less historic importance, but perhaps equal interest, is the local legend which claims that Germany's first flush toilet was introduced to the country by Queen Victoria when she paid a visit to Albert's family. The Prince Consort is remembered in a statue on Coburg' main square – and in a Pilsener beer named after him and brewed by Brauerei Sturm, one of Coburg's two medium-sized surviving breweries. A third brewery, once part of the Saxe-Coburg royal household, has been taken over by Paulaner of Munich.

Just 15 km (9 miles) northeast of Coburg, stood the Iron Curtain fortified border between former West and East Germany. Traces of the No-Man's land are still visible between the Neustadt (one brewery, Geussen) and Sonneberg. The collapse of the Iron Curtain has given a new lease of life to many small breweries in this far northern corner of Bavaria, who now have a new market to ply, but these "border" breweries still face big commercial competition from the encroaching Kulmbach giants. Coburg tourist office: Herrngasse 4, tel: 09561 74180.

Schmittner's Gaststätte

Ahornberger-str. 11
Tel: 09561 6751

Sturm's Pilsener on draught. Bottled Prince Albert Pils, Anton Sturm's Privat, Alt Coburger Dunkel.
Ⓕ *Hot food*
Thu-Tue 1600-0100; closed Wed

There are more historic pubs in the centre of Coburg, but this is the best place to sample Sturm beer. Evening meals available.

Brauereigasthof Scheidmantel

Rosenauer-str. 98
Tel: 09561 6747

Scheidmantel Coburg Pilsener on draught. Bottled Veste Pilsener, Silber Bock and Scheidmantel Hefeweisse (pale unfiltered wheat).
Tue-Sun 0930-2300; Closed Mon
✤ *Beer garden*

A traditional tap which forms part of a lovely redbrick 19th-century tower brewery overlooked by the Veste Coburg castle which forms part of the brewery's symbol. The pub has a skittle alley. Scheidmantel, enterprisingly run by three women, participates in a town festival in the Veste castle in mid-July when the brewery's wheat beer is also served on draught.

EBING

15 km (9 miles) north of Bamberg on B-173.

Gastwirtschaft Schwanen

Marktplatz 11
Tel: 09547 481

Schwanen Dunkel Vollbier on draught.
Fri-Wed 0900-2300; closed Thu

A traditional, quiet rural pub which has been in the same farming family since 1859. Brewer Andreas Hübner also make a beer schnapps called Gambrinus (the patron saint of brewers in northern Europe).

EGGOLSHEIM

Off the U-42 road and parallel A-73, north of Forcheim.

Schwarzes Kreuz

Haupt-str. 33
Tel: 09545 843

Schwarzes Kreuz Vollbier on draught.
Daily 0900-2400

A simple one-pub village brewery, the Brauerei Schwarzes Kreuz (Black Cross) produces a single beer. Although it is called Vollbier, this deliciously bitter brew more closely resembles a Pilsener. The beer is served straight from a wooden cask in the single-roomed pub on the main street. Another one-pub brewery, Witzgall, is in nearby Schlammersdorf.

ELTMANN

B-26, 19km (12 miles) northwest of Bamberg.

Gasthof Lammbräu

Marktplatz 11
Tel: 09522 5959

Lamm Dunkel, pale Lagerbier and Pilsener on draught. Bottled Märzen and pale unfiltered wheat beer.
Tue-Sun 0800-2300; Mon 1900-2300

A pleasant country town brewery pub. An indication of the small scale level of brewing activity hereabouts is the fact that Lammbräu, with production of about 25 barrels a week, is one of the biggest local breweries. Yet despite that small output, Lammbräu has an interesting and broad portfolio of beers. Perhaps a sign of the times is to be found in another local fact: ten years ago there were three other little breweries in Eltmann, mixing brewing with farming and other family activities.

ESCHENBACH

B-26, near Eltmann, northwest of Bamberg Bräustüble

Wagnerbräu

Haupt-str. 3
Tel: 09522 288

Wagner Pilsener and Märzen on draught. Bottled Hell, Dunkel, Rauchbier, pale Export, Hefeweissbier and Festbier.
Tue-Sun 0900-2300; closed Mon
Beer garden

Tiny hamlet, big brewery. Founded in 1750, Wagnerbräu is one of several traditional Franconian family breweries which have taken the path of expansion rather than just supplying one or two pubs. Now their 60,000 barrels a year reach into Berlin to the north and Italy in the south. Inevitably, Pilsener is the big seller but the Wagners still also maintain an interesting selection of eight beers. The brewery tap is in the village main street. Lively early evenings.

FORCHEIM

A-73 midway between Nuremberg and Bamberg. Frequent trains.

How does a market town of 25,000 people sustain five breweries in the mid 1990s? Four of Forcheim's breweries are virtually next door to each other; three - Greif, Neder and Hebendanz - are basic boozers which many finicky modern Germans would probably disdain to enter. They are clearly small, old- fashioned family businesses, just ticking over. Their bottled products cannot be bought in the local shops, although plenty of beers from outside town can. They appear to rely on local home deliveries, limited free trade in the surrounding district and summer beer gardens, known locally as kellers, on the edge of town. I would not like to bet all these breweries surviving the decade, but while they do, each produces some noteworthy beers, although the full range is difficult to obtain all the time and there is a confusing mix of names. Märzen is sometimes marketed as Annafestbier (brewed for a town festival in the last week of July), and Kellerbier sometimes masquerades as Lagerbier. This is a challenging town for the beer purist. Forcheim's biggest brewery, Brauhaus, has a more up-market profile, is more expansionist and, not surprisingly, produces less variety. The five breweries together produce just under 10,000 barrels a year. The town has a moated castle, and is noted for baked carp.

Brauereigasthof Greif

Serlbacher-str. 10
Tel: 09191 2971

Greif Hell on draught. Bottled Lagerbier (really a Kellerbier), pale unfiltered wheat beer, Pilsener and Märzen. Weihnachtsbier (Christmas beer).
Mon and Fri 090-2300; Tue and Sun 0900-1300; Wed, Thu and Sat 0900-1900

A small town-centre pub, run down by German standards, but with an atmosphere of past glories. Ask about the Grief Keller beer garden across town. Complicated opening hours.

Brauereigasthof Neder

Sattlertor-str. 10
Tel: 09191 2400

Neder pale Export served direct from a wooden cask. Bottled Pilsener, Kellerbier and Märzen.
Wed-Mon 0900-1900; closed Tue

Similar pub to neighbouring Greif but livelier, especially late afternoon until closing time, which is 7pm! Shades of Australia's infamous 6 o'clock swill. But here they go quietly.

Brauereigasthof Hebendanz

Sattlertor-str. 14
Tel: 09191 2619

Hebendanz pale Export on draught, direct from wooden casks. Bottled Märzen, pale unfiltered wheat beer.
Mon-Wed and Sat 0800-2000; Thu 0800-1300; Fri 0800-2300; Sun 1300-2000

A half-timbered Elizabethan-style facade camouflages a Greif Neder style interior. This old pub also has complicated opening and closing times, and is similarly at its liveliest close to chucking out time.

Brauereigaststätte Eichhorn

Bamberger-str. 9
Tel: 09191 2379

Eichhorn Vollbier and Pilsener on draught. Bottled Märzen and Erdinger wheat beers.
Ⓕ *Food*
Tue-Sun 0900-2100; closed Mon

Forcheim's smallest brewery also has the most comfortable pub in town, even if it is fitted out in the ubiquitous pine. An unusual feature is the bar at which customers can sit or lean. Good menu. Eichhorn operates Forcheim's biggest beer garden, the Eichhorn Keller, with seating for 1,800 people; open daily, May-September.

Brauhaus Stuberl

Bad-str. 13
Tel: 09191 2078

Ⓕ *Hot food*
◕ *Daily*
✤ *Small beer garden*

This comfortable brewery tap concentrates on promoting its premium product, Brauhaus Pils, and a large Bavarian menu.

GRÄFENBERG

Two-brewery village just off the B-2 Nuremberg to Bayreuth road.

Brauereigaststätte Lindenbräu

Am Bach 3
Tel: 09192 348

Linden Vollbier on draught. Maibock in season.
Ⓕ *Hot food*
◕ *Sat-Thu 0900-2200; closed Fri*

Brewer George Brehmer is the life and soul of this cheery village pub where the beer is dispensed straight from a wooden cask propped on the bar. Sunday lunch is the high point of the week when the locals crowd in for Mrs Brehmer's special roast lunches. The Linden has its own maltings and is noted in the district for its little distillery which produces a beer schnapps as well as a variety of fruit brandies.

Friedmann's Bräustüberl

Jägersberg 16
Tel: 09192 381

Friedmann Vollbier and Pilsener on draught. Bottled Dunkel, and a Christmas beer (Weihnachtsfestbier).
Ⓕ *Hot food*
◕ *Wed-Mon 0900-2200; closed Tue*
✤ *Beer garden*
Accommodation

The colourful blue and white wooden window shutters makes this 18th-century building seem more like a French country house than a German pub. But inside there can be no mistaking the Teutonic influences: hoppy Pilsener and a variety of roast pork. Fish dishes, in particular carp, are a house speciality.

GREUTH

Brauereigasthof Fischer

14 km (9.5 miles) south of Bamberg, off the B-505
Tel: 09502 545

Fischer Lagerbier and Rauchbier on draught. Bottled Weihnachtsbock (Christmas season strong beer), and Althausbrauer, a dark lager.
Ⓕ *Cold snacks*
◕ *Tue-Sun 0900-2200; closed Mon*
✤ *Beer garden*

At first sight, there is little to attract visitors to this sleepy hamlet off the beaten track. Yet quite a lot of people do drive or cycle here, especially in summer. They sit in the tree shaded beer garden and sip the lightly smoked house beer at budget prices. The distinctive Lagerbier also has a surprisingly large following.

Greuth's annual knees-up is on Ascension Day when there is a brewery open day and pub festival. Hot meals are only served on Sundays (speciality duck and carp).

HERRNSDORF

Off the B-505, 12 km (7 miles) south of Bamberg.

Brauereigaststätte Barnikel

Haus 28
Tel: 09502 293

Barnikel Lagerbier on draught. Bottled Rauchbier, Bock and a Festbier called Kerwabier which is available on draught during the two weeks after Whit Sunday.
Ⓕ *Food*
Thu-Tue 0900-2300; closed Wed
✤ *Beer garden*

History records that beer was first served on this site in 1366, but exactly what style we will never know. The present pub is a lovely, lived-in ramshackle country inn, run by the farming Barnikel family who will delight in history-telling. Ask first for a large slice of home-made onion cake (Zwiebelkuchen) which goes well with the Rauchbier.

KREUZBERG

Off the B-279 near Bischofsheim. 85 km (53 miles) northwest of Bamberg.

Klosterschenke

Kloster Kreuzberg
Tel: 09772 216

Dunkel Vollbier on draught, plus a dark Bock in winter (November-March).
Ⓕ *Hot food lunchtime; cold snacks*
Daily 0800-2000; closed 1 November-10 December
✤ *Large beer garden*
Accommodation

One of the few surviving genuine monastery breweries, Kloster Kreuzberg is also one of the least accessible. Kreuzberg is numbered among the 1,000-metre (3,000-foot) peaks of the scenic Rhön mountain range dividing the northwest corner of Bavaria from neighbouring Hessen state. The monastery's stone-vaulted inn and delightful, old, chestnut tree beer garden is a favourite resting place for walkers and others who come to watch the gliding and hang-gliding over the Rhön. The Franciscan fathers serve their rich, dark beers direct from wooden casks. Hot food is available at lunchtime only, but the best accompaniment to the beer is a wedge of the monks' own rich, spicy cheese, Schweizerkäse. The monastery can be reached by car and has simple overnight accommodation. Note that the pub shuts at 8pm.

KULMBACH

No beer tour of Franconia would be complete without visiting Kulmbach, which holds two German brewing records.

First, its four breweries (there were five until 1991) produce more beer per head of population than anywhere else in Germany: 14,500 pints per year for every one of the 30,000 inhabitants; one quarter of Kulmbach's workforce earns a living from the town's brewing industry. Second, Kulmbach produces Germany's strongest beer, the intimidatingly named Kulminator 28. If you drink much of this doppelbock you will certainly culminate in calamity; it has an alcohol (by volume) content of 11 per cent. The brewer, Erste Kulmbacher Union or EKU, has a regular tussle with a Swiss brewery to lay claim to the "strongest beer in the world" title. In Kulmbach, breweries tower over the urban landscape and an unmistakably malty smell hangs in the air. But the drinking scene, at least in the cobbled old town centre, is surprisingly disappointing. You have to head out northeast 3 km (2 miles) along Hofer-str. to Mönchshof Brewery's beer keller and garden (see below) to be convinced that the townsfolk enjoy the product of their labours.

However, Kulmbach's breweries (EKU, Mönchshof, Reichelsbräu and Sandlerbräu – the last three are linked commercially) organise a big nine-day beerfest in the town every summer. With a dig at nearby rival brewing town Bayreuth's cultural pretensions, the main beer tent at the fest is called the Festspulhaus (literally, festival swallowing house); the home of Bayreuth's annual Wagner music festival is the Festspielhaus - festival playhouse. It is certainly easier, and cheaper, to get a seat in the Festspulhaus. The Kulmbach festival starts on the last Saturday in July. Towering above everything in Kulmbach is one of the best examples of a German Renaissance style castle. The Plassenburg dates from the mid 16th century. A visit is well worth the stiff 15-minute walk up the commanding hill where it stands, and back at the bottom you can quench your thirst at the Zunftstube pub (see below). Apart from its architectural delights, the castle houses the world's biggest collection of miniature tin figures, some 300,000 pieces. Kulmbach's tourist office is at Stadthalle, Sutte 2, 8650 Kulmbach. Tel: 09221 802-216. The Schweizerhof pub (see below) has comfortable rooms.

Zunftstube

Oberestadt 4
Tel: 09221 83377

EKU Pilsener on draught. Bottled pale and dark unfiltered wheat beer, Bock, Rubin Dunkel and EKU 28.
Ⓕ *Food*
Daily 1000-2300

The small, plain Zunftsube is very much an evening beer-drinking haunt in the centre of the cobbled old town. It is also very much a thirst-quenching station at the bottom of the hill housing the Plassenburg Castle. There is a limited menu and only snacks in the evening.

Stadtschänke

Holzmarkt 3
Tel: 09221 4507

Mönchshof Pilsener on draught. Bottled Klosterschwarzbier Dunkel; pale and dark unfiltered wheat, and a pale filtered variety – all sold under the name Kapuziner; dark Klosterbock (on draught in Spring).
Ⓕ *Hot food all day*
Thu-Tue 1130-1400 and 1800-2230; closed Wed

Mönchshof brewery's town centre tap is a fashionable, up-market pub-restaurant where you are handed the menu before being asked what you want to drink. Despite that approach, it is the second best place to sample this brewery's interesting selection. One of the rooms has cubicles, shielding customers from one another with wood partitions. Another curiosity is the old-style English opening hours.

Mönchshof Braugaststätte

Hofer-str. 20
Tel: 09221 8050

Mönchshof Pilsener, Klosterschwarz, pale unfiltered wheat on draught. The Klosterbock is also on draught during Spring, otherwise bottled.
Ⓕ *Food*
Summer daily 1000-2300; winter liable to close early evening Mon-Wed
✤ *Beer garden*

Here is a real brewery font, a rambling beer hall and beer garden complex attached to the brewery 3 km (2 miles) northeast of the town centre. The tree-shaded beer garden is a local favourite, in summer. Beer is served in traditional litre-sized stone jugs (known as a Krug, NOT a Stein, which is an Americanism), and you can take your own picnic along.

Schweizerhof

Ziegelhüttener-str. 38
Tel: 09221 3985

EKU and Reichelbräu Pilseners on draught. Bottled wheat beers and EKU's Rubin Dunkel.
Ⓕ *Hot food 1100-1400 and 1700-2200*
Daily 1000-2400
Accommodation

Until late 1991, this was the location of Kulmbach's smallest brewery. It was closed by multiple brewery owner Gerd Borges (producer of the unusual Rauchenfels Steinbier) and demolished to make way for other commercial development. The only reminder of the 19th-century tower brewery is the name, retained by this former brewery tap. The Schweizerhof has a lively bar and a twee candlelit restaurant section which nonetheless serves traditional Bavarian dishes. The pub also has comfortable, reasonably priced rooms. The pub is in the Ziegelhütten suburb, 5 km (3 miles) northwest of the centre. And if you are a light sleeper be warned: the nearby church starts calling the faithful at 6am.

LAUF

15 km (9 miles) northeast of Nuremberg on the B-14.

A small town with four breweries should hold much promise for the beer hunter. But the bigger breweries from Nuremberg have captured most of the pubs which have escaped being turned into pizzerias or cafes. The local breweries: Arnold, Brauhaus, Dreykorn, and Simon are left to scratch for the home delivery market and countryside free trade. However, divert here if only to try the local wheat beer, and to visit what may be the smallest pub in Bavaria. Lauf also has a pretty cobbled square housing a "gingerbread" medieval Rathaus (town hall).

Bräustübla Weissbierbraueri Simon

Faulkner-str. 2
Tel: 09123 3134

Simon bottled wheat beer. Guest beers from other breweries.
Ⓕ *Hot food*
Tue-Sun 1100-1500 and 1730-2400; closed Mon

A newish pub in a renovated old stone building just off the town square. Good place to eat lunch.

Turmstüberl

Mauer-gasse 2
Tel: 09123 14065

Brauhaus Hell and Pilsener on draught. Bottled Dunkel.
Mon-Wed and Fri-Sat 1100-1400 annd 1700-2300; Sun 1100-1400; closed Thu

Large people might have trouble squeezing into this novel bar and onetime guard room built into a 16th-century town wall gate. It may well be the smallest pub in Bavaria.

NB Dreykorn Dunkel is worth seeking out (see Tasting Notes). Try the Cafe am Markt, Marktplatz; or the railway station bar.

LICHTENFELS

B-173, 30 km (19 miles) north of Bamberg. Frequent trains.

Brauereigasthof Mahr

Kronacher-str. 8
Tel: 09571 2462

Mahr Pilsener on draught. Weihnachtsbier at Christmas.
Ⓕ *Hot food*
Thu-Tue 0900-2200; closed Wed
Courtyard
Accommodation

Lovely old drinking pub where the beer, which does not really resemble a Pils, is dispensed straight from a wooden cask around which the locals sit. There is a beer "garden" in the brewery courtyard. Limited hot menu.

Brauereigasthof Wichert

Alte Reich-str. 50
Tel: 09571 3317

Wichert Pilsener and Kellerbier on draught.
Ⓕ *Hot food*
Tue-Sun 1100-2300; closed Mon

A modern, single storey flat-roofed hostelry which, from

the outside, might be mistaken for a doctor's surgery. Inside there is a cosy ambience, although lacking the sit-round-the-barrel atmosphere of Mahr's pub down the road. The kitchen offers a solid menu of pan-fried pork dishes.

LOFFELD

Hamlet 3 km (2 miles) east of Staffelstein, off the B-173, between Lichtenfels and Bamberg.

Bräustüberl Staffelberg

Loffeld 8
Tel: 09573 5925

Staffelbergbräu Märzen and Pilsener on draught. Bottled Vollbier. At Christmas there is a Weihnachtsbockbier, also on draught.
Tue-Sun 0900-2300; closed Mon

A charming little black and white Elizbethan-style half-timbered building which could sit prettily in a Cheshire market town like Nantwich. The beers are brewed with water from a spring which rises up in the brewery compound.

MEMMELSDORF

A three-brewery village 6 km (4 miles) northeast Bamberg off the B-505.

Gasthof Drei Kronen

Haupt-str. 19
Tel: 0951 43001

Straub unfiltered Lagerbier, Pilsener and a dark Märzen-Rauchbier on draught.
Ⓕ *Hot food*
Tue-Sat 1100-2300; Sun 1100-1500; Mon 1700-2300
✤ *Beer garden*
Accommodation

A friendly family brew pub where brewer Hans-Ludwig Straub takes a fierce pride in his products which include his colloquially-named Stöffla, a curious mix of Kellerbier-Märzen-Rauchbier - and there are certainly elements of all three. It goes well with the wild venison. Fresh carp might also be on the menu. Stöffla is Straub's biggest seller and is well seeking out, with or without the food.

Brauereigaststätte Leicht

Haupt-str. 27
Tel: 0951 44237

Leicht Pilsener, Export and Lagerbier on draught.
Ⓕ *Hot food*
Thu-Tue 0900-2300; closed Wed
✤ *Beer garden*

The big brother of Memmelsdorf's three breweries; Robert Leicht sells his beers in three other pubs outside the village. He also does his own pig slaughtering for the pub kitchen, and every first Tuesday of the month a special meat dish is on offer: Schlachtschüssel. Do not miss it.

NB Memmelsdorf's third brewery, the brew pub Brauerei Höhn, Haupt-str. 11, tel: 0951 44374, produces one draught beer, a dark amber Export. There is also reasonably priced accommodation at the pub (closed Tuesday).

NEUHAUS

Three-brewery village on the River Pegnitz, midway between Bayreuth and Nuremburg, a couple of miles from the Plech junction on the A-9.

Brewing is a varied but major occupation in this village of 2,000 people on the River Pegnitz. The small, Franconian family brewery Falkenloch caters for a few pubs. Kaiserbräu produces 150,000 barrels a year, exports 10 per cent of it and supplies 1,000 pubs. For the good burghers of Neuhaus that is not enough; the village also supports a communal brewhouse which has existed since 1556. Four families still regularly brew there, and take turns to have an open house when they convert a kitchen or living room into a makeshift pub for a few days (see Zoigl chapter).

Kommunbrauhaus

Plecher-str. 5.
Tel: 09156 561

Families Paul Reindl (Gaststube Reindl, Unterer Markt), George Bennaburger (Gaststube Bennaburger, Unterer Markt), George Döth (Gaststube Döth, Burg-str.) and Paul Müller (Gaststube Müller, Hafnerberg-str.) brew a different Märzen beer each. One is usually on sale every week at one of the above addresses when the star-shaped Zoigl sign is hung out. For best results, call the brewery, or be in the village on the first Sunday in October for the village fest.

Brauerei Gasthof Falkenloch

Marktplatz 3
Tel: 09156 234

Falkenloch Vollbier and Pilsener on draught. Bottled Märzen and Festbier.
Ⓕ *Hot food*
Tue-Sun 0900-2400; closed Mon

A quiet village square pub which prides itself on its ten different roast pork dishes from the family slaughterhouse.

Brauerei Gasthof Kaiser

Burg Veldenstein
Burg-str. 12
Tel: 09156 633

Kaiser Pilsener and Veldensteiner Landbier (dark lager) on draught. Bottled Export, Festbier and filtered and unfiltered wheat beers.
Tue-Sun 0900-2400; closed Mon
✤ *Spacious beer garden*
Accommodation

Treat yourself and stay overnight here; rooms are not cheap, but then it is not every day one has the chance to bed down in a 17th-century castle. The baronial setting is the showpiece "tap" of the Kaiser family, who opted out of the village communal brewhouse in 1929, and have been expanding ever since.

NUREMBERG

Few German cities are more closely associated with Hitler's Third Reich than Nuremberg, in foreign minds anyway. It was here that the Nazi bosses staged huge rallies of the party faithful in the 1930s, and it was here that many of the surviving hierarchy were tried for war crimes by the Allied victors in 1945-46. But Nuremberg's history runs much deeper than its tarnished image of the mid-20th century. The fortress castle dominating the inner city skyline dates from the 11th century, and was home to a succession of Holy Roman Emperors who held court there. Nuremberg played a key role in the German Renaissance period through artists and intellectuals such as painter Albrecht Dürer – whose home can be visited (Albrecht Dürer-str. 39). The old town of medieval buildings and winding cobbled streets, carefully restored with typical German precision after bomb damage in World War Two, is much more extensive than Munich's. Other sights worth seeing include the large German National Museum (Kornmarkt) and, for train enthusiasts, the Verkehrsmuseum (Transport Museum), site of the departure point of the first train journey in Germany (Lessing-str. 6). For the really curious, the parade ground where those huge Nazi rallies were held is still there, along with the podium where Hitler made his screaming speeches. The Zeppelin Wiese, close to the suburban railway station called Bahnhof-Dutzendteich, southeast of the city centre, is used today for rock concerts.

Nuremberg is famous for spicy finger-sized sausages (Nürmberger Bratwurstl), and for spicy gingerbread (Lebkuchen). The sausages are available year round, but the best time to buy the local gingerbread is in December at the colourful Christkindlmarkt, a pre-Christmas outdoor market where townsfolk gather to drink mulled wine, eat roasted chestnuts and the inevitable sausages, and buy Christmas presents.

Nuremberg has four breweries: Patrizier and Tucher are the largest, producing 1.2 million barrels a year between them and supplying thousands of pubs in the region; the much smaller Lederer; and the tiny Hausbrauerei Altstadthof, which produces just 730 barrels for two pubs.

B&B is mostly in the big city price range, but it is still possible to find simple accommodation at reasonable prices (under 100 Marks for a twin-bedded room). Try the Deutscher Kaiser, a few minutes' walk from the main train station in the old town. Königstr. 55, tel: 0911 203-341, fax: 0911 241-8982; or the Kronfleischküche pub, Kaiserstr. 22, tel: 0911 227-845, fax: 0911 241-9746. For the simpler life, and a terrific location to put your head down, seek out the local youth hostel (Jugendherberge) occupying the castle's former royal stables (tel: 0911 221-024). The city tourist office can provide more detailed lodging and sightseeing advice: Frauentorgraben 3, 8500 Nürnberg 70, tel: 0911 23360.

Zum Schuldturm Heubrücke

Vordere Insel Schütt 4
Tel: 0911 225-171

Lederer Pilsener and Patrizier Königstrunk Dunkel on draught. Bottled Patrizier unfiltered wheat beers.
Ⓕ *Hot food*
Daily 1100-2300
Beer garden

This pub-restaurant has just about the best beer garden setting in the old town district. The Schuldturm is on an elongated island in the River Pegnitz, and the garden has a pleasant waterfront. Inside, the pub has a slightly contrived country Bavarian pinewood style. The pub's name is borrowed from the adjoining medieval round tower - a former debtors' prison. There is a solid Bavarian menu.

Zunftstube

Obstmarkt 5
Tel: 0911 221-478

Tucher Pilsener and pale unfiltered wheat beers, and Jever Pils on draught. Bottled Tucher Alt Franken Dunkel, Hell and a dark unfiltered wheat.
Ⓕ *Hot food*
Daily 1000-2300

A traditional town local, where the emphasis is on drinking, smoking and card-playing. There are also some good basic Bavarian meals and an inexpensive lunchtime menu.

Alte Küch'n

Albrecht Dürer-str. 3
Tel: 0911 203-826

St. Georgenbräu Kellerbier and Pilsener (Buttenheim), and Schlenkerla Rauchbier (Bamberg) on draught. Several varieties of bottled wheat beer.
Ⓕ *Hot food*
Daily 1800-0100

A fashionable, snug little night cafe-bar tucked into a cobbled street corner. Popular with students. Note the late opening time. The kitchen stays open until midnight.

Bierkeller Zum Landsknecht

Albrecht Dürer-str. 24
Tel: 0911 204-400

Ⓕ *Hot food*
Mon-Sat 0800-0100; closed Sun

It is a bit touristy, but this small beer keller offers the chance to sample some interesting beers. On draught is Fürstenberg Pilsener (from Donaueschingen in the Black Forest), plus a changing guest draught beer. There is also bottled Tucher wheat beer, Mönchhof's "Black Pils", Schlenkerla smoked beer, and Erdinger dark, unfiltered wheat beer. Beef steaks are the accompaniment here, but they are expensive.

Gaststätte Schranke

Beim Tiergärtnertor 3
Tel: 0911 225-474

Ⓕ *Hot food*
Mon-Sat 1100-2200; closed Sun

This simple little pub, slotted among the tourist haunts on the narrow cobbled streets beneath the castle walls, is Nuremberg's best bet for beer lovers. Landlord Franz Gerber operates a guest beer policy which includes seasonal changes such as Mönchhof Doppelbock on draught. Regulars on tap include Schlenkerla smoked Rauchbier, Erdinger unfiltered pale wheat beer, König Pils, and Tucher pale export. The bottled selection includes Erdinger Pikantus bock wheat beer and Tucher dark unfiltered wheat beer. The kitchen speciality is Bratwurstl – finger-sized, roasted spicy sausages synonymous with Nuremberg.

Schwarzer Bauer

Berg-str. 19
Tel: 0911 227-217

Altstadthof beer, and Lammsbräu Pilsener and Dunkel (from Neumarkt, south of Nuremberg) on draught.
Ⓕ *Snacks*
Daily 1100-0100

This cramped bar, where most customers stand to drink, is the tap of Nuremberg's only micro brewery, the Hausbrauerei Altstadthof. It is a few doors down the hill from the Gaststätte Schranke, beside the entrance to caves cut into the cliffs hundreds of years ago by medieval brewers who needed somewhere cool to keep their beer in summer. The brewery uses old wooden fermentation vessels and wooden maturation barrels. The house beer is served in stone pots so your eyes will not be offended by the cloudiness. Sometimes, the brewer produces a stronger Bock version. The brewery was set up in 1984 by out of town Lammsbräu. Only organically grown ingredients are used. The cliff caves can be visited.

POTTENSTEIN

Three-brewery village on the B-470 between Forcheim and Bayreuth.

In the heart of what the locals call the Fränkische Schweiz (Swiss Franconia) there are numerous pretty villages with their own brewery. Pottenstein, in the winding Wiesent River valley, is among the most attractive for several reasons. Many Germans like to go down into the huge, damp Devil's Cave (Teufelshöhle) to inspect the stalagmites and stalactites (some health freaks pay to sit down there for hours on end, allegedly to improve their respiration). Other visitors are drawn to Pottenstein by the castle and the eerily-shaped rock formations, some of which look like giant stalagmites. But the beer connoisseur is lured to the village to seek out a trio of the finest dark beers in northern Bavaria. Pottenstein has three breweries, each producing an excellent Dunkel. All are in the High Street (Haupt-str.) in Elizabethan-style black and white half timbered buildings; all offer accommodation, making the village an ideal overnight stopover. Tourist office: Verkehrsbüro, Postfach 61, 8573 Pottenstein. Tel: 09243 833.

Brauereigasthof Wagner-Bräu

Haupt-str. 1
Tel: 09243 205

Wagner Altfränkisch Dunkel, Pilsener and pale export on draught. Plus out of town bottled wheat beers
Ⓕ *Hot food*
Summer daily 0900-2300; November-April closed Tue and sometimes other afternoons
Accommodation

This is the biggest of Pottenstein's three little breweries. It has the swankiest pub and the biggest food menu, plus what can best be described as a kind of altar to the European patron saint of brewing: Gambrinus. For gourmets, the pub has twice-monthly Franconian speciality buffet evenings. The waitresses are a bit glum. Eighty beds.

Gaststätte Brauerei Georg Mager

Haupt-str. 17
Tel: 09243 333

Mager Dunkel, Pilsener and pale Export on draught. Bottled Märzen.
Ⓕ *Food*
Daily 0900-2400
Accommodation

The Mager family have been brewing behind this neat and trim old inn on the sleepy High Street since two years before the American Declaration of Independence in 1776. Herr Mager brews only 1,500 barrels of beer a year, but 12 other pubs in the district are customers, mainly of the Pilsener unfortunately. You can get warm meals at lunchtime and cold dishes anytime. Eleven beds.

Gasthausbrauerei Hufeisen

Haupt-str. 38
Tel: 09243 260

Hufeisen Urdunkel and unfiltered pale wheat beer on draught.
Ⓕ *Food*
Tue-Sun 0900-2400
Accommodation

Brewer Josef Wiegärtner brews what he calls Pottenstein's Urdunkel, or the village's original dark beer. It is certainly different: almost as black as British stout, unfiltered and served straight from the cask without any CO_2 dispense. He recently began brewing an unfiltered pale wheat beer. Both beers are available only on draught and only in Wiegärtner's atmospheric brew pub, where the small copper brew-kettle stands in a corner emitting a delightful malty aroma. The Hufeisen dark beer is fermented in open vessels, then matured for about four weeks. Wiegärtner also operates a small distillery producing a beer schnapps. Cold snacks served anytime; hot meals at lunch. Two holiday apartments are available.

SCHEDERNDORF

Near Schesslitz off the B-505 between Bamberg and Bayreuth.

Brauereigasthof Will
Haus 69
Tel: 09504 262

Willbräu dark unfiltered Lagerbier.
Wed-Mon 0900-2300; closed Tue

The one beer brewed by the Will family, who have been here since 1742, is a classic traditional Franconian dark which owes little or nothing to the 20th century. It is an almost black unfiltered Kellerbier style beer, matured in oak casks. The brew is available only in the Wills' pleasant, old-fashioned pub which is an integral part of a family business embracing a small farm, a schnapps distillery (including a beer schnapps) and a slaughterhouse. Little has changed here since the Industrial Revolution apart from the addition of electricity.

SCHESSLITZ
Three-brewery village on the B-505 Bayreuth-Bamberg road.

Brauereigaststätte Senger
Oberend 11
Tel: 09542 1064

Vollbier Dunkel on draught.
Sun-Fri 0900-2400; Sat 0900-1700

An earlier era is evoked when you step inside this brew pub which has been in the same family since the mid 19th century. The delicious dark beer is served direct from a wooden cask in the gnarled taproom - where customers can, and do, bring their own snacks, or Brotzeit as the Germans call it. Brewer Hans Senger's only beer is also sold in old-fashioned flip-top bottles.

Drei Kronen
Haupt-str. 39
Tel: 09542 1564

Drei Kronen pale Vollbier on draught.
Ⓕ *Hot food*
Thu-Tue 0900-0100; Wed 0900-1300

The house beer is still served here straight from a wooden cask too. Apart from the electric light, not much else has changed since the Lindner family opened up shop in 1776. Try the home-made spicy pork sausages.

Brauereigaststätte Schmitt
Oberend 19
Tel: 09542 563

Schmittbräu Hell and Pilsener on draught. Bottled Märzen, Dunkel and a dark doppelbock Weihnachtsbier (Xmas beer).
Mon-Sat 0800-2100; closed Sun

This is Schesslitz's equivalent of a "big brewer", producing five different beers and selling them outside the village. The old brewery tap is no more commercialised because of it, though. The locals still bring their own food.

SCHLAMMERSDORF

6km (4 miles) north of Forcheim off the U-42 or parallel A-73 Bamberg-Nuremburg autobahn (exit Buttenheim or Forcheim).

Brauerei Witzgall

Schlammersdorfer-str. 17
Tel: 09545 7452

Fri-Wed 0900-2300; closed Thu

Blink as you turn the corner into this undistinguished village and you could easily miss the unsigned pub and its ramshackle brewery behind, with wooden casks piled high. Brewer Helmut Witzgall is no longer bemused by groups of British beer enthusiasts who wander in each summer, since a party of CAMRA explorers stumbled into his domain in the mid 1980s and put him on the map. The attraction has nothing to do with Witzgall's spartan, basic boozer, but with his rich, full-bodied Vollbier. Shy, unassuming Witzgall is one of that endangered Franconian species: a one-man craft brewer. In a region where so much good beer is taken for granted, he blushes when praise is heaped on him. He brews a stronger, maltier version, Kirchweihbier, for the village annual festival, always held on the Sunday after June 26.

SESSLACH

Off the B-303, 10 km (6 miles) southwest of Coburg.

The picture postcard image of medieval Germany belongs to the tourist-infested Hollywood set of Rothenburg ob der Tauber, west of Nuremburg. But there are other equally quaint and genuinely historic leftovers from the Hans and Gretel age. One such is Sesslach, which is not only a fully preserved medieval walled village but also boasts a communal brewery managed by the local council. The Kommunbrauhaus is in a 450-year-old half-timbered house on the cobbled square (Maximiliansplatz) and upholds brewing rights first bestowed on the local inhabitants in 1335. The brewhouse is next to the Gasthof Reinwand pub, one of several holders of ancient brewing licences. Visits round the brewery are part of a village tour arranged by the local mayor, or Burgermeister (Tel: 09569 718). If they kept cars out of the walled precincts, little would betray the 20th century.

Gasthof Reinwand

Maximiliansplatz 99
Tel: 09569 304

Hausbrauerbier on draught.
Thu-Tue 0900-2400; closed Wed
Accommodation

A big old coaching inn with several old fashioned overnight rooms, and a taproom from another age.

Zum Roten Ochsen

Flender-str. 95
Tel: 09569 1220

Hausbrauerbier on draught, plus guest beers, usually a Pilsener and a Dunkel.

Ⓕ *Hot food*
◔ *Fri-Wed 1000-2400; closed Thu*
✤ *Beer garden*

Slightly closer to the 20th century than the Reinwand.

STAFFELBACH

12 km (7 miles) northwest of Bamberg off the B-26.

Brauerei Hertlein

Hallstädter-str. 12
Tel: 09503 7890

Hertlein Dunkel on draught.
◔ *Sun-Fri 1500-2400; Sat 1500-1800*

A lively village community pub run by an old farming family who barely seem to have time to brew, but do. The village annual knees-up, with a special beer for the occasion, is the last weekend in July.

STAFFELSTEIN

Pretty three-brewery town on B-173 Hof-Bamberg road, just south of Lichtenfels.

Staffelstein has an impressive 17th-century half-timbered town hall (best views are from the front bedrooms at the Schwarzen Bären brewery-pub). In the hills nearby is one of the most revered of German pilgrimage churches, the Vierzehnheiligen which, surprise, surprise, has a brewery (see below).

Zum Schwarzen Bären

Marktplatz 17
Tel: 09573 274

Bärenbräu Vollbier on draught. Bottled Pilsener.
Ⓕ *Hot food*
◔ *Wed-Mon 0900-2300; closed Tue*
Accommodation

A simple former coaching inn, with its own brewery and butchery. The pub's records are traceable back to 1480, although the present half-timbered, steep-roofed building is late 17th century. In summer 1993, the brewery was due to begin producing a new, strong dark lager called St. Veit Trunk. Budget priced meals and rooms.

Grüner Baum

Bamberger-str. 33
Tel: 09573 293

Ambros-Brüttingbräu Pilsener and dark Kloster Altbier on draught. Bottled Märzen, Hell, Bock (November-March only).
Ⓕ *Hot food*
◔ *Thu-Tue 1000-2300; closed Wed*
✤ *Beer garden*
Accommodation

Renovated brewery tap with a bustling restaurant section which boasts 80 main course dishes and specialises in fresh fish. The beer garden overlooks the brewery, which resumed brewing again in 1992 after closing for a time.

Brauerei Meixner

Lichtenfelser-str.1

Eccentric one-man, one beer brewery, and a pub which opens and closes on a whim, but generally after 6pm (1800) Tuesday-Saturday. Rudolf

Meixner's beer is a dark brown Dunkel, available only at the brewery tap. This writer did not find him open, and unfortunately there is no 'phone to allow you to check in advance of a visit.

STUBLANG

Two-brewery village just off the B-173, near Staffelstein. 27 km (17 miles) north of Bamberg.

Brauereigasthof Dinkel

Stubland 76
Tel: 09573 6424

Dinkel Dunkel on draught.
Ⓕ *Hot food*
Thu-Tue 0900-2300; closed Wed
Accommodation

A big, modern roadside pub which holds no romantic images - but the only place you can try Andreas Dinkel's delicious dark lager. He brews just three times a month and spends much of the rest of his time farming and running the hotel-pub, which is a favourite stop for pensioners' bus outings. The menu includes wild venison, bagged on the Dinkel farmland.

Pension Löwen-Bräu

Stubland 45
Tel: 09573 6436

Löwenbräu Vollbier on draught.
Ⓕ *Food*
Tue-Sun 0900-2300; closed Mon
Accommodation

A rival for the Dinkel Dunkel across the street, this is another brew pub combining an old family tradition with other business. The pub kitchen bakes its own bread in a wood-fired oven.

UNTERHAID

8 km (5 miles) northwest of Bamberg, off the B-26.

Brau-Gaststätte Gambrinus

Haupt-str. 76
Tel: 09503 334

Gambrinus unfiltered Lagerbier on draught.
Ⓕ *Hot food*
Wed-Mon 1100-2400; closed Tue
✤ *Beer garden*

If the word "tradition" means anything in this hyped-up heritage age, then the Laubender family are steeped in it. They have been brewing here since 1451 when they acquired the farmland around the present-day Gambrinus pub and were granted a brewing licence by the ruling prince-bishops. This is a one-man, one-brew, one-pub operation where bottom fermenting yeast seems to be the only concession to modern methods. And if you really want to sample genuine simple Franconian fare, ask for the mixed cold plate: much aspic and offal; strong stomachs only need apply.

UNTERLEITERBACH

Two-brewery village on the B-173 midway between Bamberg and Lichtenfels.

Brauerei Hennemann

Schloss-str. 2
Tel: 09547 261

Hennemann Dunkel Export on draught. A paler Festbier is brewed for an annual village festival on the last weekend of August.
Ⓕ Hot food
Fri-Wed 0900-2400; closed Thu
Accommodation

A big rambling pub with overnight accommodation, which forms part of a family duck-breeding farm (look out for Enten on the menu). The family also has a distillery producing a beer schnapps and a plum brandy which matures in oak casks.

Brauereigaststätte Mahkorn

Schloss-str. 17
Tel: 09547 1624

Mahkorn Lagerbier on draught.
Wed-Mon 1000-0100; closed Tue
Accommodation

A small friendly pub full of inquisitive locals tickled pink that anyone beyond the village might be interested in "their" beer. Simple overnight lodging.

UNTERNEUSES

Brauereigasthof Martin

Viehtriebweg 3 (beside the B173)
Tel: 09573 4382

Martin Vollbier on draught
Ⓕ Hot food
Thu-Tue 1000-2300; closed Wed
Accommodation

Hans Martin brews only once a month and serves his fruity dark brown beer only in his own pub, which also doubles up as the local butcher's shop. Try the pub's Bierhax'n: knuckle of pork in a beer sauce.

VIERZEHNHEILIGEN

Alte Klosterbrauerei

Vierzehnheiligen 6
Tel: 09571 3488
Close to the village of Grundfeld, off B-173, south of Lichtenfels.

Klosterbier Nothelfertrunk Dunkel on draught. Bottled Vollbier and Pilsener.
Daily 1100-2000
✤ Tree-shaded garden

Monks settled on this hilltop, building a shrine church and brewing beer to refresh pilgrims, after a peasant reported visions of Jesus and the Fourteen Saints of Intercession, or Vierzehnheiligen, in 1445. Not for nothing is the local draught dubbed Nothelfertrunk – literally emergency aid drink (pronounced: Note-hell-fer-trunk). Medieval pilgrims must have been gasping after struggling to this out of the way spot. The present church dates from 1743 and is noted for its extravagant Rococo art. You can take your own picnic to the modernised and secularised pub.

VOHENSTRAUSS

South of Weiden on the B-14; 45 km (28) miles east of Amberg.

In the heart of the Oberfalz, north of the Bavarian Forest and east of the wealthier Franconia region, this corner of western Germany suffered from the blight of being right up against both the closed Czech and East German borders of the Iron Curtain for 40 years. Even today its poverty relative to other parts of Bavaria is visible. This is also Zoigl beer country (see Zoigl chapter), but the beer hunter's chief interest in the market town of Vohenstrauss is Behringer wheat beer. Overnight accommodation possible up the hill at the nearby Drei Lilien pub, Friedrich-str. 15, tel: 09651 2361, which serves beers from the tiny castle brewery at Friedenfels, west of Bayreuth, including a bottled Zoigl beer.

Behringer Weissbierstuben

Martplatz 35
Tel: 09651 2304

Behringer pale, unfiltered wheat beer on draught. Bottled Warsteiner Pils and Kloster Weltenburg beers.
Tue-Fri 1100-0100; Sat 1000-0100; Sun 0915-1200 and 1800-0100; closed Mon
✤ *Beer garden*

The hours of opening, the no-frills nicotine-coated tap room, and the ever-active barman tell all: this is a serious beer drinking establishment. The locals were drinking wheat beer here long before it became a fashionable drink once again from the mid-1980s. Everyone drinks from half-litre earthenware mugs with pewter lids. The house custom is to leave the lid sticking up when you are ready for a refill. The house wheat beer is still automatically served with a slice of lemon - a quaint but unnecessary practice which has virtually died out elsewhere in Bavaria (probably on cost grounds).

WEIGELSHOFEN

6 km (4 miles) north of Forcheim, near Buttenheim.

Brauereigasthaus Pfister

Eggerbach-str. 22
Tel: 09545 297

Pfister Vollbier on draught. Bottled pale unfiltered wheat beer. A bock is produced for Christmas and during March, also on draught.
Ⓕ *Hot food (not served Sunday)*
Wed-Mon 0700-2300; closed Tue
✤ *Beer garden*
Accommodation

A friendly, lively country pub, popular as a base for cyclists and walkers exploring the Franconian hills. Excellent food (hot meals from 5pm only) and accommodation. Brewer Josef Pfister also runs a schnapps distillery.

WUNSIEDEL

33 km (21 miles) east of Bayreuth, on B-303.

Keen newspaper readers may recall that this small, pretty and quiet market town of early Victorian terraces has reluctantly secured a footnote in Germany's Nazi history. Wunsiedel is the last resting place of Rudolph Hess, the deputy to Adolf Hitler who mysteriously flew to Britain from Germany at the height of the war in 1941. He was the last person to be imprisoned in the Tower of London, and later spent 40 years behind bars in a Berlin prison. After his death in 1987, he was secretly buried by relatives in Wunsiedel's cemetery - along with the answers to many questions surrounding his 1941 escapade. The spotlight turns on Wunsiedel every August when neo Nazis try to stage Hess commemorative rallies.

Ratsstub'n

Maximilian-str. 22
Tel: 09232 2770

Hönicka Luisenberger Pilsener on draught. Bottled Hönicka wheat beers, plus Erdinger unfiltered wheat beers. A special beer is brewed for the town festival held on the first Sunday in July.

Ⓕ *Hot food*

Mon-Sat 1000-1400 and 1730-2400

Wunsiedel's small family brewery - Hönicka Bräu - has survived both world wars, as has the Ratsstub'n, a jolly pub in the town centre where landlady Sigrid Reichenberger has erected a sign at the door inviting people to "step inside from the stresses out there". The pub name has nothing to do with rats; Rathaus means town hall, which is round the corner from the Ratsstub'n. Tasty and inexpensive meals.

ZAPFENDORF

12 km (7.5 miles) north of Bamberg on B-173.

Brauerei Drei Kronen

Haupt-str. 26
Tel: 09547 6239

Drei Kronen Lagerbier and Pilsener on draught. A dark Festbier is brewed for a village festival on the first weekend in July.

Tue-Fri 0900-1400 and 1700-0100; Sat-Sun 0900-0100; closed Mon

Beer garden

Accommodation

Lively pub which draws extra custom on days when its "Top Act" concert room is in action. There is a quiet beer garden at the back overlooking the brewery yard.

ZENTBECHHOFEN

12 km (7.5 mile) south of Bamberg, off the B-505.

Brauereigasthof Friedel

Höchstädter-str. 1
Tel: 09502 209

Friedel Vollbier on draught. Bottled Märzen.

Ⓕ *Hot food*

◔ *Tue-Sun 0900-2300; closed Mon*
✤ *Beer garden*

This tiny two-pub brewery with an annual output of 1200 barrels celebrated its 500th anniversary in 1967. The family owners are also pig farmers and produce an excellent selection of sausages, which is about as sophisticated as the pub cuisine gets. It may be difficult to get a seat on the second Sunday in July, that's when the pub is the focus of a local church fete.

NB There is also a tiny brewery in the next door village of Schnaid.

Revellers at the Oktoberfest *Photo: Robert Hetz*

Zoigl

elusive ancient Bavarian beer

One of the most mysterious and elusive of Bavarian beers is Zoigl, a pecularity of the Oberfalz area — east of Bayreuth towards the Czech Republic border in the northeast corner of the state.

Zoigl (pronounced Zoi-gull) is mysterious because no two brews are said to be alike, and elusive because it is difficult to track down. I have been able to sample a genuine Zoigl beer just once, and that was only when an old woman took pity on me after I had banged on her kitchen door at dusk in desperation.

Zoigl beer can be top fermented or bottom fermented and is an all-barley malt brew. It is usually unfiltered. It can resemble a heavily hopped amber Franconian Kellerbier, but it can also be a dark Märzen style.

Sometimes Zoigl is served straight from wooden barrels, sometimes only from bottles. It is invariably dispensed in somebody's kitchen or parlour, and this helps explain the origin of the name Zoigl, which is a dialectical version of the German word zeigen, meaning to display, or Zeichen, a sign or signal. It is only via the sign of the Zoigl — a star-shaped symbol, sometimes made from conifer twigs and with the outline of a foaming beer mug in the middle, that this tantalising beer can be found.

Zoigl beer is a hangover from medieval times when brewing rights were bestowed on private households by the lord of the manor or the church hierarchy in return for payment of a special tax. Over the centuries, the right to brew has been passed on to successive house owners, together with the secret brewing recipes.

This custom has survived in several districts of the Oberfalz and since the mid-late 1980s has enjoyed a small revival with more people resuming their right to brew.

Nowadays, the brewing is done in communal brewhouses, sometimes by the individuals with the brewing title, sometimes by a journeyman brewer who is paid. There is only one brewing kettle per commune, usually open-topped and sometimes still fired by wood, and when each wort has been mashed it is usually carted home by the owner to ferment and mature in his or her cellar.

This is where the elusiveness takes over. Zoigl beer is sold in the homes of those with the ancient licences. Simple Bavarian cold dishes are served up as well, although one Zoigl brewer-cum-farmer in the village of Falkenberg is renowned for slaughtering a pig to celebrate the tapping of a barrel. There is virtually no prior announcement, apart from word of mouth, and the star sign which is usually hung out of an upstairs window, or over a door.

I attempted to carry out my Zoigl research midweek, only to discover that the beer is usually tapped at weekends, and then with certain provisos, such as every third weekend following Lent. The best way to find out when and where Zoigl can be drunk is to enquire at local pubs (which do not sell it themselves), or the village shop. The local tourist office might also help.

The one Zoigl I tracked down and tasted was in the small town of Windisch-Eschenbach. It was drawn straight from a wooden cask, was amber in colour with a rich, full-bodied flavour and a very dry finish. Finding Frau Sperber's kitchen tap was well worth the hunt.

Two other definite main centres of Zoigl brewing are Falkenberg and nearby Mitterteich; both places have recently re-built their communal brewhouses. Reports suggests Zoigl brewing is also continuing regularly in Neuhaus, next to Windisch-Eschenbach; at Reuth near Friedenfels, and at Waldershof near Marktredwitz. There is also a communal brewery used by several families at Neuhaus an der Pegnitz, south of Pottenstein just off the A9 (see Franconia).

In Mitterteich, the communal brewhouse, renovated in 1986, is at Vorstadt 13, just off the main square. Call the local Verkehrsamt (tourist office) for guidance, tel: 09633 8919. In tiny Falkenberg, more than a dozen families are said to use the communal brewery there. It stands in the shadow of a castle on a craggy peak — once the family home of Count von Falkenberg, the man who tried to assassinate Adolf Hitler with a bomb in 1944. Call at the house in Tirschenreuth-str. next door to the Edeka grocery shop and ask for Herr Gustl, or ring 09637 328. It was the wrong time when I called. Falkenberg's Zum Roten Ochsen pub (closed Tuesday), has rooms. Tel: 09637 272.

Those with the Zoigl brewing rights pay a modest tax on their brews, and modestly charge those who crowd into their kitchens.

One commercial brewer in the area, the Schlossbrauerei Friedenfels in the village of the same name, now produces a commercial Zoigl, which some locals say is not the real thing. But since the "real thing" is often so elusive, it is well worth trying a bottle of Schwarzer Ritter Zoigl. It is brown in colour, roughly filtered, and has low carbonation. The initial taste is fruity, with some bitterness which expands to give a very dry aftertaste. It has an ABV of 5.2 per cent.

Beer Styles

The Germans are probably more fastidious in their classification of beers than any other country. Colour, strength and methods of production all help determine styles. Several varieties of beer are exclusive to Bavaria, or else are predominantly produced there.

Munich is noteworthy for its strong Bock and Doppelbock brews, and shares with Franconia in northern Bavaria a taste for dark, sometimes coal black, lager-style beers.

The deep amber Doppelbocks, which can be of formidable strength, celebrate the end of the long, cold winter. The paler Bocks — sometimes called Maibocks after the month of May — herald spring.

Munich and east of the city is the traditional home of wheat beers, Weissbier, although this style is now being produced throughout Bavaria in response to mushrooming demand.

Franconia is the home of Rauchbier, a darkish, smoky-flavoured beer once comonplace across central Europe, but now confined to the Bamberg area.

Northern Bavaria is also the natural home of Kellerbier, a sometimes fiercely hoppy beer traditionally made that way to ward off infection.

Munich, eastern, central and northern parts of Bavaria all produce varieties of Märzen, a richly flavoured style which offers spiciness, maltiness and sometimes a bitter-dry character.

Most of the Bavarian styles are bottom fermented, that is they are brewed with varieties of yeast which drop to the bottom of the fermenting vessel. Traditional British beer is made with top growing yeasts which form great foamy "crusts" atop the fermenting vessel. Bottom yeasts function at much lower temperatures than British ale yeasts and generally lead to the cleaner, sharper flavours associated with Continental beers, or lagers. But some Bavarian beers are top fermented — all the wheat beers, for instance.

Most, but not all, Bavarian beers are filtered, that is brewery conditioned. General exceptions are Weissbier and Kellerbier, and increasingly (in response to German back-to-nature health conscious fads) unfiltered versions of other styles are appearing, even unfiltered Pilseners. Unlike in Britain, where the sight of cloudy beer causes apoplexy, the Bavarians cheerfully drink their unfiltered beers in a turbid state. In the case of wheat beer, the pourer will actually roll or shake the almost empty bottle to draw out the last murky dregs. There are no side effects.

According to the Reinheitsgebot, or Purity Law, Bavarian beers must be brewed only from malted barley, hops and yeast. Weissbier is made with a mixture of barley and wheat malts. Bavarian beers are usually pasteurised only for export.

Beers in southern Bavaria tend towards a malty-sweet character. Central areas between Munich and Nuremberg have a hoppier style, reflecting the influence of the great hopfields surrounding the breweries. In the north, especially Franconia, the taste is often drier. To the east, through the Bavarian Forest, the tastes reflect the great Bohemian traditions just across the Czech Republic border.

BOCK

Strong bottom fermented malty beer, sometimes dark amber but can also be quite pale as with Maibocks. Strength varies, but is usually 6 to 8 per cent alcohol by volume (abv). In the Munich area they are usually associated with springtime, April-May. In Franconia, bocks are most frequently produced in mid-winter to coincide with Christmas. The classic pale Maibock is produced by Munich's Hofbräu and is generally only on tap from mid April to mid May. Other fine examples are Paulaner's Hubertus, also served in April-May, and Ayinger's Maibock.

DOPPELBOCK

Students of German would be excused for thinking that Doppelbock is double the strength of a Bock, but it is not. Alcohol content starts around 6.5 but can reach as high as 10 or 12 per cent abv. In Munich, Doppelbock is also called Starkbier and is generally served on draught by several breweries during the Starkbierzeit (literally, strong beer time) in March. The daddy of Doppelbocks is called Salvator from Munich's Paulaner brewery. All other beers of this style acknowledge the original by adding "ator" to their name. Despite their strength — Salvator is 7.5 per cent abv — Munich Doppelbocks are traditionally served by the litre. Several Munich producers hold their own Starkbier fests during March. The biggest is at the Salvator Keller, where the infectious jolly atmosphere helps make such heady beer dangerously easy to drink. These beers are lagered for up to three months.

DUNKEL

Dark lager, or Dunkel is a speciality of Munich and parts of Franconia. They have more individual character than ordinary pale Bavarian beers (the Helles type) but tend to be malty. They can also be quite dry and, in places such as Kulmbach and Pottenstein, very dry and hoppy. Dunkel beers vary in colour from reddish-brown to coal black and are generally slightly stronger than their pale relatives — 5 to 5.5 per cent abv. Before World War Two, dark lager was the common everyday beer of Munich and pale lager less popular. But with the trend towards lighter coloured beers, Dunkel today is often available only in bottled form. When ordering, ask for "Dunkles". Good examples of the type in and around Munich are: Spaten's Ludwig Thoma Dunkel, Kaltenberg's König Ludwig, Maisacher's Rauber Kneissl Dunkel; in Kulmbach, Mönchshof's Klosterschwarzbier (known as the Black Pils); in Pottenstein, the Dunkel varieties from all three of the little town's breweries.

HELL

This is a generic term for all ordinary strength, pale golden lagers. In southern Bavaria, in particular, if you simply order a beer in a pub you will be served a "Helles". They are generally malt accented, but there are also quite dry, hoppy examples, especially north and west of Munich. Strength is generally 4.5 to 5 per cent abv. One excellent pale lager which sits uneasily in this group but defies any other classification is Pilsissimus (5.4% abv) from Munich's Forschungbrauerei. Other good examples include: Hacker-Pschorr, Munich; Schlossbräu in Au in der Hallertau; Witzgall in Schlammersdorf; Maisacher Hell-Export. In Franconia, ordinary pale lagers are often referred to as Vollbier.

KELLERBIER

A style now confined to central Franconia around Bamberg, it is a bottom fermented beer but is unfiltered or only roughly filtered. Because of the method of maturation, which sometimes involves "bleeding" away some of the natural carbon dioxide during the conditioning period, Kellerbier has low carbonation compared with most bottom fermented beers. It is also very heavily hopped, traditionally as an added protection against infection. Kellerbier is very dry; around 4.5 to 5 per cent abv. The best exponents of the style are the two breweries in Buttenheim, south of Bamberg — St. Georgen and Löwenbrauerei.

MÄRZEN

Traditionally this reddish-brown, bottom fermented beer is associated with Munich's Oktoberfest, and varieties of it are still produced by some Munich breweries during that two-week drinking orgy. At the Oktoberfest itself however, Märzen has been replaced by paler, less potent beer. The name Märzen comes from the German word for March, which was when — in pre-refrigeration days — the last batches of beer were brewed before summer weather made production unsuccessful. Märzen is stronger than ordinary Hell and Dunkel beers but weaker than the Bocks. Classically, it is around 5.5 per cent abv. Apart from Munich, numerous small breweries east of the city as well as in Franconia continue to produce Märzen, but usually only in small quantities and in bottled form, making it perhaps the most threatened of the Bavarian styles. Märzen is always a rich, full-bodied beer and is well worth seeking out. Ask for it by name if it is not advertised on a menu. Good examples: Hofbräu, Munich; Klosterbräu, Au am Inn; Müller, Altötting; Pfefferbräu, Zwiesel; Plank in Laaber near Regensburg.

PILSENER

This beer is not indigenous to Bavaria, although there are many local varieties. Many Bavarian examples have a heavier, more malt accented character than the classic Pilsener and sometimes a deeper golden colour. Usually around 4.8 to a little over 5 per cent abv. The best Munich-made examples are Paulaner, Spaten and Löwenbräu. Many smaller Bavarian breweries also produce excellent varieties, including Maisel of Bayreuth; Kuchlbauer, Abensberg; Dimpflbräu in Fürth im Wald on the Czech border; Bischofshof, Regensburg.

RAUCHBIER

Rauchbier, or smoked beer, is now a strictly Franconian speciality. The barley malt is infused with the aroma of beechwood smoke to give the finished beer a burnt, slightly fishy flavour. Bottom fermented Rauchbier varies in colour from dark brown to coal black. The strength hovers around 5 per cent abv. The style is an accident of pre-industrial age practices which were once quite common across central Europe. Beechwood was plentiful in the region and brewers lit fires of chopped beech to dry their germinating barley to prepare it for brewing. When technical advances produced alternative ways of drying barley, the method was mostly abandoned, partly because it was time consuming, but also because many drinkers did not like the smoky taste. The method lingered in and around Bamberg and is now carried out specifically to create the smoky taste. Bock strength varieties are produced in winter.

WEISSBIER OR WEIZENBIER

After almost dying out earlier this century, wheat beer is now the fastest growing style in Bavaria. Wheat beer was once the fashionable drink of the medieval aristocracy who controlled the brewing industry and left the poorer quality brown beers to the peasantry. Nineteenth-century technical advances brought new choice and by the early 20th century only a handful of breweries continued to make wheat beer. However, since the early 1980s its popularity, especially among young people, has expanded to capture 30 per cent of the total Bavarian beer market. Wheat beers are top fermented and in southern Germany are usually 50 per cent wheat and 50 per cent barley malt. It is characteristically fruity and sour, and usually copper coloured, although more recent, dark varieties tend to be sweeter and softer. There are filtered versions — known as Kristall Weissbier, or ohne hefe (without yeast) — but the unfiltered varieties are more popular. It is customary to drink the unfiltered variety in a turbid form. Classically, unfiltered wheat beer is bottle conditioned and therefore heavily carbonated, but there is a trend towards draught dispense by bigger breweries. Purists say draught versions lack the full flavour of bottled varieties, which can be "laid down" for up to a month before leaving the brewery.

Strengths are in the 5 to 5.5 per cent abv range, but Bock or Doppelbock varieties can be 8 per cent. The range of taste is considerable. Good examples include: Schneider of Kelheim and Munich; Erdinger, near Munich; Maisel of Bayreuth; Karg of Murnau; Andorfer of Passau.

ODDITIES

Bavaria also has a couple of one-off eccentric beers, both of which are top fermented and have considerable character:

Dampfbier

A fruity beer which has nothing to do with steam processes, even though the word "Dampf" is German for steam. The use of particular barley malts and a special yeast gives Dampfbier an English beer flavour. See Maisel of Bayreuth, and Pfefferbräu of Zweisel.

Rauchenfels Steinbier

Translated, Steinbier means stone beer. Special rocks are used in the brewing process to create an unusual flavour. The beer gets its burnt or smoky flavour because the wort is poured over red-hot rocks heated to 1,200 degrees centigrade, a process which caramelises the malt. This is a modern version of an old central European brewing method, pre-dating the use of metal kettles for heating the wort. See under Altenmünster in the Southern Bavaria section.

Tasting notes

KEY TO QUALITY

✪✪✪✪	*Outstanding*
✪✪✪	*Excellent*
✪✪	*Good*
✪	*Average*

ALBRECHT
Regensburg

Kupfer Dunkel (5.1%)
Copper coloured unfiltered lager. Gentle and smooth malty beer. Sweet. ✪

Messing Hell (5.1%)
Honey coloured unfiltered pale lager. Sharp and tangy, mixing malt and fruitiness. Bitter-sweet finish. ✪✪

ALTENMÜNSTER-KRONENBRAÜ
near Augsburg

Rauchenfels Steinbier (4.9%)
Brown coloured, top fermented and filtered. Slightly perfumed nose with a hint of vanilla. A quite bitter and very dry beer in which the smoky flavour dominates but is not overbearing. A one off. ✪✪✪✪

Dunkelweissbier (5%)
Dark brown, unfiltered wheat beer. The slightly burnt malt taste has a sour tinge but finally becomes quite bitter. ✪✪✪

Jubelbier (5%)
Very dark lager. The rich, creamy head leads into a smooth, sweet-malt flavour but the final taste is quite dry. ✪✪

Pilsener (4.8%)
An unusually dry and bitter Pils for a south German version of this style. The very hoppy head holds well over a full-bodied, but always sharp and dry beer. ✪✪✪

ALTE KLOSTER
Vierzehnheiligen

Nothelfertrunk (5.2%)
A dark brown Export style. Rich, creamy head with a malty aroma. Slightly bitter-tart taste ending quite dry. Sturdy but refreshing pilgrim's beer. ✪✪✪

ALTSTADTHOF
Nuremberg

Hausbier (4.8%)
Reddish-brown and unfiltered. A Kellerbier style with low carbonation and hop bitterness, but there is also some fruitiness before a dry finish. ✪✪

AMBROS-BRÜTTING
Staffelstein

Pilsener (5%)
Full-bodied but well-hopped with a very dry finish and aftertaste. ✪✪✪

Kloster Altbier (5.2%)
Dark brown lager. Rich malty aroma giving a hint of sweetness, but a strong hop content which forces a dry finish. ✪✪

Hell (4.6%)
Amber, fruity, with a dryish finish. ✪✪

ANDECHS
Ammersee lake, south of Munich

Export Dunkel (5%)
Reddish brown. Big malty aroma off a dense creamy head. Rich nutty-malt flavour with a dryish finish. ✪✪

Doppelbock Dunkel (7%)
Dark ruby. Thick creamy head with a very burnt malt nose. Rich and thick with a Christmas cake malt-fruit taste which is initially sweetish but becomes remarkably dry, with a bitterish aftertaste. ✪✪✪

ANDORFER
Passau

Weissbier (5.3%)
Amber, unfiltered wheat. Rounded taste, nicely balancing a malty sweetness with a tart, dryish finish. ✪✪✪

Weizenbock (6.2%)
Dark brown and unfiltered. A very rich, malty wheat beer with a smooth chocolaty taste. ✪✪

AUER
Rosenheim

Hell (5%)
Pale golden. Big hop-fruit aroma. Slightly tart flavour with a bitter-sweet finish. ✪✪

Rosenheimer Hefeweissbier (5.5%)
Rusty brown. Yeast head with a background aroma of vanilla. Rich mix of fruit and clove spice flavours before a sparkling, dry finish. ✪✪✪

AUGUSTINER
Munich

Dunkel (5%)
Very dark with reddish tints. Malty aroma. Nutty flavour which sweetens slightly and then dries out. ✪✪

Pale Weissbier (5.2%)
Rusty-brown. Unfiltered. Yeasty aroma with a malt palate before a sweet-sour finish. ✪✪

Hell (5.2%)
Very pale. A delicate malty aroma with a light malty-sweet taste and a smooth finish. ✪✪

AUKOFER
Kelheim

Hell (4.8%)
Straw coloured. Very soft, fruity taste, typical of the Altmühltal valley. Light hoppiness which gives a dryish finish. ✪✪

Pilsener (4.8%)
Hoppy head gives way to a very malty bitter-sweet flavour and sharp bitterish finish. ✪✪

Dunkel (5.1%)
Light brown. Over-maltiness gives a rather sweetish taste and finish. Anaemic. ✪

AYINGER
Aying

Hell (5%)
Golden. Light malty flavour which mellows in a fruity finish. ✪

Pilsener (4.9%)
Good hoppy nose. The fullsome flavour is a refreshing balance between hop and malt influences. Smooth, bitter-sweet finish. ✪✪

Dunkel (5.2%)
Reddish-brown, loose headed beer with a nutty-malt taste and smooth sweetish finish. ✪

Maibock (7.2%)
Straw coloured. Firm, dense head and heavy hop aroma. Clean, apple taste ahead of a dryish finish. Dangerously easy to drink, despite its strength. ✪✪✪

Fortunator (7.5%)
Dark Doppelbock. Rich and heavy like Christmas cake. Bitter malt overtones mellow to a smooth, warm finish and a surprisingly dry aftertaste. ✪✪✪

BACHMAYER
Dorfen, near Erding

Dunkel (5%)
Tawny coloured. Rich and fruity with a burnt malt finish. ✪✪

Hell (4.7%)
Very pale. Fruity aroma and flavour, finishing untypically dry. ✪✪

BALS
Oberaudorf

Hefeweissbier (5.1%)
Darkish, unfiltered. Strong yeasty nose before a long malty body, imparting a background of sour fruit. Dryish finish. ✪✪✪

BAMBERGERHAUS
Home brew pub, Munich

Brauhausbier (4.9%)
A dirty yellowish, unfiltered beer which is difficult to categorise but is hardly a Pilsener as implied by the brewer. Initially sour, then fruity; the taste progresses to yeastiness and finally a dryish finish. ✪✪

Dunkel Weissbier (5.2%)
A dark brown, malty brew which lacks the sparkle and bite of a wheat beer. ✪

BÄRENBRÄU
Berching

Bären Pilsener (4.8%)
Fine balance between malt and hop produces a light-bodied, crisp, dry beer of the style. Slightly fruity aftertaste. ✪✪

Berchinger-Weisse (5.3%)
Rusty-yellow, unfiltered wheat. Coarse, with a robust yeast element with spice and fruit influences before a classic sweet and sour finish. ✪✪✪

Alt-Berchinger Dunkel (5.3%)
Almost black lager. Creamy head, malt-hop aroma. Slightly burnt flavour which enhances a dryish taste. ✪✪✪

BÄRENBRÄU
Nesselwang

Hell (5%).
Amber. Gentle malty taste. Bitter-sweet. ✪

Dunkel (5.2%)
Reddish-brown. Firm malt aroma off a loose, fluffy head. Fruity-sweet with a tingle of bitterness round the edges. ✪

Weissbier (5.5%)
Rust coloured, unfiltered. Firm yeasty head and aroma. Sharp initial sourness which becomes fruity and ends bitter-sweet. ✪✪

BÄRENBRÄU
Staffelstein

Vollbier (4.8%)
Amber and Kellerbier-like, although filtered. Quite hoppy and dry. Low carbonation. ✪✪

Pilsener (4.8%)
Dark for a Pilsener but hoppy and dry with a hint of maltiness in the background. ✪✪

BARNIKEL
Herrnsdorf

Lagerbier (4.7%)
Unusually pale for these parts. Big hoppy head, a hint of apples, but a long dry bitterish finish. ✪✪

Rauchbier (5.2%)
Light brown. A firm malty body with a light smoky flavour filtering through and a bitter, dry end. ✪✪

BAUER
St. Wolfgang

Hell (4.9%)
Golden coloured. Clean and sharp with hints of fruit. Bitter-sweet finish. ✪✪

Pilsener (4.7%)
Hoppy nose, descending into a strong malt flavour. ✪

Weissbier (5.2%)
Lemon coloured and unfiltered. Very fruity taste, before a tangy sweet-sour finish. ✪✪

BAYREUTHER BIERBRAUEREI
Bayreuth

Pilsener (4.7%)
Big hoppy head. Firm malt feature, but also hints of fruitiness before finishing dry and bitterish. ✪✪

Zwickel (4.7%)
Rusty-yellow in colour, unfiltered. Yeasty aroma and flavour which becomes fruity. Sweetish aftertaste. ✪✪

BECHER
Bayreuth

Pilsener (4.7%)
Rusty-yellow. The unfiltered condition gives a yeasty tang to a quite hoppy beer, which is distinctive but detracts from the Pilsener style. ✪✪

Dunkel (5%)
Red-brown. Hop aroma rises from the nose and a firm hoppiness remains throughout the malty-tang taste. ✪✪✪

BEHRINGER
Vohenstrauss

Weissbier (5.2%)
Amber. Loose, fluffy head offers initial fruitiness giving way to a sharp, sour flavour. Slightly bitter, dry finish. ✪✪✪

BIERBICHLER
Rosenheim

Weissbier (5.2%)
Orange-yellow, unfiltered. Massive yeast aroma. Very turbid but also very smooth. Fine balance of pale wheat beer flavours. Sweet and sour finish. ✪✪✪

BISCHOFSHOF
Regensburg

Prälat Pilsener (4.9%)
Initial hoppy head mixes with a slight maltiness and fruit; finally dry and bitter. ✪✪

Dunkel (5.2%)
Reddish brown. Malty aroma off a creamy head. Malt mingles with a firm hoppiness. Dry.✪✪

Weissbier (5.2%)
Yellowy-brown, unfiltered wheat. Fluffy head reveals a

lemony aroma. The taste is of sour fruit and spice. Sharp, dry aftertaste.✪✪

BRAUHAUS
Amberg

Vollbier (4.6%)
Very pale. No aroma in the head, but a clean crisp beer mixing fruitiness with some hoppiness. Finishes quite dry.✪✪

Pilsener (4.7%)
Very hoppy and sharp. Some background maltiness before a bitter finish.✪✪✪

BRAUHAUS
Forcheim

Hell (4.9%)
A rich pale beer. Hints of fruitiness but with a robust hoppiness, ending bitter-sweet.✪✪

Pilsener (4.9%)
Very pale. Sharply hopped aroma. A sharp, clean-tasting, lean beer with a dry finish.✪✪

BRÄUHAUS
Fussen

Hell-Export (5.1%)
Amber. Full-bodied and slightly fruity.✪✪

Pilsener (4.9%)
Light-bodied, but with a strong hop character and a refreshingly dry finish.✪✪

Märzen (5.5%)
Dark red. A remarkable clover honey nose belies the rich, fruity flavour and malt-dry finish.✪✪

BRAUHAUS
Gunzenhausen

Pilsener (4.8%)
A strong hop character counter-balances a rather malty taste.✪

Bock (6.2%)
Pale amber. A rich initial mix of hops and malt leads into a surprisingly clean-tasting, sharp beer with a bitterish finish and dry after taste.✪✪✪

BRAUHAUS
Hausham

Märzen (5.6%)
Copper coloured. A creamy head offers an aroma of malt and hops; full-bodied flavour with some fruit sweetness. A bitter-sweet finish.✪✪

Hell (5%)
Gentle malt flavour and some hop character, with a sweetish finish.✪

Weissbier (5.2%)
Honey coloured unfiltered wheat. The dense head has much fruit character leading to a rich, rounded and finally tart aftertaste.✪✪✪

BRAUHAUS
Lauf

Brauhaus Pilsener (4.8%)
Light malt aroma. Fruity, light-bodied taste with a smooth, clean finish.✪✪

Dunkel (5.1%)
Dark brown. Malty aroma. Sharp, malty body with a liquorice bitter-sweet aftertaste.✪✪

KEY TO QUALITY

✪✪✪✪	*Outstanding*
✪✪✪	*Excellent*
✪✪	*Good*
✪	*Average*

BRAUHAUS
Tegernsee

Spezial (5.5%)
Gold-amber. Crisp Export style beer. Full-bodied with both hops and malt flavour. Sparkling bitter-sweet finish.✪✪

Dunkel Bock (6.4%)
Fullsome malty beer with a sweetish character balanced by some hop bitterness.✪

BRÄUWASTL
Weilheim

Hefeweissbier (5.3%)
Medium-brown, unfiltered. A coarse, yeasty cross between a pale and a dark wheat beer. Initially sharp and slightly sour, becoming sweeter.✪✪

BRUCKMAYER
Drachselsried

Hell (4.9%)
Very pale gold. Fruity aroma which extends into a rich, fruity flavour and a dryish finish.✪✪

Pilsener (4.9%)
Strong hop nose, firm body and a long dry taste with a bitter finish.✪✪✪

Respektator (6.3%)
Reddish-brown with a powerful fruit-malt aroma. Smooth, malty taste with a cherry-fruit background, but finishing surprisingly dry for its strength.✪✪✪

BRÜCKMÜLLER
Amberg

Vollbier (4.9%)
Very pale. Very hoppy. Dry.✪✪✪

Pilsener (4.9%)
Drier than its sister Vollbier, finishing surprisingly sharp and tart.✪✪✪

BÜRGERBRAÜ
Augsburg

Augsburger Braunbier (5.2%)
Unfiltered bottom fermented dark beer supposedly brewed to a style common between 1750-1850. Chestnut brown in colour. A malty, slightly sour flavour through the lasting thick creamy head. The aftertaste is dry.✪✪

BÜRGERBRÄU-KAISERDOM
Bamberg

Dunkel (5.2%)
Red-brown. Hoppy nose, light malt-sweet flavour. Thin, sweetish finish.✪

Rauchbier (4.8%)
Amber. Dryish beer with a lightly smoked flavour mingling with malt.✪✪

Hefeweissbier (5.2%)
Honey coloured, sparkling wheat beer. Flavours of yeast and apple. Sharp and bitter-sweet at the end.✪✪

BÜRGERBRÄU
Regen, Bavarian Forest

Alt Regener Dunkel (4.8%)
Dark brown. Strong malty aroma, a bitter, coffee-like taste moving to a dryish finish.✪✪✪

Pilsener (4.8%)
Hoppy head but an overly malty taste for this style of beer.✪

Weissbier (5.1%)
Rusty red. Hint of apples in the nose. Quite sour tasting with a

very sharp bitter-sweet finish.✪✪

Hell (4.6%)

Pale golden. Initial fruitiness fades to a bitter-sweet finish.✪

CHARLYBRÄU
Augsburg

Weissen (5.4%)

Amber and unfiltered. Similar to Munich's Isarbräu pale wheat beer, but slightly drier and less fruity.✪✪

Weizenbock (6.2%)

Dark brown, unfiltered wheat bock. Rich and malty with a hint of cinnamon spice. Fruity edge in the smooth finish.✪✪✪

DACHS
Weilheim, south of Munich

Dachsweizen (5%)

Dark wheat, unfiltered. Strong malty aroma but a sourish taste which ends in a mix of yeast and sweetness.✪✪

Dunkel (5%)

Reddish-brown. Malty and slightly spicy. Crisp and dry.✪✪

DEININGER-KRONENBRÄU
Hof (subsidiary of Kulmbach's EKU)

Dunkel Hefeweissbier (5.1%)

Very dark brown, unfiltered. Rich, sour-dry flavour with a liquorice aftertaste.✪✪✪

DIMPFL
Fürth im Wald

Hell (4.8%)

Golden coloured. A very dry, sharp beer for the style, almost like a Pils.✪✪✪

Pilsener (4.8%)

Perhaps comes nearest in this area to mimicking a Czech pale beer. Rich with a touch of malt, but dry and clean.✪✪✪

DINKEL
Stublang

Dunkel (5.2%)

Dark brown with a fluffy creamy head. A wonderfully hoppy, dry beer.✪✪✪

DREI KRONEN
Schesslitz

Vollbier (4.9%)

Amber coloured pale Export style lager. Complex mix of fruit and malt; full-bodied but with a dryish aftertaste.✪✪

DREI KRONEN
Zapfendorf

Lagerbier (4.6%)

Amber, fruity but with a slightly tart finish.✪✪

Pilsener (4.8%)

Big fluffy head, big firm body with a malt background which ends dry.✪✪✪

DREYKORN
Lauf, near Nuremburg

Dunkel (4.8%)

Very dark, almost black colour. Yeasty nose. A strong malty start which becomes hoppy and dryish in the end.✪✪

ECK
Böbrach

Wilderer Dunkel (5.3%)

Almost black lager. Hops play a big part in the flavour, in good balance with a malt influence which is not overpowering. Firm dry finish.✪✪✪

Pilsener (4.8%)
Pale golden. Heavy hop character in both head and body. Clean, crisp. dry.✪✪✪

Magistrator Doppelbock (7%)
Black strong beer which strikes a highly palatable balance between hop and malt. A bitter-chocolate taste. Bitter-sweet finish.✪✪

EHRNTHALLER
Kelheim

Pilsener (4.9%)
Golden amber colour. Firm hoppy aroma, firm malty body. The hop influence grows towards the finish, which is quite crisp dry.✪✪

Hell (5%)
Very pale golden lager. Keen vanilla aroma over a light, fruit-malt body. Bitter-sweet.✪

EICHHORN
Forcheim

Märzen (5.7%)
Unusually pale for the type. The nose has a strong aroma of apples ahead of rich flavour of malt and hops. A rounded dry finish.✪✪✪

Pilsener (4.8%)
A richly hopped beer but with a fruity body which pushes the bitterness back to give a quite mellow finish.✪✪

Vollbier (5.1%)
Copper coloured. A fullsome, rather rich Export style beer with a bitter-sweet aftertaste.✪✪

EKU (ERSTE KULMBACHER UNION)
Kulmbach

Rubin Dunkel (4.8%)
Reddish-brown. Rich and malty with a hint of cherry fruit. Dry finish.✪✪

Pilsener (4.9%)
A firm hoppy bouquet. Bitter taste balanced by a meaty malt background. Smooth, malty finish.✪✪

Kulminator (7.5%)
Dark brown doppelbock with a strong malt aroma. A heavy malt-sweet taste is balanced at the end with a slightly bitter aftertaste.✪✪

Kulminator 28, or EKU 28 (13.5%)
Amber doppelbock of premium barley wine strength, claiming to be one of the two strongest beers in the world (its chief rival is in Switzerland). A powerful sweet malt aroma is balanced in the taste with tinges of hops. A warming "glow" accompanies the smooth, bitter-sweet aftertaste.✪✪

ERDINGER
Erding, near Munich

Hell Weissbier (5.3%)
Unfiltered. Big fruity palate moving to a sweet-sour finish.✪✪

Dunkel Weissbier (5.6%)
Dark brown, unfiltered. An attractive liquorice flavour comes through the dense, rich head. Surprisingly dry for a beer of this type.✪✪

Pikantus Bock (7.3%)
Chocolaty-brown colour. The dense fruity head has an aroma of raisins. This rich fruitiness mixes with a smooth malty palate, ending deceptively dry for a beer of such strength.✪✪✪✪

ERHARTINGER
between Mühldorf and Altötting near the Austrian border

Hefeweissbier (5.2%)
Pale, with a dense and lasting bitter head which influences the beer through to the distinctive sour-dry finish.✪✪

Hell (4.7%)
Pale golden. Crisp and slightly fruity with a dryish taste and clean finish.✪✪

ETTL
Teisnach

Bayerisch Dunkel (5.4%)
Blackcurrant coloured. Slightly yeasty head leads into a dry but malt-flavoured dark lager. A fruity influences expands to give a tangy aftertaste.✪✪✪

FALKENLOCH
Neuhaus a.d. Pegnitz

Vollbier (4.8%)
Golden coloured. Lots of apple and a slightly tart finish.✪✪

Pilsener (4.8%)
Big hop aroma descends into a firm malty body and a quite dry finish.✪✪

Märzen (5.4%)
Amber. Strong malt influence in the aroma and the coarse, bitter-sweet flavour.✪✪

FALTER
Drachselsried

Dunkel (5%)
Reddish-brown. Big malty nose. Chocolaty taste, but a final dryness which overrides the sweet edges.✪✪

Arber Pilsener (4.7%)
Thick malty flavour which almost submerges the hop content. Bitterish finish but a sweetish aftertaste.✪

Hell (4.7%)
Golden lager, classically combining the regional maltiness with a fine hop balance. Bitter-sweet finish.✪✪

FÄSSLA
Bamberg

Lagerbier (4.9%)
Copper coloured. Hoppy-malt flavour with some fruitiness in the background and a bitter-sweet finish.✪✪

Pils (5%)
More an Export beer than a true Pilsener. Full-bodied with a firm initial hoppiness which fades into sweetish finish.✪

Märzen (5.3%)
Also known as Zwergla. Dark amber. A nuttiness in the malt nose combines with a firm hop character. Bitter-sweet.✪✪

FISCHER
Greuth

Lagerbier (5%)
Golden coloured with a rich, full-bodied malt-fruit flavour which gradually gets bitter and finishes dry.✪✪✪

Rauchbier (4.8%)
Light brown and lightly smoked. Aroma of kippers. Dry and slightly bitter.✪✪

FLETZINGER
Wasserburg

Pilsener (5%)
Typical south German malt influence, but drying out to a quite hoppy, rounded beer.✪✪

Dunkel (5%)
Red-brown. Rather excessive malty taste and a little thin. Sweetish aftertaste.✪

FLIEGER
Munich

Flieger-Weisse (5.4%)
Copper coloured and unfiltered. Bags of fruitiness in this rich wheat beer with a tangy, slightly bitter finish.✪✪

FLOTZINGER
Rosenheim

Pilsener (5%)
Strongly hopped aroma. Meaty, tangy body with a slight fruity character. Hoppiness predominates into the crisp, dry finish✪✪✪

Weissbier (5.3%)
Rusty-yellow coloured, unfiltered wheat beer. The head has a tangy bitter yeast character. Sharp, fruity flavour and a sour-sweet aftertaste.✪✪

FORSCHUNG
Perlach, Munich

Pilsissimus (5.4%)
Copper coloured and highly characterful. The pronounced hoppy aroma follows through into the initial taste which then moves to a softer maltiness before drying out in a smooth finish tinged with bitterness.✪✪✪✪

St. Jakobus Bock (7.8%)
A soft amber brew which, like many Munich beers of this strength, is very deceptive (even so, it is customarily drunk by the litre mug). Strong malty flavour with a smooth, sweet finish which is nevertheless moreish.✪✪✪

FRIEDEL
Zentbechhofen

Vollbier (5.1%)
Honey coloured. Fruity with a spicy flavour reminiscent of cinnamon. Dryish aftertaste.✪✪

Märzen (5%)
Dark amber with a rich fruit-malt loaf taste which dries out.✪✪

FRIEDMANN
Gräfenberg

Vollbier (5%)
Copper coloured. Coarse and hoppy with a fruity-dry finish.✪✪

Pilsener (4.7%)
Big hop aroma and a meaty body combines to make this a powerful tasting beer with a bitter-sweet finish.✪✪✪

Dunkel (5.2%)
Reddish-brown. Good mix of hop and malt aroma with a curious peppery finish.✪✪

FÜRSTENBERG

Export (5.2%)
Deep golden. Elements of fruit in a big bodied, crisp-tasting beer with a clean, dry finish.✪✪✪

Pilsener (5%)
Strong hoppy head, full-bodied with considerable bitterness and a crisp dry finish.✪✪✪

GAMBRINUS
Unterhaid

Lagerbier (4.9%)
Unfiltered muddy brown. Low carbonation. Firm fruity-malt aroma, strong fruity-spice taste. Dryish finish.✪✪✪

GENOSSENSCHAFT
Holzkirchen

Hell (4.9%)
Very pale, with a big yeasty aroma. Firm malty body, but with a surprisingly hoppy influence for the style, Some fruitiness in the finish.✪✪

Dunkel (5.2%)
Dark brown lager. Strong malty aroma off a dense, firm head. The malt flavour tends to crowd out the hop character. Brown ale sweetness.✪

Festbier Märzen (5.5%)
Dark amber. Rich and full-bodied, balancing a strong malt character with a firm hop influence. Dryish flavour, ending bitter-sweet.✪✪✪

GLENK
Bayreuth

Pilsener (4.8%)
Good hoppy head over a firm-bodied tasting beer which has malt and bitterness and a hoppy-dry finish.✪✪

GMEINDER
Deisenhofen, Munich

Gmeinder Weissbier (4.9%)
Dark brown. A soft and surprisingly mellow taste for a wheat beer. Hints of yeastiness, becoming bitter-sweet and finishing dry. Unusually low carbonation when served draught.✪✪

GOLDENER GANS
Augsburg

Urhell (5%)
Rich and full-bodied pale lager; some initial sweetness mellows to a mildly, fruity finish.✪✪

Pilsener (4.8%)
Dense hoppy head. Light, clean body. Slight fruit character before drying out in a crisp finish.✪✪

GOSS
Deuerling

Märzen (5.5%)
Quite pale for the style. Hops dominate throughout rather than malt, which is in the background along with some fruitiness. A superbly dry beer for the style, ending with a clean, crisp palate.✪✪✪

Hell (5.1%)
Very pale. Full-bodied with some maltiness in the background, but the dominant taste is fruity.✪✪

GRAF ARCO
Valley, south of Munich

Hell (4.9%)
Copper coloured. Marvellously attractive strong malt taste which contrives to be quite dry.✪✪✪

Dunkel (5.1%)
Dark brown, light malt flavour. Unexceptional.✪

Weissbier (5.3%)
Honey coloured and unfiltered. Light-tasting, some fruit and slight sourness in the crisp, clean finish.✪

GREIF
Forcheim

Edel-Märzen (5.3%)
Golden colour. Vanilla aroma with a rich sweet-malt flavour which dries out in a bitter aftertaste.✪✪

Lagerbier (4.5%)
Copper coloured, unfiltered

beer with all the characteristics of a Kellerbier: very hoppy with a dry aftertaste. Bottled only.✪✪

Hell (4.9%)

Golden colour. An interestingly fruity beer for the style.✪✪

GRÜNERBRÄU

Bad Tölz

Kräusen-Pils (4.9%)

Pale amber, unfiltered. The aroma has yeast and hops. Well-hopped, firm-bodied dry beer, with a slightly yeasty aftertaste.✪✪

Hefeweizen (5.4%)

Copper coloured, unfiltered wheat. Tart, lemony taste with a gentle, mellowing sweet note which balances the sour-dry finish.✪✪✪

HACKER-PSCHORR

Munich

Hubertusbock (Maibock, 6.8%)

Copper coloured. Mix of hops and fruit in the strong dense head. Initial maltiness swings to a big explosion of hoppiness, and back again to a touch of sweetness before a big dry finish. A gem.✪✪✪✪

Dunkel (5.2%)

Dark brown. A malty aroma in the tight head leading to an almost chocolaty taste but becoming dry in the finish.✪✪✪

Pschorr Weisse (5.5%)

Unfiltered. Pale and heavy yeastiness in the aroma which carries through into an otherwise undemanding ride over the tastebuds.✪

Hell (5%)

Golden amber. Distinctly fruity beer with a clear taste of apples and a dry finish.✪✪

HACKLBERG

Passau

Zwicklbier (4.5%)

Copper coloured and unfiltered. A big yeasty flavour which lacks the firm hoppiness of a true Kellerbier, but sharp and tangy.✪✪

Hochfürst Pilsener (4.1%)

Bitter dense head with a firm hoppiness which dominates the smooth, surprisingly fullsome body for this beer's low strength. Very dry.✪✪✪

Jacobi Hefeweizen (4.1%)

A pale unfiltered wheat beer which relies on a too sour, bitter-sweet taste, perhaps hiding a thin body.✪

HASEN

Augsburg

Weisser Hase (5.2%)

Pale, unfiltered wheat beer. Good balance of sweetness and sourness, with a tinge of bitterness at the end.✪✪

Pilsener (5%)

Malt and hop aroma comes through the dense head, but the hop character dominates. Quite a bitter finish.✪✪✪

Fortissimo Hell Bock (6.5%)

Golden coloured with a hop-yeast aroma, bitter-sweet palate and a hard dry finish with a bitter aftertaste.✪✪

HAUSBRAUER

Sesslach

Hausbrauerbier

(as at the Gasthof Reinwand pub).

Dark brown, roughly filtered, low carbonation. Strongly hopped but the dark malt character pushes in to make it bitter-sweet. Dryish aftertaste.✪✪✪

HEBENDANZ
Forcheim

Annafestbier (Märzen, 5.3%)
Medium brown. Mix of fruit and malt in the complex nose. The malty flavour has a liquorice edge moving to a bitter-sweet finish and dryish aftertaste.✪✪✪

Hell-Export (5.1%)
Pale, full-bodied beer with a strong fruity finish.✪✪

HELLBRÄU
Altötting

Pale Export (5.1%)
Yellowish coloured, with a mix of fruit and malt and a bitter-sweet finish.✪

Dunkel (5.4%)
Dark brown and unfiltered lager. A yeasty head gives way to a well-hopped, heavy but dry-tasting beer.✪✪✪

Märzen (5.6%)
Dark amber. A thick, heavy brew with a sweet malt emphasis, although some hoppiness helps dry it a little.✪✪

HELM
Landshut

Dunkel (4.4%)
Dark brown with reddish lights. Distinctly burnt malt aroma which bursts through the strong, lasting head into the taste. Slowly, the flavour becomes more tart with a crisp refreshing finish.✪✪✪

Pilsener (4.5%)
An unusually tart, dry flavour for the style, with a surprisingly fruity finish. An interesting taste.✪✪✪

HENNEMANN
Unterleiterbach

Dunkel Export (5.2%)
Reddish brown. Low carbonation. Smooth and mellow beer with an initial maltiness submerging in a firm hop character. Dry finish.✪✪

HERRNBRÄU
Ingolstadt

Hell (4.9%)
Pale golden. A good balance of malt and hop, plus some fruitiness. Bitter-sweet aftertaste.✪✪

Hefeweissbier (5.4%)
Honey coloured and unfiltered. Powerful yeasty head and initial taste, giving way to a fruity-dry finish.✪✪

Dunkel (5.2%)
Dark brown with red tints. A nutty-malt flavour tinged with sweetness, finishing bitter-sweet.✪✪

HERTLEIN
Staffelbach

Dunkel Lagerbier (5.2%)
Dark brown, unfiltered. Big malty aroma and body, but any hint of sweetness fades into a crisp dry finish.✪✪

HOFBRÄU
Abensberg

Pilsener (4.7%)
Correct, dense head but little aroma. Rich, malty flavour with

a background bitterness expanding in the mouth. Quite sharp and slightly peppery.

Dunkelweissbier (5.2%)
Reddish-brown, unfiltered wheat beer. Yeast and malt aroma off a creamy head. Sparkling but thinnish body and sweetish finish.

HOFBRÄU
Berchtesgaden

Hell-Export (5.2%)
Pale golden. Malty nose fades to a rather dull bitter-sweet finish

Dunkel (5.2%)
Reddish-brown. Firm malt-fruit aroma. Good full body; slightly sweet finish.

Pilsener (4.7%)
Hoppy aroma over a quite malty, full-bodied taste. Quite dry but with a slightly cloying aftertaste.

HOFBRÄU
Munich

Export (5.2%)
A coppery coloured lager with a malty taste, a hint of fruit but a bitter-sweet finish.

Münchner Kindl Weissbier (5.1%)
Muddy brown, unfiltered. Malty-sweet with a slightly sour aftertaste.

Maibock (7.2%)
Deep copper colour. Rich malt and hops aroma from the dense creamy head of Munich's original pale bock. The malty flavour is laced with a big hoppy background which comes through into the lip-smacking malty-dry finish. A princely beer.

Dunkel (5.2%)
Coffee-brown. A vanilla-fruit aroma, tart fruit palate and a smooth, dryish finish.

Märzen (5.7%)
Reddish-brown. Heavy malt aroma gives way to a surprisingly light, drinkable malt-accent taste. Soft dry finish.

HOFER
Fürth im Wald

Hell (4.6%)
Very pale and rich, with a fruity tinge and bitter-sweet finish.

Pilsener (4.8%)
Tight, lasting head oozes hops and malt. A full-bodied taste, ending bitter.

Dunkel (5%)
Red-brown. Creamy head has a hoppy aroma. Dry-malty taste which has firm lasting bitterness.

HOFMARK
Loifling, Cham

Herb Würzig (5.1%)
Amber with a hoppy aroma. Dry with some bitterness and a quite sharp finish.

Mild Würzig (5.1%)
Amber but less hoppy and bitter flavoured than its brother Herb Würzig. Rounded and mellow finish.

HÖNICKA
Wunsiedel

Luisenberg Pilsener (4.9%)
Hoppy nose. Slightly acidic taste mixed with bitterness.

Hönicka Weisse (5.2%)
Lemon coloured, unfiltered wheat. Fullsome yeasty head, fruity-sour palate with some bitterness. Dry aftertaste.

HOPF
Miesbach

Weisse (5.2%)
Pale and unfiltered. A fine balance between fruity sweetness and tart dryness. Quite sour.✪✪

Dunkel-Spezial (5.3%)
Reddish-brown, unfiltered wheat. Malt-chocolate sweet flavour which turns a little tart.✪✪

Dunkler-Bock (6.3%)
A dark brown bock wheat. Initial chocolate taste gives way to a rich fruit loaf maltiness. A spicy-sour background combines to make the finish malty-dry.✪✪✪

HUFEISEN
Pottenstein

Dunkel (5.4%)
Coal black and unfiltered. Strong malt flavour with a dry, coffee-ish tang which helps to rein in a slightly sweet finish.✪✪✪

Weissbier (5.2%)
Honey coloured and unfiltered. A fine balance of fruitiness and sourness, finishing with a bitter, refreshing edge.✪✪

INNSTADT
Passau

Dunkel (5%)
Dark brown. Fruity, malty. A curious tangy-fruit and bitter-sweet finish.✪✪

Pilsener (4.7%)
Very hoppy, rich and smooth. Bitter aftertaste.✪✪✪

ISARBRÄU
Munich

Isartal Weisse (5.4%)
Dark amber, unfiltered wheat beer. Smooth body (it is dispensed on draught) with a good balance of fruit and sourness.✪✪

JANKA
Zwiesel

Kupfer Spezial (5.6%)
Dark copper. Hoppy aroma leads into a rich, very fruity flavour culminating in a long dry finish.✪✪✪✪

Böheme Pilsener (4.6%)
Very pale golden. A sharp, hoppy variety of the style with a very dry, clean and refreshing palate.✪✪✪

Böhmisches Schwarzweizen (5.2%)
Reddish-brown, filtered dark wheat beer. Sharp, slightly sour taste with a mildly burnt malt background.✪✪

KAISER
Neuhaus an der Pegnitz

Veldensteiner Landbier (5%)
Light brown. Smooth, rich malt taste. Bitter-sweet finish.✪

Pilsener (4.7%)
Light-bodied, with a hint of fruitiness and a sharp, bitter finish.✪✪

Hefeweissbier (5.2%)
Honey coloured, unfiltered. Big vanilla aroma and considerable apple fruitiness, with a good sour-dry finish.✪✪

KALTENBERG

Prinzregent Luitpold Hell Weissbier (5.5%)
Unfiltered. Rusty brown. Yeasty

head over a tart bitter-sour flavour which ends very dry.✪✪

Prinzregent Luitpold Dunkel Weissbier (5.5%)
Unfiltered. Dark brown. Fruity malt loaf flavour with some sourness at the end.✪✪

Hell (4.8%)
Very pale. Crisp and dry, with hints of fruit which give way to bitterness. More like a Dortmund Export than a south German Helles.✪✪

König Ludwig Dunkel (5.1%)
Very dark, almost black. A solid, yeasty head leads into a thick malty body and a bitterness which never subsides. The aftertaste is remarkably dry for a dark lager.✪✪✪

Ritterbock (6.8%)
Almost black, almost doppelbock. Coffee-malt aroma in the thick creamy head. Rich brew with a combination of malt fruitiness and hop bitterness but with a quite dry, clean finish, making it dangerously moreish.✪✪✪

KARMELITEN
Straubing, Bavarian Forest, but served in Schneider pubs

Dunkel (5.2%)
Reddish-brown. Soft and malty with a mix of sweetness and hops in the finish.✪

Donau Pilsener (4.7%)
Gentle hop nose over a full-bodied, malt-accented taste with a dry, clean aftertaste.✪✪

KARG
Murnau, southwest of Munich

Hell Weissbier (5%)
Copper coloured and unfiltered. Dense yeasty head which leads into a coarse yeasty flavour with a fruity background. Very tart with a dry aftertaste. One of the best of its kind.✪✪✪

Kaltenberg's Prinz Luitpold outside his castle

Schwarzer Woiperlinger dark wheat beer (5.3%)
Dark brown, unfiltered. Extremely turbid and tart with a cooked apples taste, ending sharp and surprisingly dry for the style.✪✪✪

KLOSTERBRÄU AU

Au am Inn, south-east of Munich

Klostergold Märzen (5.5%)
Light brown. A hazelnut aroma and malt taste mingling with hops. A wonderfully coarse, dry finish.✪✪✪

Dunkel (5.1%)
Reddish-brown. Firm creamy head and malty body which has a dry finish.✪✪

Hell (4.7%)
Golden coloured, but rather thin and bland.

KLOSTERBRÄU BAMBERG

Ächd Bambärcha Schwärzla (5.3%)
Very dark brown, almost black. Both malt and hops in the nose. Thick brew with coffee and fruit flavours. Smooth, mellow, slightly sweet aftertaste.✪✪✪

Märzen (5.6%)
Golden coloured, filtered. A robust, fruity beer with a smooth finish which has an apple-like, dryness.✪✪

KLOSTERBRÄU ETTAL

Dunkel Export (5%)
Dark brown with reddish tints. Strong malt taste with coffee-ish background. Smooth body, quite dry finish. An excellent example of south German dark lager.✪✪✪

Pilsener (5%)
Initial maltiness typical of south German Pilseners yields to a firm and sharp hoppy character which gives a bitter, dry finish.✪✪

Curator (7.3%)
Reddish-black doppelbock. A heavy, malty brew with a rich and warming port-like body. Background hops burst through to sharpen the finish and provide a long bitter aftertaste.✪✪

KLOSTERBRÄU IRSEE

Irsee, southwest of Munich

Kloster-Urtrunk (5.6%)
Deep copper colour. Unfiltered, but bottom fermented beer which contrives to be a cross between a Kellerbier and a Märzen. The thick creamy head has a vanilla aroma over a rich mix of hoppiness and fruit, with some malt in the background. The aftertaste is bitter and very dry. A magnificent beer.✪✪✪✪

Abtstrunk (11.5%)
Dark, thick and slightly oily. An unusual brew which despite the aroma and taste of both hop and malt resembles a liqueur in character. Rich, smooth, warming and surprisingly dry.✪✪✪

Kloster Starkbier (6.8%)
Dark brown and unfiltered. Yeast and malt flavours in a surprisingly light-bodied beer for its strength. An expanding hop character leads to a dryish, mellow finish.✪✪

Kloster Weizen (5.2%)
Pale amber, unfiltered wheat. Coarse and yeasty with a prominent bitter palate and a sour, dry end.✪✪✪

KLOSTER KREUZBERG

Dunkel Vollbier (5.2%)
Very dark brown. Rich malty aroma which mingles sweetly with a slight liquorice flavour. Bitter-sweet.✪✪✪

KLOSTER MALLERSDORF

Hell (5%)
Copper coloured. A pale, fruity lager with a clean, dryish finish. Hops are clearly evident in the palate, reflecting the hop-growing region where it is brewed.✪✪

KLOSTER RAITENHASLACH

Raitenhaslach

Kellerbier (4.8%)
Honey coloured and unfiltered. Initial fruitiness gives way to a stout hoppiness and a dryish finish✪✪

Dunkel (5.2%)
Dark brown. A solid dry-malt flavour throughout, with a hint of liquorice in the aftertaste.✪✪

Weissbier (5.4%)
Very pale unfiltered wheat. A big fruity aroma and taste, with some background yeastiness before ending dry and tart.✪✪

Schwarzerweisse (5.4%)
Dark brown and unfiltered. Rich creamy head with a coffee-ish aroma. Strong, malty taste, drying out in a slightly sour finish.✪✪✪

Pilsener (4.7%)
A good, hoppy example of the style.✪✪

KLOSTER WELTENBURG

between Ingolstadt and Regensburg

Asam Doppelbock (6.5%)
Black with reddish tints. A hint of liquorice in the nose. A rich but dry malty flavour which somehow avoids becoming sweet.✪✪✪

Spezial Export-Dunkel (5.1%)
Near black, full-bodied and well balanced dark lager. Creamy, malty head leads into a burnt-malt taste where an element of hop bitterness lasts through to the finish.✪✪✪

KNEITINGER

Regensburg

Export Dunkel (5.4%)
Dark brown. A malty brew with a big, rich body. Hop taste in the background combines finally to give a dryish finish.✪✪✪

Pilsener (4.8%)
Big malt character which masks the hops perhaps too much. A bitter-sweet finish.✪

KUCHLBAUER

Abensberg

Weissbier (5.2%)
Honey coloured, unfiltered. Yeasty aroma which carries through into the initial taste, becoming sour and slightly bitter.✪✪

Pilsener (4.8%)
Very hoppy and dry; the heavy maltiness which often accompanies south German Pilseners is absent.✪✪✪

Hell (4.7%)
Amber. Mix of fruitiness and malt, but a dry finish.✪✪

LAMM

Eltmann

Lagerbier (4.7%)
Surprisingly pale, light-bodied but a firm hop flavour and refreshing dry finish.✪✪

Dunkel (5.3%)
Almost black, with a distinctive nutty flavour which finishes dry. Unlike other dark lagers west of Bamberg.✪✪✪

Pilsener (4.9%)
A very rich, full-bodied Pilsener with a sharp, bitter ending.✪✪✪

LEDERER
Nuremburg

Pilsener (5.3%)
The higher than usual strength makes for a richer, fuller beer, but rather too malty. Bitter-sweet finish.✪

LEICHT
Memmelsdorf

Pilsener (4.7%)
Dense, hoppy head, firm malty body. Rounded finish, with a bitter-sweet aftertaste.✪✪

Lagerbier (4.5%)
Amber coloured beer with little head. Low carbonation. Quite hoppy, but with a fruity body and finish.✪✪

Export (5.1%)
Quite pale for a Franconian beer. Malty aroma, full-bodied with a fruity-dry ending.✪✪

LINDENBRÄU
Gräfenberg

Vollbier (4.9%)
Amber. Rich, full-bodied lager with a strong hop flavour ending dry with a hint of apples.✪✪✪

Maibock (6.3%)
A big burst of hops gives way to a chewy, fruit malt loaf taste, ending considerably dry for a beer of this strength.✪✪✪

LÖWENBRAUEREI
Buttenheim

Pilsener (5%)
A very hoppy, flowery head before a rich body, mixing some malt-sweetness with bitterness which becomes dominant into the dry finish.✪✪✪

Kellerbier (4.7%)
Copper coloured and filtered. Little head but an enormous burst of hops and fruitiness ending very dry.✪✪✪

LÖWENBRÄU
Munich

Hell Weissbier (5.3%)
Pale honey coloured, unfiltered wheat. Strong vanilla aroma in the fluffy head; light tasting but producing a good sour-dry finish.✪✪

Pilsener (5.4%)
Pale yellow. A tinge of lemon mingles with the hugely hoppy head. An unwavering bitterness lasts through the light body to produce a tangy, dry finish. Malt seeps into the aftertaste.✪✪✪

Dunkel (5.3%)
Dark brown. Firm malty bouquet through a creamy head. A tart, sharp taste which ends quite dry.✪✪✪

Hell (5.3%)
Pale golden. A malty, cloyingly-sweet beer.

LÖWENBRÄU
Passau

Pilsener (4.9%)
Hoppy aroma. Strong malty flavour, but drying out in a smooth, slightly bitter finish.✪✪

Weissbier (5.5%)
Rusty red, unfiltered. Complex aroma of cinnamon, yeast and apples in a big dense head. Sour and dry.✪✪

LÖWENBRÄU
Stublang

Vollbier (5%)
A deep amber beer with a rich fruity flavour which ends very dry.✪✪✪

MAGER
Pottenstein

Dunkel (5.2%)
Very dark, Guinness-like in its smoothness. A remarkably hoppy beer with a bitterness which expands in the mouth to give a long, very dry finish. Gives the lie to any notion that dark lagers are sweet.✪✪✪✪

MAHKORN
Unterneuses

Lagerbier (4.7%)
A coppery coloured Kellerbier style, well hopped and dry with low carbonation.✪✪

MAHRS
Bamberg

Pilsener (4.7%)
A meaty beer whose fullsome hop character strikes a good balance with the malty influences to give a deliciously dry and bitter taste.✪✪✪

Vollbier (5.1%)
A full-bodied amber beer. The initial apple fruit taste gives way to a firm hop content mixing with a soft maltiness. A bitter-sweet finish.✪✪

MAHR
Lichtenfels

Pilsener (4.9%)
More like a filtered Kellerbier than a Pilsener style. A big taste of hops and some fruitiness combine to provide an amazingly dry beer.✪✪✪

MAISACHER
near Munich

Rauber Kneissl Dunkel (5%)
Reddish-brown. Initial maltiness gives way to a bitterness in the long, dry finish.✪✪✪

Pilsener (4.8%)
Straw coloured. Hoppy nose. Again, initially malty, but breaking into a quite hoppy finish.✪✪

Pale Export (5.5%)
Straw coloured and full-bodied. Pronounced vanilla nose. Considerable bitterness in the taste which carries through into a very dry finish.✪✪✪

MAISEL
Bayreuth

Pilsener (4.8%)
Straw coloured. Strongly perfumed, hoppy aroma. A crisp, light and dry beer with a long bitter finish. Good example of the style.✪✪✪

Dunkel (5.1%)
Tawny colour. A nutty flavour with a hint of hops.✪✪

Dampfbier (4.9%)
A rusty red, top fermented but filtered bottled beer. Big fruity

flavour with a smooth dry finish. An unusual Bavarian beer, which manages to mimic some English bitters.✪✪✪

Maisel's Hefe-Weisse (5.2%)

Deep amber, almost rust red, unfiltered wheat beer. Lively, yeasty head over an apple taste with a sharp, dry sourness to the finish.✪✪

MALTESER

Amberg

Hell (4.6%)

Fruity sweet. Sticky aftertaste.

Pilsener (4.6%)

Thin tasting and a bitter-sweet finish.✪

Rittertrunk Bock (6.5%)

Reddish-brown. Rich, creamy head and a malt and hops aroma. The maltiness fades into the background as the taste progresses to a more fruity character with a dryish finish.✪✪✪

MARIABRUNN

near Munich

Hell (4.7%)

A full-bodied pale lager which has strong vanilla aroma followed by a dryish palate.✪✪

Dunkel (5.1%)

Reddish-brown, smooth beer with a flavour which manages to be both fruity and nutty.✪✪

MARTIN

Unterneuses

Vollbier (5%)

Dark brown, rich and fruity. Dryish aftertaste.✪✪

MÖNCHSHOF

Kulmbach

Klosterschwarz (4.7%)

Known locally as the "Black Pils" because of its unusually hoppy character for a dark lager. Robust malt and yeast taste which becomes hoppy and dry with a firm bitter aftertaste.✪✪✪✪

Klosterbock (6.3%)

Reddish-brown. The full-bodied malty flavour is well balanced with a hop element which provides a dryish finish.✪✪

Pilsener (4.8%)

A rather malty beer for the style, lacking hop character.✪

Kapuziner Dunkel (5.2%)

Dark brown, unfiltered wheat beer. Big malt and yeast aroma. Smooth malty body, and an oddly sweet-sour finish.✪✪

NB Mönchshof also produces two other wheat beers under the Kapuziner name: Kapuziner Kristalklar (pale filtered), and Kapuziner Hefetrüb (pale unfiltered).

MOY

Haag and Freising

Hell (4.9%)

Pale golden lager of sweet, undistinguished character.

Weissbier (5.5%)

Honey coloured and unfiltered. A yeasty head and tart taste with sweet edges.✪✪

Dunkelweissbier (5.5%)

Dark brown and unfiltered. Strong malty aroma and coarse, chewy, chocolate taste. Some tartness is finally masked by a malty sweetness.✪✪

MÜLLER

Altötting

Dunkel (5.2%)
Dark brown. Rich malty aroma and flavour. Smooth bitter-chocolate finish.✪✪

Märzen (5.5%)
Bronze coloured. Strong, creamy head with a powerful hop aroma. Firm-bodied beer balancing a subtle fruitiness with a dry-malt flavour. Smooth dryish finish and a slightly bitter tinge.✪✪✪

MÜLLER
Pfaffenhofen

Weissbier (5.4%)
Pale and unfiltered. Rusty brown colour. A very fruity beer, from the nose to the finish, tasting of cherries.✪✪

Hell (5%)
Very pale. Fruity aroma, soft smooth body hinting of both malt and hops. Dry, clean finish.✪✪

Hopfenland Pilsener (4.9%)
The name is descriptive: a hoppy beer. But the taste is well balanced with some maltiness, drying out in a smooth, bitter finish.✪✪

NEDER
Forcheim

Pilsener (4.7%)
A very hoppy aroma from a firm head. The clean, dry taste makes the mouth tingle with uncompromising hoppiness.✪✪

Kellerbier (4.6%)
Amber. Low carbonation and quickly fading head. Initial taste of hops gives way to an apple-like fruitiness. Dry aftertaste.✪✪

OBERBRÄU
Holzkirchen

Holkirchner Weisse (5.2%)
Rusty red, unfiltered. Complex mix of fruit and spice, with a hint of cinnamon. Very fruity palate, finishing dry.✪✪✪

Laurenzi Export Dunkel (5%)
Ruby coloured. Dark chocolaty flavour, malty-sweet finish.✪✪

Pilsener (4.9%)
Strong hop aroma off a dense, lasting head. Rich, dry mix of malt and bitterness with a hint of fruitiness. Dry finish.✪✪✪

ODELZHAUSEN
Village northwest of Munich

Operator doppelbock (7%)
Tawny coloured with a burnt malt aroma and a sherry-like richness which becomes bitter in the aftertaste.✪✪

OTTENBRÄU
Abensberg

Märzen (5.2%)
Copper coloured. A big malty flavour with a smack of liquorice. The maltiness mellows at the finish to allow a dryish aftertaste.✪✪

Hell (4.7%)
Deep golden. Hop and vanilla nose. Tinge of fruity sweetness in the taste but drying out in a clean, crisp finish.✪✪

PATRIZIER
Nuremberg

Hefeweissbier (5.3%)
Pale and very lightly flavoured, with a sour finish.✪

Dunkel Weissbier (5.1%)
Brownish colour. Light malt taste with a hint of coffee. Fizzling to a sweetish finish.✪

PAULANER
Munich

Original Münchner Hell (4.9%)
Golden coloured. Driest of the Munich style, combining the city's famed maltiness with a distinct hoppiness and a bitter-tinged finish.✪✪

Dunkel (5.2%)
Almost black. Prominent malty nose but hoppiness comes through in the finally dry taste.✪✪

Pale Hefeweissbier (5.4%)
Copper colour. The fruity aroma leads to a coarsely-textured yeasty taste with a sour finish.✪✪

Salvator Doppelbock (7.5%)
Very dark. A dense, creamy head oozing a big malt and hops aroma. The thick, malty flavour never veers away from the astonishing dryness achieved with a brew of this strength. A king among beers.✪✪✪✪

Pilsener (4.8%)
Very pale. Hoppy, perfumed aroma. Smooth and firm-bodied with a hop bitterness which runs to the very dry. Fully justifies the brewer's epithet "Extra Trocken" - Extra Dry.✪✪✪

PESCHL
Passau

Hell (4.8%)
Unexceptional copper coloured, south Bavarian pale lager.

Dunkel (5.1%)
Ruby-brown. A moreish, rich beer producing a very dry finish through the firm malt body.✪✪✪

PFEFFERBRÄU
Zwiesel

Märzen (5.5%)
Copper-brown colour. A rich blend of malt and hops, with a slightly burnt flavour before a rounded dry finish.✪✪✪

Export Hell (4.5%)
Pale and very fruity with a dry finish.✪✪

Dampfbier (5%)
Copper coloured and top fermented. A strong background aroma of raspberries to this remarkably fruity, sharp beer which has a refreshingly dry, biting finish.✪✪✪✪

Weissbier (5.3%)
Honey coloured, unfiltered wheat. A strongly sour-sweet taste with a pear-like fruitiness which grows quite dry in the aftertaste.✪✪✪

PFISTER
Weigelshofen

Vollbier (5.1%)
Dark copper. Fruity, full-bodied flavour with a very dry finish.✪✪✪

Hefeweissbier (5.4%)
Honey coloured. Strong apple taste with a classic sweet-sour finish.✪✪✪

PLANK
Laaber, near Regensburg

Märzen (4.8%)
Golden. Amazing apple aroma which mingles with a lightly malt and hops flavour. The final taste is very dry.✪✪✪

Hell (4.5%)
Very pale. Lots of fruity character which ends surprisingly hoppy and dry for the style.✪✪

PLOTZBRÄU
Peissenberg

Dunkel (5.2%)
Dark reddish-brown. A complicated beer which offers initially a mellow burnt malt flavour, then becomes quite bitter before a tangy, dry finish.✪✪✪

Rigi-Weizen (5.4%)
Rusty red, unfiltered wheat. Hops and yeast rise off the head, but the body is spicy with a lemon-fruit tang ahead of a sour-dry finish.✪✪

Schützenkönig (4.9%)
Port coloured, unfiltered dark wheat beer. A yeasty, tangy start which develops into a smooth, malt-sweet finish.✪✪

POSTBRÄU
Nesselwang (Alps region)

Zwickel (4.9%)
Copper coloured, unfiltered. Described by the brewer as a Kellerbier. Initial malt sweetness is overtaken by a hoppiness which influences the dryish aftertaste.✪✪

Dunkel (5.3%)
Dark brown. A malty brew with a sweet finish.✪

Der Postillion (5.3%)
A dark, unfiltered wheat beer. Firm coffee-malt aroma and flavour. Bitter-sweet finish.✪✪✪

Gold (5.3%)
A pale Export-style. Less full-bodied than most Export beers, less hoppy than the Zwickel with a bitter-sweet finish.✪

Pilsener (4.8%)
A pleasant hop aroma gives way to a south German malty flavour. Some dryness in the finish.✪✪

POSTBRÄU
Thannhausen

Hell (4.7%)
Typical south Bavarian style with perhaps more fruitiness than normal, with a sweetish finish.✪

Dunkel (5.1%)
Dark brown. Soft flavoured, dark lager with a malty-sweet finish✪

Weissbier (5.4%)
Honey coloured. The fluffy head quickly fades to a sweetish taste. Sweet and sour finish.✪✪

Pilsener (4.7%)
Well balanced mix of malt and hoppiness gives a full-bodied flavour and dryish finish.✪✪✪

PRÖSSL
Adlersberg

Dunkel (5.3%)
Near black lager. Malty aroma which stays with the taste, combined with a raisin-like fruitiness. Mellow and bitter-sweet.✪✪

Adlersberger Pilsener (5%)
Deep golden. Strong hop aroma off a thick, lasting head which laces the glass. Full-bodied but not heavy. Bitterness dominates hints of malt sweetness. Dry.✪✪✪

REICHELBRÄU
Kulmbach

Edelherb Pilsener (4.9%)
Sharp, hoppy aroma from a firm head over a quite malty beer which nevertheless produces a dry, bitter finish.✪✪

Eisbock (10%)
Ruby coloured doppelbock of exceptional strength. A thick, warming brew which has a mellow bitter aftertaste.✪✪✪

RIEDENBURGER
Riedenburg, Altmühltal Valley

Pale wheat beer (4.9%)
Honey coloured, unfiltered. Very sharp, tart taste, ending crisp and dry.✪✪✪

Pilsener (4.9%)
Plenty of hops in the aroma and the palate. The background malt taste is finally lost in the expanding hop bitterness.✪✪

REUTBERG
Near Holzkirchen

Dunkel (4.8%)
Dark brown. Little in the nose, but a big malty taste with some hoppiness penetrating to give a dryish finish.✪✪

Pale Bock (6.9%)
Initial bitterness leads into heavy malty-sweetness which lingers to the end and can be cloying.✪✪

RIEMHOFER
Riedenburg, Altmühltal

Schwanen Weisse (5%)
Pale, unfiltered wheat. A sour fruit aroma with a surprisingly light taste which finishes classically sweet and sour.✪✪✪

Dunkel Weisse (5.2%)
Chestnut brown, unfiltered wheat. Yeast aroma followed by a thickish, sweet malt taste, turning slightly sour in the finish.✪✪

ST. GEORGEN
Buttenheim

Kellerbier (4.9%)
Rusty red, unfiltered. Massive hop aroma, like rubbing dried hops in the hand. A taste of apple fruitiness gives way to an explosion of hops in the mouth and an extremely dry finish.✪✪✪

Vollbier (4.6%)
Copper coloured. A fruity aroma; more rounded, softer flavour than the Kellerbier but also very dry.✪✪

Pilsener (4.8%)
More full-bodied and darker than many German Pils, more hoppy than the Czech Urquell. But the clean, sharp, dry finish makes it a moreish beer.✪✪✪

Gold Märzen (5.6%)
Amber coloured. Powerful hop aroma in the dense firm head. Strong hoppy taste, typical of Buttenheim beers, gives way to a more malty rounded flavour. Finally very dry, with a hint of apple in the aftertaste. A tremendously flavoursome beer.✪✪✪✪

SCHALLER
Bayreuth

Pilsener (5%)
Flowery nose. Full-bodied with a good balance between south German maltiness and hop character. A crisp, clean and dry finish.✪✪

Spezial (5.3%)
Pale brown. Creamy, malty head leads into a full-bodied mix of malt and hops. Bitter-sweet.✪✪

SCHATTENHOFER
Beilngries

Dunkel (5.2%)
Reddish-brown. Fluffy head offering little aroma. Malt flavour with a peppery tang and an expanding gentle bitterness. Some sweetness in the smooth finish.✪✪

Pilsener (5%)
Robust, malty body which gradually gives way to a firm hop character and a dry finish. Bitter aftertaste.✪✪

SCHEIDMANTEL
Coburg

Coburg Pilsener (4.8%)
Firm-bodied with a strong hop character and a good dry finish.✪✪

Silber Bock (6.2%)
Deep amber. Heady malt aroma, but a deliciously fruity flavour. Bitter-sweet finish.✪✪✪

Hefeweisse (5.4%)
Pale, unfiltered wheat beer. Turbid with a yeasty initial taste which blossoms into a fruity-sour finish.✪✪

SCHEYERN
now brewed in Augsburg

Kloster-Gold Hell (5.4%)
Golden-coloured. A full-bodied Export style brew with some background fruitiness. Crisp, dry finish.✪✪✪

Dunkel (5.4%)
Almost black lager. Hop and malt in the buoyant aroma carries right through to a deliciously dry finish.✪✪✪

SCHIERLINGER
between Abensburg and Straubing

Roggenbier (4.7%)
Dark brown, unfiltered and top fermented rye beer. Similar taste to wheat beer, but softer and sweeter. English brown ale with a tang.✪✪

SCHIESSL
Amberg

Vollbier (4.8%)
Amber coloured. Fruity with a sweet accent.✪

Bock (6.3%)
Copper coloured. Complex nose contrives to offer a lemon aroma overlaid with hops. Very fruity with a bitter-sweet finish.✪✪

Weissbier (5.3%)
Honey coloured, unfiltered wheat. Spicy aroma from the fluffy head which laces the glass well. Strong background of cooking apples and a tart finish.✪✪✪

SCHINNER
Bayreuth

Altbayreuther Braunbier (5.1%)
Deep brown colour. Full-bodied. Malty flavour, slightly tart finish.✪✪

SCHLENKERLA
Bamberg

Märzen, or Rauchbier (4.8%)
Virtually black as coal. A big aroma of burnt malt which erupts into the mouth in a rich, thick, almost too-dry taste. A mysterious and appealing fishy

flavour lends an oiliness to the final palate. An unusual, powerfully attractive beer in a class of its own.✪✪✪✪

SCHLOSSBRÄU
Au in der Hallertau

Hell (4.7%)
Honey coloured and unfiltered. A wonderfully distinctive, fruity beer, with a sharp, sour and dry finish.✪✪✪

Dunkel (5.3%)
Dark brown and unfiltered. A rich, coffee-malt taste with a dryness which lasts right through into the aftertaste.✪✪✪

Auer-Weisse (5.5%)
Yellowish, unfiltered pale wheat. A cinnamon spicy beer with hints of apples. Fruity-sour finish.✪✪

Pilsener (4.9%)
Very hoppy head which laces well through the glass. Soft but dry body and only a faint hint of malt before finishing bitter.✪✪✪

SCHLOSSBRÄU
Maxlrain

Schlossherrentrunk (5.5%)
Amber. A rich, well balanced, Märzen style beer, offering delicate fruitiness and malt ahead of an expanding dryness.✪✪✪

Bock (6.3%)
Golden coloured. A hint of pear fruit in the hoppy aroma. A background maltiness competes with a rising hop character. Smooth and rounded.✪✪✪

SCHMITT
Schesslitz

Jura Hell (4.7%)
Amber, tart, fruity beer with a bitter-sweet aftertaste.✪✪

Märzen (5.4%)
Dark copper colour. A powerful combination of malt and hops. Fruitiness with a flavour of cooking apples gives way to a bitter-sweet finish.✪✪

Pilsener (4.7%)
Heavy malt flavour dominates with some fruitiness at the edges. Bitterish aftertaste.✪

Dunkel (5%)
Rusty red, with a strong malt aroma. Bitter-sweet finish.✪

SCHNEIDER
Essing

Dunkel (5.2%)
Black with red lights. A complex beer which starts malty, becomes a little fruity before an expanding bitterness fills the mouth in the dry finish.✪✪✪

Schneider's Privat (5.5%)
A rusty red, big-bodied beer with a malty accent and a bitter-sweet finish.✪✪

Weissbier (5.2%)
Light brown cross between a pale and dark unfiltered wheat beer. Very sour and smooth with low carbonation for a wheat style, ending surprisingly dry.✪✪✪

SCHNEIDER
Kelheim

Schneiderweisse (5.4%)
A classic wheat beer. Bottle conditioned only. Darker than the average pale wheat. Strong vanilla nose. Rich malt and fruit taste which moves to a tart, dry finish.✪✪✪✪

Aventinus (8%)
Dark brown, unfiltered doppelbock wheat beer. Dense, creamy head yields a blackcurrant fruit aroma. Rich, fruity taste which is at first slightly sweet then a little sour, heightened by a gentle sparkle. Dries out to a smooth finish which, at this strength, deceives when served chilled, as it should be. Bottle conditioned only.✪✪✪✪

SCHNEIDER
Weissenburg

Vollbier (5%)
Dark amber. Full-bodied, malty flavoured beer with a fruity-dry finish.✪✪

Märzen (5.5%)
Reddish-brown, with a dense malty aroma but quite a hoppy flavour. Bitter-sweet finish.✪✪✪

SCHNITZLBAUMER
Traunstein

Hell (5%)
Deep golden. Surprisingly hoppy nose leads into an unusually bitter beer for the style.✪✪

Pilsener (4.8%)
Strong hoppy nose. The hop character overrides any malty influence in the firm, meaty body. A long, dry finish.✪✪✪

Georgitrunk (5.4%)
Copper coloured Märzen. Big hoppy aroma. Rich body, balancing a fruit maltiness and bitterish background. Smooth finish.✪✪✪

SCHWANEN
Ebing

Dunkel Vollbier (4.8%)
A dark brown, full-bodied, malty brew with a fruity dry finish.✪✪✪

SCHWARZES KREUZ
Eggolsheim

Vollbier (5%)
Straw-coloured. Only partially filtered. Very hoppy aroma. Full-bodied flavour with a smooth, dry and bitter finish.✪✪✪

SCHWEIGER
Markt Schwaben

Hell Export (5.1%)
Copper coloured lager; slightly fruity but a sweetish finish.✪

Dunkel (5.1%)
Reddish-brown. Full-bodied with a sweet-malt finish.✪

Schmankerlweisse (5.3%)
Honey coloured and unfiltered. The dense head has a strong yeast and hop aroma. Rather thin bodied, but a good tart finish.✪✪

Hell Bock (6.8%)
Amber colour. A rich mix of malt, fruit and hops. Full-bodied with a bitter-sweet finish.✪✪

SENGER
Schesslitz

Vollbier Dunkel (5.3%)
A dark brown, thick and rich malty beer but with a strong hop influence. The finish is firmly dry.✪✪✪

SIGWART
Weissenburg

Pilsener (4.6%)
Light-bodied, firmly hopped and a strong bitter finish.✪✪

Märzen (5.2%)
Copper coloured. Heavy malty aroma from a thick creamy head. The flavour mixes fruitiness with a slightly bitter background and a dryish aftertaste.✪✪✪

Hell Hefeweissbier (5%)
Rusty red, turbid and coarse. Strong yeasty flavour and hints of vanilla before a dry-sour finish.✪✪

SIMON
Lauf, near Nuremburg

Erster Laufer Weissbier (5.2%)
Light brown, unfiltered. Coarsely textured and very sour, with a sharp bitterish finish.✪✪✪

SONNE
Ebermannstadt, Franconia

Kellerbier (4.7%)
Dark copper colour. A surprisingly sweet start which quickly becomes quite fruity before the expected hoppiness of this style breaks through to give a dry finish.✪✪✪

SPATEN
Munich

Ludwig Thoma Dunkel (5.5%)
Very dark. Slightly fruity nose, but a smooth malty-dry flavour with an edge of bitterness in the aftertaste.✪✪✪

Premium Bock (6.5%)
A golden Maibock. A burst of hops at the beginning gives way to a rich maltiness tinged with bitterness and a dryish finish.✪✪✪

Franziskaner Hell Weissbier (5%)
Pale, unfiltered wheat beer. One of the original survivors of the style. A fine balance of fruitiness and tart dryness.✪✪✪

Franziskaner Dunkel (5%)
Reddish brown, unfiltered wheat. Yeasty aroma and a quite bitter palate with a sharp, tart finish.✪✪

Hell (4.8%)
A golden pale lager with the classic bitter-sweet, malty taste, typical of the south Bavarian style.✪✪

Pilsener (5%)
A big burst of hops in the mouth through the rich dense head gives way to a malty background so typical of the south German Pilsener style, but which manages to finish bitter-dry.✪✪✪

Ur-Märzen (5.6%)
Reddish-brown. Big malty aroma. The smooth, rich full-bodied malt taste is balanced by some hop character, ending bitter-sweet but quite clean on the palate.✪✪✪

SPEZIAL
Bamberg

Lagerbier (4.9%)
Light brown Rauchbier. A malty, lightly smoked beer which has a fruity-dry finish.✪✪✪

SPITAL
Regensburg

Hell (4.9%)
Golden coloured. Full-bodied, with heaps of fruit character. The finish is quite dry and clean-tasting.✪✪

Dunkel (5.2%)
Reddish-brown. Light malty flavour with a sweetish aftertaste.✪

STADTBRAUEREI
Roth

Märzen (5.2%)
A lusty, amber brew with a strong fruit-malt flavour and a hoppy background. Fruity-dry finish.✪✪✪

Dunkel (5%)
Reddish brown. Dense malty head and a dry, nutty flavour.✪✪

Dunkelweissbier (5.2%)
Chocolate brown, malty, spicy. A sweet-sour finish.✪✪

STAFFELBERG
Loffeld

Märzen (5.2%)
Dark brown, with a malty nose but a slightly spicy, cooking apples flavour and a bitter-sweet finish.✪✪✪

Pilsener (4.6%)
Darker than normal for a Pils, but a dense creamy head, a light, hoppy body and a very dry finish.✪✪✪

STIFTUNGSBRÄU
Erding

Dunkel (5.1%)
Brown lager with a mild, malty taste and a sweetish finish.✪

Hell (4.9%)
Very pale with a fruity character and typical bitter-sweet finish.✪

Prosper doppelbock (7.1%)
Dark brown. A complex aroma of malt and cinnamon-like spiciness. The heavy malt flavour is balanced by firm hoppiness which gives a bitter-sweet aftertaste.✪✪✪

STRAUB
Memmelsdorf

Stöffla (5.2%)
Dark brown with red tints. Unfiltered. A fullsome beer which mixes the heavy hoppiness of a Kellerbier with the sweetness of a Märzen, plus a slight smoky-fish flavour. Dry finish.✪✪✪

Lagerbier (4.6%)
Dark amber. Unfiltered. Fruity with a bitter-sweet flavour.✪

Pilsener (4.9%)
Dark for a Pilsener style but well-hopped and bitter with a good firm body.✪✪

STURM
Coburg

Sturm's Pilsener (4.6%)
Thin-bodied, but heavily hopped with a dryish end.✪

Prince Albert Pils (4.9%)
Good firm, hoppy head. Very full-bodied with the malt taste eventually overpowered by the strong bitter finish.✪✪

Anton Sturm's Privat (5.2%)
A heavy Export style brew, but rather full-bodied with a bitter-sweet ending.✪

Alt Coburger Dunkel (5%)
Reddish-brown. Despite a tradition-tugging name, a newish beer which at least catches some flavour of the past. Full-bodied, malty, with a curious tanginess. Medium dry.✪✪

THURN UND TAXIS
Regensburg

Pilsener (4.9%)
Mix of hops and malt in the firm, lasting head. A long, dry flavour which leaves a lip-smacking bitter aftertaste.✪✪

Pale Export (5.5%)
Succeeds in being more than just a typical south Bavarian pale lager. A thick, perfumed head over a dry, full-bodied palate, with bitterness in the finish.✪✪✪

Hell Hefeweissbier (5.5%)
Honey coloured. Firm yeasty head. Fine balance between fruit and maltiness leads into a good sweet-sour tangy finish.✪✪

TUCHER
Nuremberg

Urfrankisch Dunkel (4.4%)
Reddish brown. Slightly burnt-malt flavour, moving to hoppiness which leads to a dryish finish.✪✪

Hell (4.7%)
Very pale and surprisingly crisp and dry for a beer of this style. A hoppy finish.✪✪

Pilsener (4.7%)
Initial malt flavour which quickly evaporates into a hoppy beer with a bitter-dry and clean tasting finish.✪✪✪

UNERTL
Haag, north of Wasserburg

Hefeweissbier (4.8%)
Deep copper colour, unfiltered. Very fruity nose: a mix of malt sweetness and sourness in the coarse finish.✪✪

Hefeweizenbock (6.2%)
Dark brown, unfiltered. A rapidly vanishing head reveals a cloying sweetness which a low carbonation over-exposes.✪

UNION
Munich

Naturtrüb Hell (4.8%)
A honey-coloured unfiltered yeasty beer, similar to a Zwickel. The yeasty flavour gives way to an over-cloying sweetness.✪

Maibock (6.3%)
An unfiltered, pale bock with a good hoppy aroma, some yeastiness in the taste which finishes bitter-sweet with a hint of nuttiness.✪✪

URBANUS
Pfaffenhofen

Hell Export (5.1%)
Straw coloured. Vanilla nose. Initial fruit-malt taste gives way to firm hoppiness. Bitter-sweet finish.✪✪

Pilsener (4.9%)
Very hoppy nose. Apple and malt flavours ahead of a gentle hoppiness and smooth finish. Firm dryness.✪✪✪

VALENTIN
Roth

Naturtrüb (4.8%)
Deep amber, unfiltered beer. Yeasty aroma and coarse initial taste, mellowing to a malty-dry finish.✪✪

Festbier Dunkel (5.2%)
Chestnut brown and chewy. Pleasant coffee-malt flavour, becoming bitter and dry.✪✪

Pilsener (4.8%)
Malty taste through a heavy, lasting bitter head.✪

VIERZEHNHEILIGEN
Grundfeld

Nothelfertrunk (5.2%)
Reddish-brown lager. Rich, creamy head, oozing malt and hop aromas. A thick brew, blending a strong malty taste with a bitter edge. Mellow, dry finish.✪✪✪

WAGNER
Eschenbach

Pilsener (4.8%)
Firm, hoppy head. Fruity flavour which ends dry.✪✪

Märzen (5.3%)
Dark amber. Rich malty aroma, lots of fruit and a spicy ending.✪✪✪

Dunkel (5%)
Dark brown. Strong malt body. Bitter-sweet.✪✪

Rauchbier or Räucherla (4.8%)
A very lightly smoked flavour which ends rather disappointingly sweet.✪

WAGNER
Pottenstein

Dunkel (5.2%)
Almost black in colour. A rich, burnt malt aroma and taste which continues through in a long, dry finish. A must for all who want to get to know bottom fermented dark beers.✪✪✪

WEIHENSTEPHAN
Freising

Hell (5.1%)
Very pale golden. Fairly typical initial malt-sweet taste, but finishes more bitter than most of the style.✪✪

Edelpils (4.9%)
Hop perfume in the strong, dense head. A good dry Pilsener with a slightly malt-accented body. Quite a bitter aftertaste.✪✪✪

Kristall-Weizenbier (5.4%)
Golden, filtered wheat beer. Original of the style. Remarkably big tart-fruit taste and sharp, dry finish.✪✪

Stephansquell (6.8%)
Amber doppelbock. Expansive hop aroma. Full-bodied malty flavour, finishing bitter-sweet.✪✪

WEISSESBRÄU
Altötting

Hefeweissbier (5.2%)
Nicotine brown, unfiltered wheat. Rich, creamy head with a spicy nose. A pear-like fruit character with a sour-dry flavour and tangy aftertaste.✪✪✪

Kirtaweissbier (6.1%)
Reddish brown, unfiltered bock wheat. Smooth, rich, malt-chocolate taste. Soft finish with a dry aftertaste.✪✪

WICHERT
Lichtenfels

Kellerbier (4.6%)
Dark amber, almost reddish brown, unfiltered. Low carbonation, a strong hoppy taste but with some fruitiness. Smooth and dry.✪✪

Pilsener (4.9%)
Sharp hop flavour, a tinge of

malt and a clean, crisp finish.✪✪✪

WIDMANN
Markt Schwaben

Dunkel (5.5%)
Ruby colour. Malty nose. Initially a rough burnt-malt flavour, smoothing into a dry, slightly bitter finish.✪✪

Hell (4.9%)
Golden colour. More fruity than normal for this style.✪✪

Lorenzi Doppelbock (7.2%)
Almost black. Rich malt with a chocolaty taste, becoming fruity. A bitter-sweet aftertaste.✪✪

Weissbier (5.2%)
Pale unfiltered. Unusually yeasty head. Some fruitiness but surprisingly bitter for a wheat beer.✪✪

WILL
Schederndorf

Lagerbier (5.3%)
Almost black and unfiltered. Low carbonation. A cross between a Kellerbier and a Franconian Märzen. The dark loose head has a malt-hop aroma, a very well balanced bitter-sweet palate and a smooth, dry finish.✪✪✪

WINKLER
Amberg

Vollbier (4.6%)
Pale yellow. A clean, sharp palate. Slightly fruit finish.✪✪

KEY TO QUALITY

✪✪✪✪	*Outstanding*
✪✪✪	*Excellent*
✪✪	*Good*
✪	*Average*

Dunkel (4.9%)
Dark brown. Nutty flavour and a malty background. Smooth, dryish finish.✪✪

Pilsener (4.6%)
Hoppy, but a metallic aftertaste.✪

WINKLER
Lengenfeld

Hefe-Pils (4.9%)
Honey yellow colour, unfiltered and cloudy. Yeast and hops in the nose. Yeast and malt dominate the taste. Dry finish with a bitter tinge in the aftertaste.✪✪

Pilsener (4.9%)
Good hoppy nose; a malty character finishing quite bitter.✪✪

Kupfer Spezial (5.7%)
Deep copper colour. Rich malty aroma and taste with some hop bitterness before a smooth, slightly burnished finish.✪✪✪

WITTMANN
Landshut

Weissbier (5.3%)
Lemon in colour, unfiltered. Very yeasty nose mixed with vanilla. A bitter-sour flavour which ends dry and sharp.✪✪

Pilsener (4.9%)
Powerful hop nose; a firm, meaty body which balances malt and hop in a smooth, rich drink with a dry, slightly bitter finish.✪✪

Dunkel (5.3%)
Reddish-brown. Malty aroma off a dense, creamy head. The taste mingles sweet-malt and hop flavours. Bitter-sweet.✪✪

WITZGALL
Schlammersdorf

Vollbier (4.6%)
Copper coloured. Much more full-bodied and richer than a typical Bavarian Hell. An initial fruity sweetness is replaced by a bitterness which gives a dry finish. A classic example of Franconia's endangered hand-crafted species.✪✪✪

The imposing Kloster Monastery at Ettal where the monks still brew

Getting there
and travelling around

BY PLANE

Both British Airways and Lufthansa run daily year-round direct services Munich-London Heathrow and Munich-Manchester. British Airways also has a Glasgow-Munich service.

Fixed date Apex fares reduce costs considerably, but vary according to the time of year; peak times always include school holiday periods. Shop around: some travel agents, Thomas Cook's for example, offer discount fares below the airlines' own Apex rates. Apex flights should be booked well in advance.

In winter, charter air travel firms operate skiing specials several days a week to Munich, but you do not have to go skiing. The charters operate out of Luton and East Midlands as well as Manchester and Gatwick. Discount fares can also be picked up on American intercontinental airlines which go to Munich via London.

Book well in advance for dates during the two week Oktoberfest, which usually starts on the third Saturday of September and always finishes on the first Sunday in October.

London-Munich takes one hour 30 minutes. Manchester-Munich about two hours.

Munich has a new airport 28 km (17 miles) north of the city centre. A train service operates every 20 minutes between the airport and the main railway station (Hauptbahnhof). The journey takes 40 minutes.

BY TRAIN

The fastest journey time London-Munich is about 13 hours, using the Dover-Ostend jetfoil, and changing trains at Cologne. The slowest journey time can take 23 hours.

In summer, the journey can be done in daylight hours by catching the 0800 train from London Victoria. On the Munich-London journey, it is possible to depart about 0730 and arrive in London that evening in time for a pint — but only if you use the jetfoil to cross the the Channel. Later departures from either end involve travelling through the night.

Ordinary return rail fares can be more expensive than travelling by plane. Enquire about deals which include regular discounted fares through Belgium and Germany.

It is worth considering a fly-rail combination, taking the shortest (and cheapest) air routes like London-Düsseldorf, or London-Frankfurt, then switching to train travel inside Germany, using heavily discounted German Rail Rovers (see below).

BY BUS

Buses offer the cheapest public transport to Bavaria. A daily service to Nuremberg and Munich is operated from London's Victoria Bus Station by Europabus. The journey time to Nuremberg is about 21 hours, and to Munich about 23 hours. Bus connections to London Victoria are available from most major cities in the UK. Call Victoria Bus Station, 071-730 3466, for details.

BY CAR

Calais, Dunkirk and Ostend offer the best European mainland access for driving to Bavaria.

The shortest journey from Ostend to Munich is 850 km (530 miles). The cheapest car ferry is Dover-Calais, and with the opening of the Channel tunnel in 1994 there are expected to be competitive half-hourly sailings with tickets transferable between the ferry lines.

From Calais and Ostend take the E40 to the German border at Aachen via Brussels and Liège. Or, from Calais and Dunkirk, take the E42 via Lille to Aachen, avoiding the heavy traffic around Brussels.

From Aachen, continue along the E40 (the German A4) towards Cologne (Köln). Either turn south onto the A61 shortly before Cologne to reach Nuremberg via the pretty city of Heidelberg and the A6, or stay on the E40/A4 through Cologne and join the A3 to reach Nuremberg via Frankfurt and Würzburg. Using the A3 route, you enter Bavaria in the far northwest corner at Aschaffenberg. From Nuremberg, take the A9 for Munich.

More scenic routes exist, through France for example, but they take longer. The fastest French routes to the German border involve expensive toll roads. There are no toll roads in Germany, although the idea is being debated.

German motorways (Autobahnen) are of a high standard and traffic generally flows more freely than in

Britain, allowing faster average speeds. Unless there are special restrictions, because of bad weather or road-works, there are no speed limits. But this unfamiliar pleasure, coupled with driving on the wrong side of the road, is not without danger. High-powered BMWs and Mercedes are apt to roar out of nowhere, so extra vigilance is required. Do not be intimidated by fast drivers arrogantly flashing you out of the fast lane. It is a common German trait, but they have no right to do so. It is more dangerous to be stampeded at high speed than to stand your ground until you have completed an overtaking manoeuvre. Smiling calmly at gesticulating apoplectic German Mercedes drivers is one of the few remaining pleasures in life.

Speed restrictions on non-motorway roads are clearly signposted. Hidden cameras are in use on many major roads to trap speeding motorists, so if you exceed the limit, you risk being caught.

Seat belts (front and rear, where fitted) are obligatory.

Drink-driving limits are similar in Germany to those in the UK, and you can be stopped and breathalysed if police suspect you are over the limit. The obvious advice is do not drink and drive, particularly in a strange country, when you are driving on the "wrong" side of the road. Beware too, that if you drive in former Eastern Germany, here the total ban on drinking and driving in some areas may still be in force.

Autobahn traffic jams are rarer than in Britain, but they often occur during peak holiday times. Bavarian school holidays roughly coincide with those in Britain.

Service and rest areas are of a high standard, but prices can be quite high too. A pull-in offering vehicle, restaurant and accommodation services is usually called a Raststätte. The Autobahns also have simple rest lay-bys where there may be nothing more than a toilet and a picnic bench. This is a Rastplatz.

It is advisable to obtain a Green Card from your insurance company for comprehensive cover abroad. You may also wish to consider taking out "Get you home" insurance cover from the AA, RAC (check local telephone directory for addresses) or Europ Assistance, 252 High Street, Croydon CR0 1NF, tel: 081-680 1234.

GETTING ABOUT IN BAVARIA

By Train

The best way of getting about on public transport is by train. There is a comprehensive network of international, national, regional and local services.

For the foreign visitor, German Federal Railways (Deutsche Bundesbahn, or DB) offers a variety of attractive national and regional rover tickets which make travelling about Bavaria quite economical. These rover tickets must be bought in Britain, prior to departure. Ordinary train tickets bought within Germany, especially for InterCity services, can be expensive. Rail users are heavily penalised for travelling on a Friday.

Even if you do not opt for a visitor's rover ticket, very worthwhile discount deals are available for three or more people travelling together. These group tickets operate on a direct A to B basis, although stopovers are allowed. They are called Minigrüppenfahrkarten, and can be bought within Germany.

Unless you have a rail rover ticket, supplements are payable on ICE (InterCity Express), IC (InterCity), FD (long distance international) trains. Regional services now operate under the category of Inter-Regio trains. "E" trains are slow stopping services.

The ICE fast track network is expanding, allowing speeds of up to 165 mph. But beware if you are a rail enthusiast and fancy a short distance high speed spin: some sections of ICE routes through Bavaria operate still on ordinary track and do not reach maximum speeds.

Full details of all special offers can be obtained from German Federal Railways in London, tel: 081-390 0066.

By Bicycle

This is not so silly as it may seem. Bavaria is the best place for making use of the DB's train and bicycle service — and is ideal for exploring some of the backwoods, small country breweries, especially in northern Bavaria. Scores of stations have bikes for hire. The hire rate is heavily discounted if you show a ticket proving you arrived at the hire station by train. Bikes can be hired at one station and returned to another for a small fee. Reserve bikes in summer holiday periods or if you are a group. Bikes can be taken on local trains but not ICE and IC services. The DB publish a booklet listing all the hire stations.

By bus

Good "post" bus services operate in country areas and always link up with railway stations. Services can be infrequent however. Buses are handy for crossing the Bavarian Alpine region east-west between train stations, since rail services operate on a north-south radial system from Munich. Rail rover tickets are valid on some of these buses too.

Long distance buses are few and far between.

CAR HIRE

Major chain hire firms, such as Hertz, Avis and Europcar, are expensive. You pay for what you get: new luxury vehicles, numerous pick-up and drop-off offices. Two Munich firms which trim the luxury and offer small car budget hire with daily and weekly rates comparable with small firms in Britain are: Swing Autovermietung, Schelling-str. 139, tel: (from UK): 010-49-89-523-2005, fax: 010-49-89-523-6388, and Chariot Autovermietung, Richard-Strauss-str. 29, tel: 010-49-89-472021, fax: 010-49-89-470-2212. Staff at both firms speak perfect English.

General Information

A SIMPLE GLOSSARY

German is a phonetic language, with a few exceptions. For example, the h in "th" is always silent; v is pronounced as "fau" and w as "vay". Just think of a VW car: in German it is a Fau-Vay. An "ei" combination in a word is always pronounced as in "eye", "ch" is mostly pronounced hard as in back. An initial k is not silent. There are no trick words like the English "though". In cities and larger towns, many people speak some English, and can often hold fluent conversations. English is a compulsory subject in all secondary schools in Bavaria. However, older people, especially in rural areas, often do not understand English. This simple guide is intended to help travellers with little or no German to find their way round German pubs and menus, and secure essentials such as a bed for the night and help in an emergency.

In The Pub or Brewery

Pale beer — Hell Bier (ask for Helles — *Hell-ess*)
Dark beer — Dunkel Bier
(ask for Dunkles — *Dunk-less*)
Wheat beer — Weissbier (pron: vice-beer)
Alcohol free beer — Alkoholfrei
Low alcohol beer — Leichtbier
Unfiltered — mit Hefe, or naturtrüb
Filtered — ohne Hefe, or klar
Top fermented — obergärig
Bottom fermented — Untergärig
Yeast — Hefe
Hops — Hopfen
Malt — Malz
Dry — trocken, or herb
Sweet — süss
Full-bodied — vollmundig, or würzig
On draught — vom Fass
Wooden barrel — Holzfass
Bottle — Flasche
Bottled only — nur Flasche
Pub — Gaststätte (pron. Gast-shteta), or Gasthof
Night Bar — Kneipe

Closed today — Heute Ruhetag
Closed Monday — Montag Ruhetag (other days of the week are: Tuesday — Dienstag, Wednesday — Mittwoch, Thursday — Donnerstag, Friday — Freitag, Saturday — Samstag, Sunday — Sonntag)
Opening times — Öffnungszeiten
We are closing — Feierabend, or Polizeistunde
I'd like to pay now, please — Zahlen, bitte.
Do you have any dark/Pilsener/wheat beer on draught, please — Haben Sie bitte Dunkles/Pils/Weissbier vom Fass?
Is there a pub near here — Gibt es eine Gaststätte in der Nähe?
How many different beers do you have on draught — Wieviele Bier Sorten vom Fass haben Sie?

Reading A Menu, Or In The Food Shop

Abendessen — dinner (evening meal)
Bratwurst — sausages (fried or roast)
Brot — bread
Brotzeit — snacks (usually cold)
Champignons — mushrooms
Ei(er) — egg(s) (Spiegeleier — fried eggs, Rühreier — scrambled eggs, gekochtes Ei — boiled egg, hartgekochtes — hard-boiled)
Eisbein — knuckle of pork (boiled)
Ente — duck
Erbsen — peas
Gans — goose
Gemüse — vegetables
Hähnchen — chicken
Hausgemacht — home-made
Hendl — chicken
Hirsch — venison (Hirschbraten — roast venison)
Kartoffeln — potatoes (Salzkartoffeln — boiled potatoes, Bratkartoffeln — roast or pan-fried potatoes)
Käse — cheese
Knoblauch — garlic
Leber — liver
Leberkäs — meat loaf (a popular Munich snack)
Meerettich — horseradish
Mittagessen — lunch
Nudeln — pasta
Obst — fruit
Pommes Frites — chips
Reis — rice
Rindfleisch — beef

Schwein — pork (Schweinebraten — roast pork)
Schweinshaxe — knuckle of pork (roasted)
Senf — mustard
Surhaxe — knuckle of pork (boiled)
Wild — Game meat dishes
Zwiebeln — onions

Looking For A Bed

In villages and the countryside, the German Bed and Breakfast sign is "Zimmerfrei". This sign is also often hung at the door of village pubs.
Room Free — Zimmer Frei
No vacancies — Zimmer Belegt, or Besetzt
Double Room — Doppelzimmer
Single Room — Einzelbettzimmer
Breakfast — Frühstück
Half board — Halbpension
Without breakfast — ohne Frühstück
Have you got a room free, please? — Haben Sie noch Zimmer frei, bitte?
A room with bath or shower — Zimmer mit Bad oder Dusche
Can we stay another night — Können wir noch eine Nacht bleiben?
Just for one night, please — Eine Übernachtung, bitte

Emergencies & General

Doctor — Arzt
Dentist — Zahnarzt
Hospital — Krankenhaus
Casualty Dept — Ambulante Behandlung
Emergency services — Nothilfe (pron: note-hellfa)
Chemist shop — Apotheke (pron. apoteka)
Headache — Kopfweh (pron. kopfvay)
Stomachache — Bauchweh (pron. bow-vay)
Toothache — Zahnschmerzen
Post Office — Postamt
Stamps — Briefmarken
How Much — Was kostet das?
Railway Station — Hauptbahnhof
Arrival — Ankunft
Departure (train or bus) — Abfahrt
Departure (from hotel guesthouse) — Abreise
Good Day, Hello — Guten Tag
Good Evening — Guten Abend

CUSTOMS AND TIPPING

Complete strangers in northern Bavaria are liable to stroll up to your table on entering a pub, or as they are departing, and rap the top with their knuckles. Do not laugh, or try to flee the imagined country halfwit. This is a centuries-old wordless way of saying hello or goodbye. In other parts of Bavaria, new arrivals at a pub will call out "Grüss Gott" to the rest of the customers. This is a peculiarly southern German/Austrian greeting of hello or good-day, although it literally means God's Greeting.

The Germans are a nation of handshakers; even close friends will shake hands warmly each time they meet, and again when they depart. It is part of the formality — some would say stiffness — of public behaviour. The pace of life in the big cities has undermined some of the old courtesies, but youngsters still give up a seat on a bus or train for an elderly person, or someone loaded with shopping bags. Older people are treated with respect in Germany.

Except in some night bars, where stand up bar service can be so blitz-schnell it gets you drunk, patience is often a necessity when waiting for a beer in a pub. First, find a seat. Second, attract the attention of the waitress serving your table — they each have their allotted tables. Apart from in the big city beer halls and gardens, it is customary to pay for your beer and food altogether when you leave. The waitress often keeps count of the number of beers you order by writing crosses, circles or slashes on your drip mat. Make sure you have a clean mat to start with. This system tends to rule out buying rounds, which has two big advantages: each person drinks at his or her own pace, and the final bill is lighter on your pocket. A good waitress will keep an eye on the level of beer in glasses, and offer refills. In pubs still using earthenware mugs, it is customary to lay your mug on its side when empty, signifying you want a refill. In one north Bavarian pub I visited, the custom was to leave the tin lid open when another beer is required.

It is often in a waitress's interest to sell more beer because wage bonuses are sometimes linked to the quantity of beer sold. Another important component of pub wages are tips, which although paid directly to the waitress or waiter are estimated and calculated by publicans as part of income. In a large, busy pub a landlord might calculate that tips represent up to one third of staff income.

It is customary to round up a pub bill. If your total comes to, say, 8.40 Marks, give the waitress 9 Marks; if 15.90, make it 16.50, or even 17 Marks if the service was efficient and friendly. If you are in a group, indicate whether you want to pay together (Zusammen), or individually (Getrennt).

If you pop into a pub or bar for a quick one before catching a train or bus, ask to pay immediately on receiving your beer, otherwise Sod's Law will apply and the waitress will disappear until the train has departed. The phrase to pay quickly is: "Gleich zahlen, bitte", or "Sofort zahlen, bitte".

Hours of opening for all day pubs can vary anywhere between 8am and midnight. In bigger towns they tend to open later and then do not shut until 1am, which is the general closing time without a licence extension. If business is slack, a landlord can choose to close early. Many pubs, especially in rural areas, close for one day in the week. This is known as the Ruhetag (literally, rest day), and a sign in the window often indicates the rest day. Most pubs, particularly in rural areas or suburbia, have a regulars' only table, called a Stammtisch. This is usually identifiable by a sign of the same name, or by being the only table without a cloth covering. It is impolite for strangers to sit at a Stammtisch uninvited.

WHAT, WHEN AND WHERE TO EAT

A tour through Bavaria, especially in country areas, is likely to be a little stomach-shrinking for vegetarians. Bavarian food is best described as robust. If you like pork, you'll eat well. Dumplings and roasts in thick gravy are the staple offering in most pubs and, although somewhat repetitive, is a good accompaniment to the local beer — or "liquid bread", as the Bavarians call it.

In Munich, Nuremberg, Bamberg and other locations which attract plenty of foreign visitors, some pub restaurants have menus in English, or an English-speaking waiter or waitress can usually be found. But if both options fail, the following tour through the staples of Bavarian cuisine, plus a brief study of the Glossary, should stop you going hungry or making the wrong choice.

The most easily recognisable food is sausage: short and fat (a red Polnische, a white Weisswurst); long and thin (Wiener), short and thin (Schweinswurstl); or the foot-long Coburger special. They come boiled, grilled or roasted. The most common is the small spicy Schweinswurstl, often served with Sauerkraut, which is finely chopped cabbage, cooked and pickled in wine, white vinegar and mixed with juniper berries. It tastes nicer than it looks; you'll either love it or hate it. German sausages are 100 per cent meat, mostly pork, with varying levels of fat content. The exception is the Munich Weisswurst, a breakfast or "Elevenses" snack made with veal and herbs and wrapped in an inedible skin. Sweet mustard and Weissbier are the traditional accompaniments. Bratwurst is a beef-pork mix, usually grilled. The Polnische is very spicy and, in Munich, is often served at snack stalls with a shake of curry powder and tomato sauce. The term Wurst generally applies to thinly sliced cold meats, similar to English tinned luncheon meat. Wurstsalat is misleading and not a good accompaniment to beer: it is a mix of "luncheon meat" and chopped onion in vinegar. Pressack is cold meat in aspic. In northern Bavaria, very fatty cold meats and liver sausage are offered in many country pubs and are regarded as a delicacy. If you know you cannot stomach such things, beware of well-meaning local recommendations.

Some dishes have completely misleading names. To an unsuspecting student of German, Leberkas sounds like a combination of liver and cheese. It is neither. Leberkas is a beef-based, spicy meat loaf. At food stalls in Munich, especially around the terrific Viktualien Markt outdoor food and drink market, door stop wedges of hot Leberkas are served on a bread roll as a substantial on-the-hoof snack at any time of day. In traditional pubs, where plain home cooking (Gutbürgerlich) is the order, even bigger wedges of Leberkas are served with a fried egg on top as a budget-priced main meal.

In pub restaurants, soups are popular at lunchtime. Some are a meal in themselves, for example Eintopf, a thick pea soup with chopped Frankfurters mixed in, or Goulasch soup, heavily flavoured with paprika; others are thin, greasy and gruel-like (Knödelsuppe and Fladlsuppe). The most generally available solid main course meal, and best eaten at lunchtime for freshness, is Schweinebraten — the classic roast pork, usually served with a dumpling and red cabbage (Blauerkraut). Other sturdy favourites are Schweinshaxe (knuckle of pork), which is usually served with a little flag planted on top of it (this tells you the weight, since price is based on size); Sauerbraten (roast pickled pork). The popular Schnitzel comes in several guises: the bread-crumbed Wienerschnitzel; Jägerschnitzel, which is served with an onion and mushroom sauce; and Cordon Bleu, wrapped in cheese and ham. A veal schnitzel is Kalbschnitzel.

Bavarian dumplings bear no comparison to the English suet-based version. The Bavarian variety are either potato or bread based (Semmelknödel), and can include herbs, egg and finely chopped bacon. Most main course meals come with a side salad. Vegetables are rare, except in more up market eating establishments.

If you are really hungry, look out for Dampfnudel on the menu. No-one feels hungry after one of these: a sweet, flour-based steamed dumpling about the size of a dinner plate and covered in vanilla sauce, the Bavarian equivalent of custard.

It isn't all bad news for vegetarians. Omelettes and main course salad dishes are becoming more commonplace, and an interesting cheese plate can always be ordered even if you cannot find one on the menu. Some of the bigger pub restaurants in Munich and Nuremberg now offer vegetarian dishes, and fish — usually trout — is increasingly on offer. South of Munich, look out for Renke, a chunky white fish found in the mountain lakes. In Franconia, carp is a speciality.

For beer garden picnics, visit a supermarket or a butcher's shop (Metzgerei). Bavaria has the best possible selection of hams, and the choice of bread is unbeatable. Hopfisterei bread shops show the rest of the world how to bake. One of the tastiest concoctions to spread on the local bread is Obatz'n, a cocktail of Camembert cheese, paprika, herbs and finely chopped onion. In the beer garden, order a plate of wafer thin sliced Radi, a giant hot white radish liberally sprinkled with salt. Add a foaming litre mug of beer, a warm sun twinkling through a shady chestnut tree, and paradise seems closer.

FROM A STUBE TO A KNEIPE: THE BAVARIAN PUB

Typical village or suburban pubs in Bavaria may not always resemble their British cousins, but they share similar traditional names. The most common term for a pub is Gaststätte (pron. Gast-shteta) or Gasthof. They bear such names as: Gaststätte Hammerschmied (The Hammersmith), Gasthof Drei Krönen (Three Crowns), Zum Schwarzen Bär (The Black Bear). Like the British pub, they are often the focal points of local community activity: sports clubs are based in the Gaststätte, business lunches are held there, weddings are celebrated, and funeral wakes are catered for. Whereas the emphasis in a British local might be to gather round the beer pumps at the bar, Bavarian pubgoers invariably sit at tables. Regulars have their own special table or corner, known as the Stammtisch; a soccer club team might reserve the same table on a regular night of the week. Old coaching inns, usually big rambling country pubs or the main watering hole in a market town square, generally carry the name Gasthof Post — a reminder of the days when post was delivered by stage coach.

The Bavarian equivalent of the British pub's snug, is the "Stube". The Stube is usually fitted out in pine, and the focal point of the room is a gaily-tiled Kachelofen, or wood-fired ceramic-tiled stove (although nowadays the wood is often replaced by oil).

The Gaststätte is usually open all day, in country areas from as early as 8am, closing between 11pm and 1am, depending on business. When there are several pubs in a village, they stagger their Ruhetag (day off) so there is always at least one pub open every day.

As in Britain, most Bavarian pubs are tied to one particular brewery's products, but also like in Britain, there is a slow trend to offer an outside choice, particularly in the burgeoning wheat beer market. The most basic country boozer will have a variety of beers on offer, from a dark lager to a Pilsener. But ask what's available: many pubs simply give you a Helles (pale draught lager) if you ask for a beer. The bottled selection is often better.

Many pubs serve food all day, although outside busy districts hot meals may be confined to 11.30am-2pm and 6pm-9pm (1130-1400 and 1800-2100). The best value is at lunch (Mittagessen) when two or three course specials (called Tageskarte) are offered at attractive prices.

In cities and larger towns, an alternative to the Gaststätte is the tiny pub known as a Kneipe, where customers sit or lean at the bar. Here the emphasis is on drinking, food is minimal and the opening hours much shorter. A Kneipe might not open until 4 or 6pm, but always remains open until 1am (the general closing time) or 3am with a licence extension. In Munich, it is possible to drink beer round the clock by pub hopping (see Munich Pubs section).

Many traditional pubs, and almost always the Post houses, offer good, basic and reasonably priced bed and breakfast accommodation. Double rooms rarely have a double bed as the British know it; a "double" is often two singles cobbled together with a small ridge down the middle, covered by separate duvets. If you are in a group of three, enquire whether a three-bed room (Dreibett Zimmer) is available. These provide the cheapest per person rate. In rural northern Bavaria, there are numerous brew pub-hotels. The innkeeper is often the brewer, while his wife changes the sheets and cooks the meals.

USEFUL ADDRESSES & EMERGENCY HELP

The British Consulate in Bavaria is at Bürkleinstrasse 10, Munich. Tel: 089 211-090.

Munich Tourist Office: Sendlingerstrasse 1, 8000 Munich 2. Tel: 089 239 1272.

Bavarian Tourist Office (Landes-Fremdenverkehrsverband Bayern): Prinzregenten-str. 18, 8000 Munich 22. Tel: 089 212 3970.

South Bavarian Tourist Office (FFV Oberbayern): Sonnen-str. 10, 8000 Munich 2. Tel: 089 597 347.

Franconian Tourist Office (FFV Franken): Am Plärrer 14, 8500 Nuremberg 81. Tel: 0911 264 202.

German Camping Club: Mandl-str. 28, 8000 Munich 40.

German Youth Hostels Association (Deutsches Jungenherbergswerk Hauptverband): Bismarck-str. 8, 4930 Detmold.

Health care

English-speaking chemists in central Munich:
Internationale Ludwigs-Apotheke, Neuhauser-str. 8, tel: 089 260-3021;

Europa-Apotheke, Schützenstr. 12 (near the Hauptbahnhof), tel: 089 595-423.

The main public hospitals in central Munich are: Klinikum rechts der Isar, Ismaninger-str. 22 (next to Max Weber Platz station, U4, U5), tel: 089 41401; Schwabinger Krankenhaus, Kölner Platz 1 (Scheidplatz station, U3, U2), tel: 089 30681.

USING THE TELEPHONE

To telephone Britain dial 0044 followed by the city or area code, minus the 0.

Coinbox telephones need five-Mark pieces for long distance calls. Many telephone boxes operate only with cards. These cost 12 Marks and 50 Marks and are sold at the Post Office (Postamt). The area code for Munich is 089, not needed when telephoning within the city itself.

To telephone Germany from Britain dial 010-49, then the area code without the 0. For example, to call ADAC in Munich (see below) dial: 010-49-89-76760.

Emergency services telephone numbers are:

Police: 110

Fire: 112

Ambulance or urgent medical help (in Munich): 55-8661.

MOTORING ORGANISATIONS

The German equivalent of the AA or RAC is ADAC, which gives free advice to tourists. The head office is in Munich at: Am Westpark 8, 8000 Munich 70. Tel: 089 76760.

NEWSPAPERS AND BOOKS

English newspapers, English-language maps and guide books are available from the Internationale Presse shop on the main concourse in front of platforms at Munich's central railway station (Hauptbahnhof).

USEFUL ADDRESSES IN BRITAIN

German National Tourist Office, Nightingale House, 65 Curzon Street, London W1Y 7PE. Tel: 071-495 3990.

German Federal Railways, Passenger Services, Suite 4, The Sanctuary, 23 Oakhill Grove, Surbiton, Surrey KT6 6DU. Tel: 081-390 0066.

Bavaria – heart of Europe

Hamburg
Berlin
Hannover
GERMANY
München
Frankfurt
CZECH
REPUBLIC
Nuremburg
BAVARIA
Stuttgart
Munich
Salzburg
Zurich
AUSTRI A

The Munich rail system

MVV
U6
Garching-Hochbrück
vsl. Ende 1995
Fröttmaning
vsl. Juni 1994
Kieferngarten
Freimann
Studentenstadt
Alte Heide
Nordfriedhof
Dietlindenstraße
Münchener Freiheit
Giselastraße
Universität
Odeonsplatz
Lehel
Max-Weber-Platz
U4
Arabellapark
Richard-Strauss-Str.
Böhmerwaldplatz
Prinzregentenplatz
S8
Flughafen München
Besucherpark
Hallbergmoos
Ismaning
Unterföhring
Johanneskirchen
Englschalking
Daglfing
S3
S4
S7
Leuchtenbergring
Berg am Laim
Isartor
Rosenheimer Platz
Marienplatz
Ostbahnhof
St-Martin-Straße
Kolumbus-platz
Untersberg-straße
U1
Innsbrucker Ring
endlinger Tor
Fraun-hofer-straße
Silberhorn-straße
Giesing
Karl-Preis-Platz
Goetheplatz
im Bau
Mangfallplatz
im Bau
Michaelibad
Quiddestraße
Neuperlach Zentrum
Therese-Giehse-Allee
Neuperlach Süd
Perlach
Fasangarten
Fasanenpark
Unterhaching
Taufkirchen
Furth
S27
Deisenhofen
Sauerlach
Otterfing
S2
Holzkirchen
U2
U5
Neubiberg
Ottobrunn
Hohenbrunn
Wächterhof
Höhenkirchen-Siegertsbrunn
Dürrnhaar
Aying
Peiß
Großhelfendorf
Kreuzstraße
S1
S6
Erding
Altenerding
Aufhausen
St Kolomann
Ottenhofen
Markt Schwaben
Poing
geplant
Grub
Heimstetten
Feldkirchen
Riem
Trudering
Gronsdorf
Haar
Vaterstetten
Baldham
Zorneding
Eglharting
Kirchseeon
Grafing Bahnhof
Grafing Stadt
Ebersberg
S5

Southern Bavaria

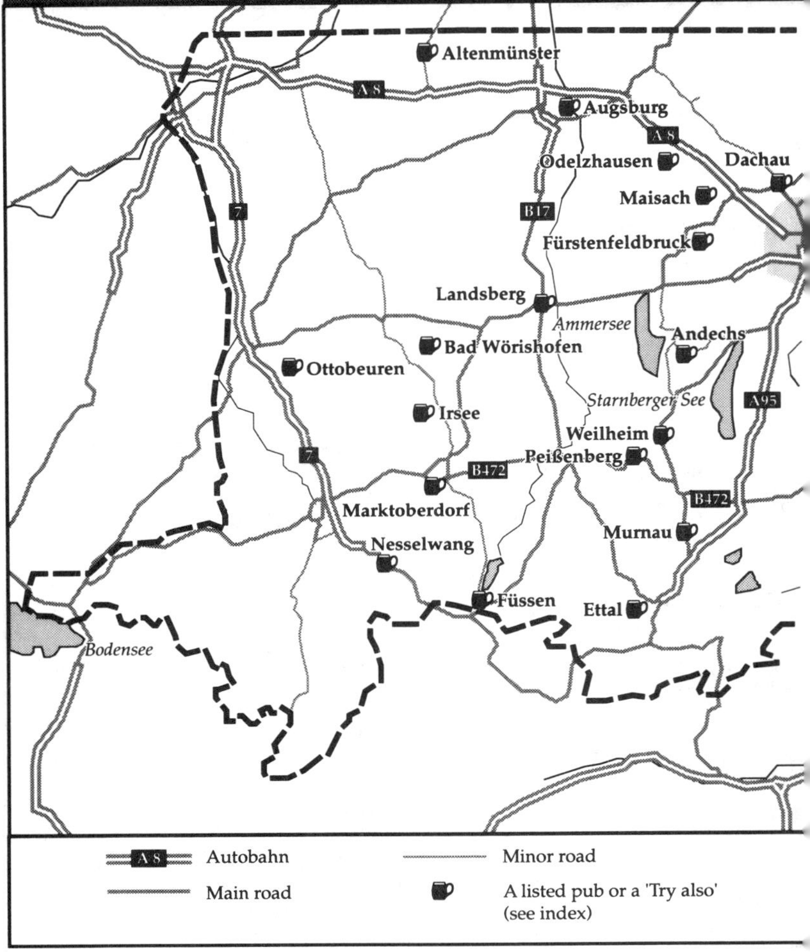

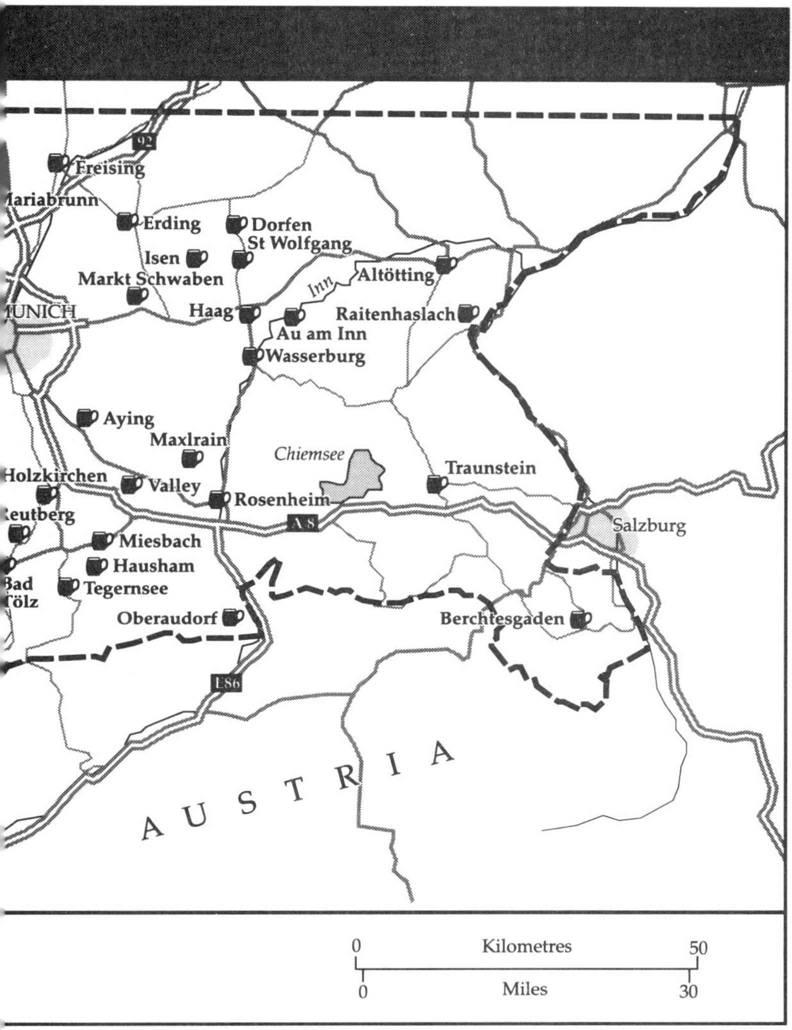
92
Freising
Mariabrunn
Erding
Dorfen
St Wolfgang
Isen
Markt Schwaben
Inn
Altötting
MUNICH
Haag
Au am Inn
Raitenhaslach
Wasserburg
Aying
Maxlrain
Chiemsee
Traunstein
Holzkirchen
Valley
Rosenheim
Reutberg
A 8
Salzburg
Miesbach
Hausham
Bad Tölz
Tegernsee
Oberaudorf
Berchtesgaden
E86
AUSTRIA
0
Kilometres
50
0
Miles
30

Central Bavaria

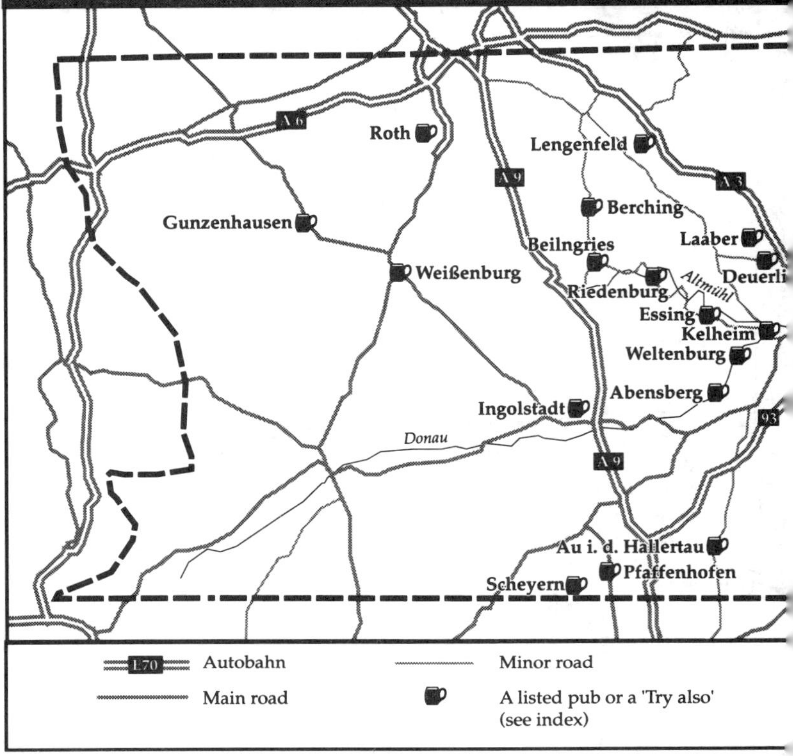

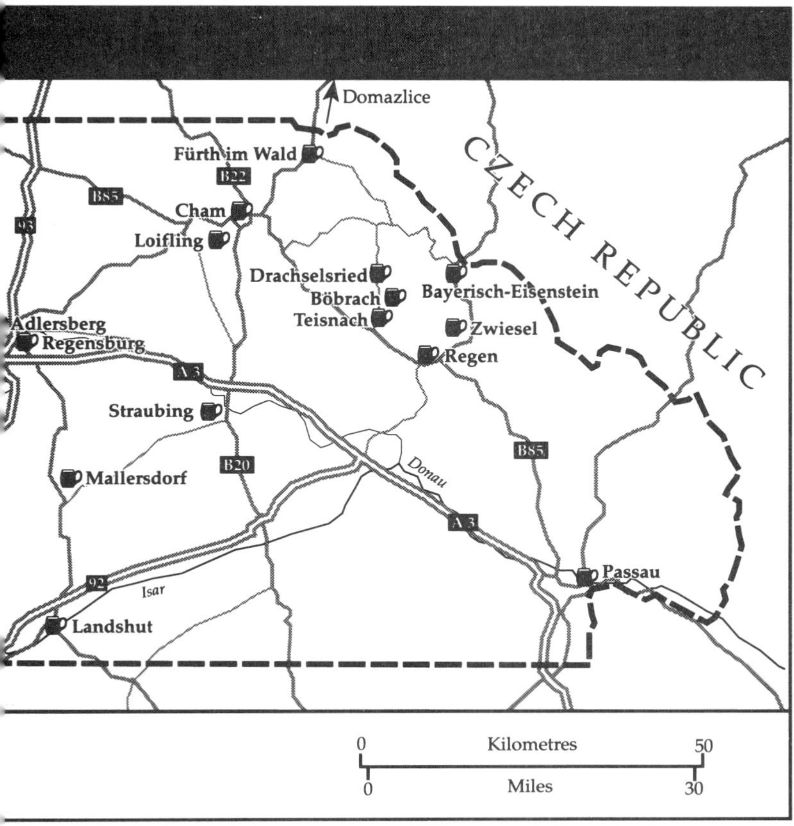

Domazlice
CZECH REPUBLIC
Fürth im Wald
B22
B85
Cham
93
Loifling
Drachselsried
Böbrach
Bayerisch-Eisenstein
Teisnach
Zwiesel
Adlersberg
Regensburg
Regen
A 3
Straubing
B85
Donau
B20
Mallersdorf
A 3
Passau
92
Isar
Landshut
0
Kilometres
50
0
Miles
30

Northern Bavaria

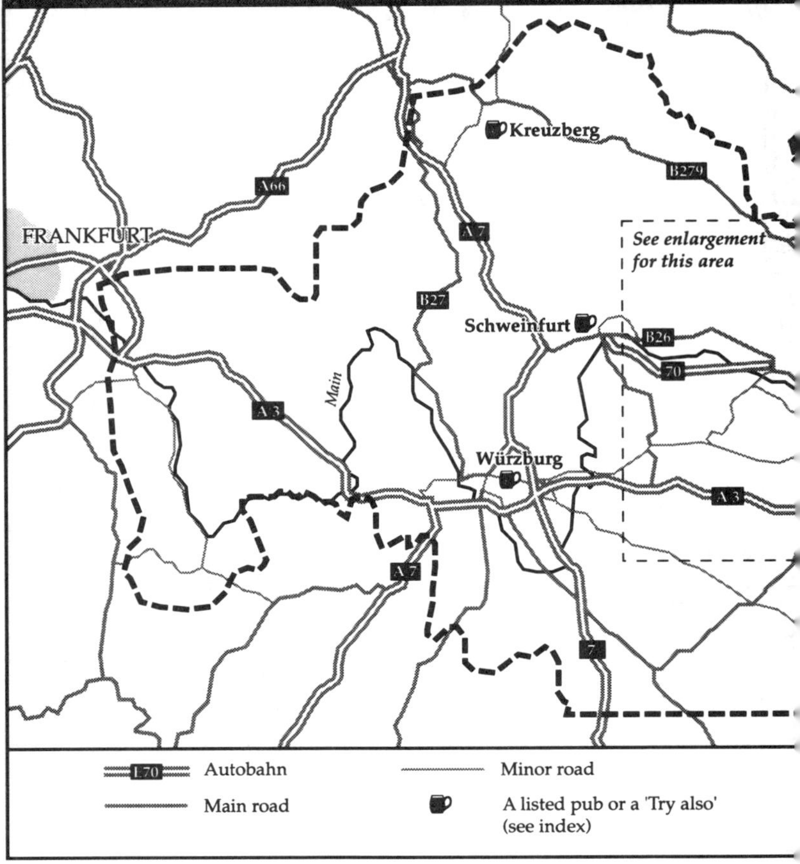

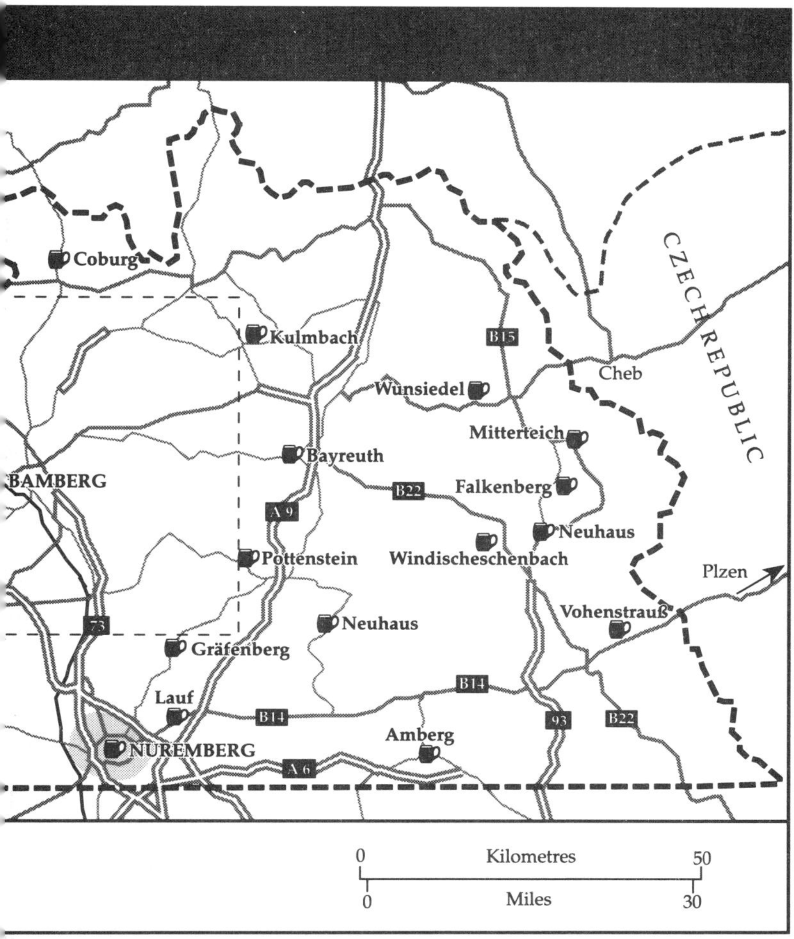

Coburg
Kulmbach
CZECH REPUBLIC
B15
Cheb
Wunsiedel
Mitterteich
Bayreuth
BAMBERG
B22
Falkenberg
A 9
Neuhaus
Pottenstein
Windischeschenbach
Plzen
Vohenstrauß
73
Neuhaus
Gräfenberg
B14
Lauf
B14
93
B22
Amberg
NUREMBERG
A 6
0
Kilometres
50
0
Miles
30

Bamberg area

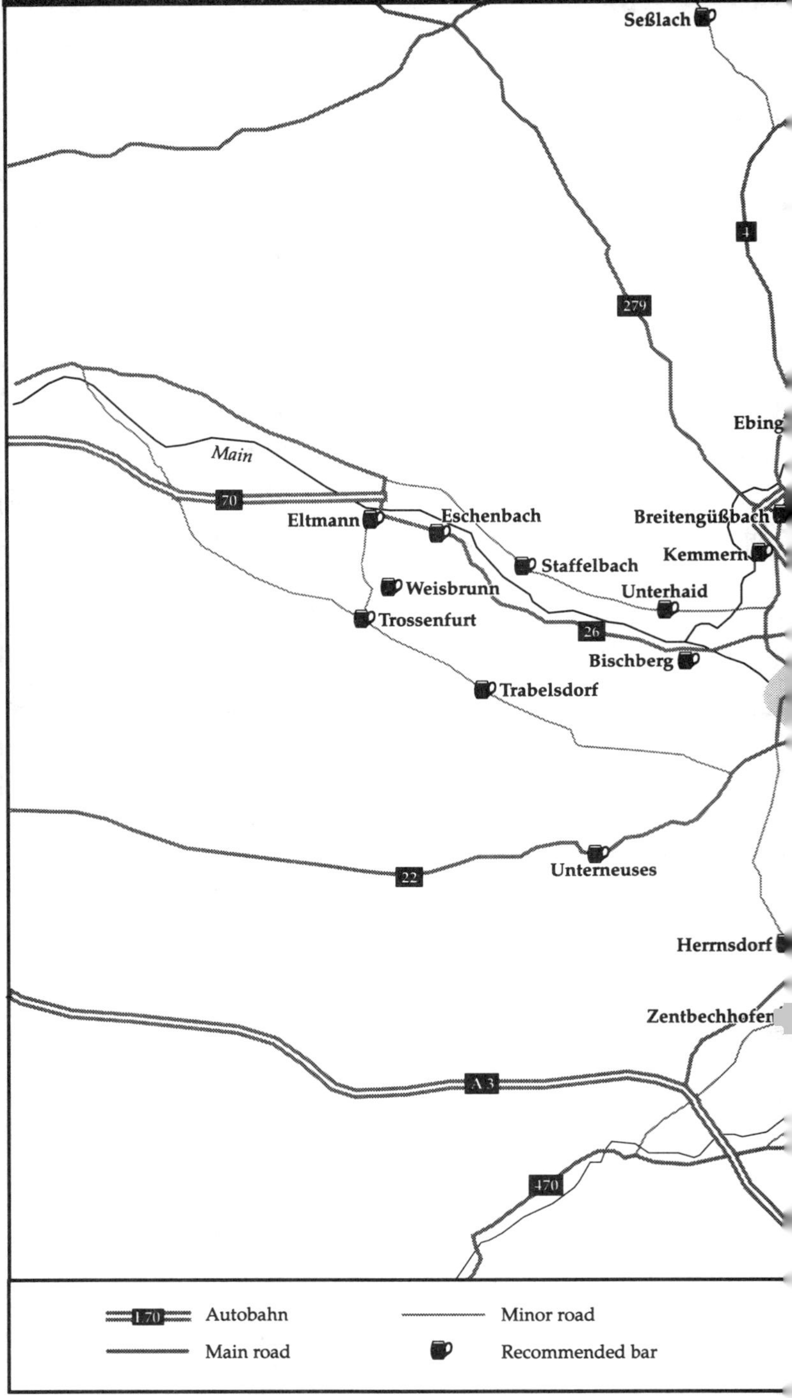

Burgkunstadt
Main
Lichtenfels
289
Herreth
Nedensdorf
Vierzehnheiligen
Staffelstein
eisen
Ützing
Stublang
Pferdsfeld
Ebensfeld
Unterleiterbach
173
Zapfendorf
Schederndorf
505
Scheßlitz
22
Memmelsdorf
BAMBERG
73
Buttenheim
505
Weigelshofen
Ebermannstadt
Eggolsheim
470
Schnaid
Schlammersdorf
Greuth
Forchheim
0
Kilometres
10
0
Miles
6

Index to place names

A

B

C

D

E

F

G

H

I

K

L

M

N

O

P

R

S

T

U

V

W

Z

NOTES

NOTES

NOTES

NOTES

NOTES

NOTES

NOTES